Adam's Gene and
the Mitochondrial Eve

Adam's Gene and the Mitochondrial Eve

The Non-incestuous Descent of Man from Adam and Eve
A Paleoanthrapologic and Scientific Synthesis

and

Evolution

Based On the Epics of Hinduism, the Bible and the Qur'an

What Are the Scriptures Saying?

Ahamed V.P. Kutty M.D.

To order additional copies of this book, contact:
Xlibris Corporation
1-888-795-4274
www.Xlibris.com
Orders@Xlibris.com
55447

CONTENTS

Acknowledgements

Samar Kutty and Layla Kutty for helping with grammar and spelling check.
Ann Wendlick for the skeletal diagrams
Karen Lafond and Ann Wendlick for the picture of the Garden of Eden.

Dedication:

This book is dedicated to my parents and my family, children and grand children-Samar,Layla and Kabir- and specifically to my late grandmother and mother who were widowed prematurely. They had to raise their children single handedly against all odds and braving all stumbling blocks, so that their children might live a better life.

This dedication is also extended to all mothers whether in the past, present or in the future who had to or will have to raise their children single handedly due to death, natural disasters or separation of their spouses. The special bond that exists between the mother and child is one of the supreme biological phenomenons that human beings possess, that enables the survival of the off springs and guarantees the survival of our species. In recognizing the importance of motherhood in the life of human beings and elevating the status of mothers (women) The Prophet *said: "The heaven lies under the feet of your mother"(Ahamed, Nasai and Tabarani.)

*   Prophet Muhammad (pbuh)

INTRODUCTION

In this book, I have made an attempt to look back in time when our ancient parents Adam and Eve were believed to have lived about ten to twelve thousand years ago. In addition, I have made an attempt to go farther back to 3.5 billion years ago when life on earth is believed to have been originated (created) according to scientific data. The mode of descent of mankind from Adam and Eve has remained murky in the fathomless depth of time. The premier intent of this book is to investigate whether the children of Adam and Eve had to commit incest to propagate humanity as there were no other human beings around for them to marry outside of their family, as the traditional theological belief goes. The Bible and Qur'an both convey the message that we, the present-day human beings, are created out of this pair, but have not elaborated on it as to how it was done, even though people have concluded that incest was the only option.

This book is based on the revealed scriptures supported by science and paleontology. The evidence will support the fact that there were human beings on earth other than Adam and Eve during their lifetime and even before, and there is no compelling reason to believe that the children of Adam and Eve had to marry each other and committed incest. These pre-Adamic people were genetically identical to us but had not given the status of the "fully developed" human beings by God, for reasons beyond our understanding, except possibly they were not deemed developed enough to understand the omnipresence of God (God consciousness).

This book will show that Adam was created to live on earth and not in heaven, contrary to the belief that Adam was created in heaven and was expelled after he violated God's commands.

Evidence for biological evolution based on the revelations in the Epics of Hinduism, the Bible, and the Qur'an is presented along with available scientific facts. In addition, the ever-increasing evidence for life originating from clay (the creation of man from clay as described in the Bible and Qur'an) is presented. Additionally it will give a glimpse into the billions of years old "life" as we know it and how it has remained unchanged. Life, a biological phenomenon, has remained in the bacteria, worms, plants, mammals, or man as the same process ever since it appeared (created) on earth 3.5 billion years ago. The different plants and animals look different not because their "life" is different but only because the physical structure is different. Like electricity the same energy can activate different machines with different results. When electricity is applied to a fan, we get cool air; when it is applied to a light bulb, it gives light. The same energy if applied to the television set, it gives sounds and sights.

Life, the metabolic process is the same in all living things, and as such, we cannot call the worms or flies as low forms of life but only their structure is low compared to the human, but not their life.

It can be construed that our life did not start in the womb of the mother, but has been there billions of years ago, long before our conception in the womb, in the seeds of our remote ancestors and transmitted through the seeds of our parents (the ova and sperms). Only our physical structure and function is made new in the mother's womb and it is unique for every individual other than identical twins. Every child born is a totally new entity the like of which will never be found unless in an identical twin, because of the shuffling of the genetic material (genes) of our parents during conception.

An overview of the formation (evolution) of the present-day universe and its contents including man from the big bang is presented; in addition, the scriptural account of the end of the World (Universe), or eschatology (Qiyama in Arabic) supported by astronomy is touched upon.

Finally the warning in the Qur'an that we may be replaced by yet another species is compared to the history of human evolution (transformation), as species after species were destroyed by God (Qur'an) or nature to eventually install mankind on earth as its overall controllers.

CHAPTER 1

Adam

The word Adam is a name, personal or generic (generic for humanity) that is remembered by billions of people of the Judeo-Christian-Islamic faith. They also believe that Adam and Eve (Hawwa) were the two Original human beings from whom all races of mankind living and dead were originated, some ten to twelve thousand years ago.

Seldom have we discussed the origin of this word (Adam) that was uttered by God to call the first human being either created de novo from mud (clay) or the first evolved human being from previous hominids.

We have no clear idea as to what was the language in which God communicated with Adam, it may have been a divine means of "communication" that enabled Adam to understand God's instructions.

As far as we can determine, the word Adam is derived from the Hebrew noun *ad amah*, which means "ground" or "earth." A literal translation of that word is "man of the red earth."

In Arabic, it means "made from the earth or clay."

In the Arabic lexicon, the word Adam or its derivatives are used to denote many circumstances and entities not necessarily pertaining to human beings alone but also referring to man and humanity. In his dictionary, E. W. Lane gives reference to man and humanity for some of the derivatives of the word Adam.

In E. W. Lane's Arabic-English Lexicon page 37 it says, "Relating to Adam and hence human." In page 36, he defines Adam, "He is the pattern, exemplar, example, or object of initiation, of his people, or family, by means of whom they are known."

In the Arabic English dictionary by J. W. Cowan, in page 10, Adam is translated as human being. Therefore, Adam simply means either a personal name given to the first man or the name of the species—the human beings.

When did this word come into being in order to refer to human creatures? In the King James Version of the Bible, the word appears for the first time in Genesis 2:19. Here it is mentioned that every beast and birds were brought to Adam on the command of God. But it is not clear who originated this word. Maybe it is a personal name or generic name used by the theologians who translated the original Hebrew language, and it does not seem to be the pronouncement of God. Until this time, the Genesis refers to this person as man. In Genesis 3:23, Adam called the female a woman. In Genesis 3:20, Adam called his wife's name as Eve. God did not refer to the woman as Eve (Eve, meaning the "mother of all humanity").

In Qur'an, the word Adam first appears in verse 2:31; this happens right after God mentioned that He is going to "create a vicegerent on earth." And He taught Adam the names of all things; this could be either a personal name given by God to this first human, or it could be the generic name for human species. Adam was asked by God to tell the names of all creatures, and he *did*. In *2:33* it says, "O Adam tell them their names." Adam told their names, the names that Adam gave must have been a generic name of a genus or species, and similarly God might have used Adam as a generic name for mankind, just like we say there is an elephant there, it only refers to the generic name of a species.

It is to be remembered that God does give specific names to his prophets, and as such, Adam could be a personal name given to the first human being by God himself. Qur'an: 3:45, God says with reference to the birth of Jesus Christ even before his birth, "O Allah (God) giveth thee glad tidings of a Word from Him: his name will be Christ Jesus. The son of Mary held in honor in this world and the Hereafter and of the company of those nearest to Allah (God)."

In Qur'an 61:6, with reference to the coming of another prophet (Prophet Muhammad), Jesus warns his people, "And remember Jesus, the son of Mary, said, 'O children of Israel! I am the messenger of Allah (God) sent to you confirming the Law which came before me and giving glad tidings of a messenger to come after me whose name shall be Ahmad (Muhammad).'"

In Qur'an, there is no mention of a name given to the first human female, Adam's wife. It is generally assumed to be Eve from the biblical description of her name as Eve. Eve is referred to as Hawa in Arabic.

By tradition, when we refer to Adam and Eve, we take it as the personal names given to the first human pair.

CHAPTER 2

The Life and Death of Adam

In the teachings of Judeo-Christian-islamic tradition, all human beings on earth today are descendents of Adam and Eve as described in the bible and Qur'an. Many believe that Adam was created de novo from clay or mud and made him alive by breathing life-giving spirit of God into him, and he became alive. There are many believers who entertain the idea that Adam was evolved from hominid species, that scientists believe had split from the Common ancestor of human beings and apes about six million years ago. Regardless of the root of his origin, after Adam appeared on earth, he is believed to have lived in the biblical Garden of Eden (1) (Gen. 2:8), (2) Qur'an 2:35. There is no clear evidence as to how long Adam and Eve lived in the garden before they were expelled from there, by God and how they lived therein.

Since all human beings on earth are believed to be the descendents of Adam and Eve, one will be curious to know how and where our remote ancestors would have lived, ten to twelve thousand years ago. Historically there is no evidence of a biography of this couple. There is indication in the Genesis that they were agriculturists.

Genesis 2:15 (3) says, "Then the Lord God placed the man in the Garden of Eden to cultivate it and guard it."

In the Qur'an 5:27 (4), there is reference to sacrifices offered to God by the sons of Adam, and commentators believe these were products of agriculture and domesticated livestock as described in the Genesis [Gen:4:3-4] (5).

Since the lifetime of the biblical Adam and Eve is generally believed to be around ten to twelve thousand years ago, it falls into the period what we call prehistory, as writing was not invented at that time.

Nevertheless, there are some documents written about a century before Christ and few decades after Christ called Pseudepigrapha and Apocrypha (6) that describe the life of Adam and Eve after they were expelled from the Garden of Eden (paradise).

Pseudepigrapha (in Greek pseudes [false], epigraphe [inscription]) refers to inscriptions whose authorship is not well founded. These inscriptions were recorded on rocks or other durable materials or cast in metal, usually for public viewing or for God's view. The authenticity or the truth of their contents are not to be discredited, but the authorship of these documents being falsely attributed to some noted figures has led to controversy.

Because of false ascription of authorship, an authentic work can become Pseudepigrapha.

These are now ascribed to Jewish theologians one hundred years before Christ and to Christian theologians a century after Christ. They were not part of the canon in Jewish or Christian religion because the rabbis did not consider them to be the product of an inspired revelation. The Apocrypha and Pseudepigrapha usually go together. Apocrypha means "hidden writings, not to be shown to the common man because of its divinity." But some of these apocryphal writings have been included in the Roman Catholic, Greek, Slovakian, and Ethiopic bibles. The authorship of these apocryphal writings is also questionable. In Judeo-Christian theology, the term apocryphal refers to any collection of scriptural writings outside the canon.

One such document is "Vita Adae et Evae" from the Apocrypha and Pseudepigrapha of the old testament translated by R. H. Charles (7). These contain some details of Adam's life with Eve after their expulsion from the Garden of Eden.

After the expulsion from the garden, they went to the eastern part of Eden and made a hut and lived there; for seven days they wept and regretted. They became hungry. Eve asked Adam to look for some food. But he did not find any food like what they were used to, in the garden. They realized that they were going to die. Eve requested Adam to kill her, but Adam admonished her, saying it will bring another punishment from God.

Then Adam discussed the process of penitence and repentance. Adam told Eve that he will have forty days of penitence, and Eve will have thirty-four days of penitence and asked Eve to go to the river Tigris and stay in the water on a stone and immerse herself up to her neck and pray and not to utter any word, and Adam went to Jordan River to pray until God gave them food.

Adam told the river Jordan to suffer with him and to assemble all animals around to pray, not for their sake but for him, as God did not withhold their food. All the cattle gathered around him. The water in the river restrained its flow. After twelve days of prayer, Satan approached Eve, in Tigris River, in the shape of an angel and tricked her to leave the water, as he told her that God had forgiven her and her husband, Adam. When Eve came out of the water, her body had withered like rotten vegetable due to the cold water. Then Satan led her to where Adam was. When Adam saw Eve, he realized that Satan had deceived her and asked her why she did not follow the rules of the penitence and asked Satan why he is deceiving them again. Then Satan described the story of his expulsion from heaven due to the fact that he did not prostrate before Adam. Satan blamed Adam for his expulsion from his dwelling (throne) and that he was angry at Adam. Satan told Adam, "When God breathed His spirit on you (Adam) had the likeness of divinity and Angel Michael made you bend before God and God proclaimed that He had created you in His image. Michael directed other angels to bow down to you". But Satan (devil) refused, and because of his refusal, he was expelled. When Adam heard this, he prayed to God to get away from Satan, and then Satan (devil) disappeared.

Adam continued his stay in the water, and Eve told Adam that she has transgressed a second time, and she left in the direction of the setting sun, and she vowed to eat grass till she dies. Eve made a hut there; by this time, she was three months pregnant, and the baby was to be Cain. When the time of parturition came, she began to tremble and called for Adam in a loud voice. Adam heard her cry from the river Jordan. Then God sent Angel Michael with some seeds and taught Adam sowing and related jobs so that they might be saved. Then Adam, upon hearing the voice of Eve, thought that Satan may be attacking her again and left the river and followed Eve's footsteps in the direction where Eve was, and when he saw Eve, she was crying for help, and Eve asked Adam to pray for God to ease her suffering. Upon hearing Adam's prayer, God sent down twelve angels and two powers from heaven to the place where Eve was.

One of the powers came to Eve and told her to prepare for labor. The power told Eve that she was a blessed person because of Adam. Then Eve gave birth to a child whose color was that of stars. He fell into the hands of the midwife (power), and the boy immediately began to pluck grass from the hut where grass was planted. The midwife then remarked, "You are Cain, the perverse one, killer of the good, for you are the one who plucks up the fruit-bearing tree and not him who plants it. You are the bearer of bitterness and not of sweetness." Then the power told Adam to stay with Eve till Eve is done with the infant what the power had taught her.

Then Adam took Eve and the child and went to the east and lived there. Then in the eighth year and second month, Eve became pregnant and bore another son named Abel.

At this time, Eve had a dream in which Eve sees Abel's blood being poured into the mouth of Cain, and he drank it without mercy. Upon hearing this, Adam told Eve, "Lest Cain plans to kill him (Abel), let us separate them from one another and let us be with them so as to provide no room for anger." God tells Angel Gabriel, "Say to Adam: do not reveal to Cain this secret plan which you know, for he is a son of wrath, because his brother will be killed by him. However, let Adam not be sad, for I will rise up Seth for him instead of Abel, and he will resemble My image and he shall teach you everything which I have a memory of. But do not reveal this to anyone but Adam."

Adam kept the word in his heart, and Adam and his spouse were sad.

Later Cain killed Abel, and Adam told Eve that God has established an end to all human beings. And the time arrived when Cain and Abel had gone up toward their fields. Two demons resembling Cain and Abel came. One demon reproached the other. He became very angry with the other and took a stone sword, then he cut his throat and killed him. And when Cain saw the blood, he went quickly and took the stone in his hands. But when Abel saw him coming upon him, he begged him, "Do not make me die, O my brother Cain!" He, however, did not accept his prayer and spilled Abel's blood in front of him.

And Adam and Eve afflicted themselves all the time with great sadness. Eve bore a third child and was named Seth who resembled Adam. After that, Adam had thirty sons and thirty daughters. And Adam lived 930 years.

Then at age 930, Adam fell ill and cried in a loud voice and said, "Gather to me all my descendents, and I will see them before my death." And all his progeny gathered to him who had settled. Then he told his children that he is sick, and the children asked Adam what his sickness was and how does a human being fall ill.

Then Seth asked if Adam is thinking of the fruit from the forbidden tree of the garden, and because of that, he became sad. If so, Seth was willing to go to the garden, and he will weep so that God might send angels to get the fruit from the forbidden tree, and if so, he will bring it to his father, Adam, to alleviate his distress. Adam told Seth that was not the reason for his sadness, and he was really sick and had pain. Then Seth asked Adam, "What is pain, and how do you get pain?"

Adam told Seth, "When God made me and your mother, we were put in the paradise to eat its fruits. But there was one plant in the middle of the paradise, very beautiful concerning which God had commanded, 'Eat not of this.' And the serpent deceived Eve, and because of that, we are going to die." And she deceived him and their children, for he did not know.

There were twelve angels to guard each of them, and they ascended each day at dawn, and at the moment of their ascent, the devil deceived Eve and caused her to eat the fruit. She also made Adam eat of it, and he did not understand.

Adam then described that God had given him the eastern and northern portions of the paradise and Eve the southern and western parts of the paradise to take care of. There were twelve angels with each of them, but the serpent (devil) deceived him, and God got angry and caused him to perish through death. Then Adam asked Eve to go with Seth to the paradise and weep before God so that God will let them have some oil from the tree of life for him to anoint and to relieve his misery.

Then God sent Angel Michael who is in charge of the souls and told Seth, "Man of God, do not labor to supplicate thus concerning the olive tree in command to anoint your father, Adam." Michael then told him about the coming of Jesus five thousand five hundred years from then, and he will anoint Adam. Then he told Seth to go to his father as his soul will leave in three days. After this, Eve and Seth departed to Adam's hut.

After they disobeyed God's commands, God entered the paradise sitting on the cherubs' back. When God entered the paradise, the trees cast off their foliage. Then God gave punishment to Adam and Eve. To Eve among other punishments also was to have increased pain in childbirth. Then God expelled them from the paradise. Then Adam repented. God refused the tree of life to Adam and told him that he will have the tree of life after resurrection.

Then Adam asked permission to take four incenses—nard, saffron, reed, and cinnamon—from the paradise.

Then Eve prayed to God in repentance. Then Michael appeared and announced that Adam's soul has gone from his body. Then Eve looked up to the sky and saw chariot of fire, and a light went up. Then Seth also saw seven firmaments open and saw Adam before God. Then God asked Michael and Gabriel to cover Adam's body in three shrouds and to bury it in the eastern part of the paradise with the body of Abel. Then God called Adam, and he answered from the grave. God told Adam, "You are soil and has returned to soil and will rise up in the resurrection." Then God sealed the grave with a triangular seal and ordered that let no person touch it during these six days until Adam's rib (Eve) returns to him.

Then Eve prayed to God not to separate her from Adam even in death and she dies. The angel Michael came down and showed how to dress Eve's body and took her body to the place where Adam was buried. Then Michael told Seth how to dress the dead until all humans die. And Michael left, telling Seth not to mourn more than five days and to rejoice on the seventh day. (This is a summary of the life and death of Adam and Eve, based on the translation of "Vitae Adae et Evae" from the Apocrypha and Pseudepigrapha of the old testament by R.H. Charles).

Did Cain marry his sister Luluwa?

There are many conflicting references as to whom did Adam's children marry? Many believe that Adam and Eve were the only two human beings when they appeared on earth, and their children have to marry each other (between brothers and sisters) as there were no other human souls at that time. Even though it is incest, they argue, that incest was allowed at that time due to the prevailing circumstances.

There are unsubstantiated stories in Judeo-Christian faith and Islamic faith (not substantiated in the Bible or Qur'an) that the sons and daughters of Adam and Eve married each other. Some believe that Adam's children were all twins, one male and one female in each pregnancy specifically for the sole purpose of marrying each other; others bring up the story that some angelic figures were deputed in the form of human beings for the purpose of marrying Adam's children. The prevailing story is that Cain married Luluwa who is the twin of Abel as she looked beautiful than his own twin, Qelima.

In one of the Pseudepigrapha-Apocrypha books (8) (Pseudepigrapha are writings by unknown authors prior to assembling the Bible and were considered non canonical by the compilers of the Bible, even though it is part of the Ethiopian bible; apocrypha are secret writings which were considered divine and were inscribed on rocks for people to view) the second book of Adam and Eve chapter 2:5 says, "After the burial of Abel, Adam and Eve were in great grief for hundred and forty days. Abel was fifteen and a half years old, and Cain was seventeen and a half."

Chapter 2:6 says , "As for Cain when the mourning for his brother was over, he took his sister Luluwa and married her, without leave from his father and mother, for they could not keep him from her, by reason of their heavy heart. He then went down to the bottom of the mountain away from the garden."

In another pseudepigrapha—the Cave of Treasures (9), under Adam's expulsion from paradise.

Note 11 says So Adam and Eve went down from the holy mountain (of Eden) to the slopes which were below it, and there Adam knew Eve, his wife (knew in this context refers to sexual relation; a marginal note in the manuscript says that Adam knew Eve thirty years after he went forth from the paradise). And Eve conceived and brought forth Cain and Lebhudha, his sister, with him. And Eve conceived again and brought forth Habhil and Kelimath, his sister, with him. "The Book of the Bees" (10) makes Kelimath the twin sister of Cain, and Lebhudha the twin sister of Abel. And when the children grew up, Adam said unto Eve, "Let Cain take to wife Kelimath who was brought forth with Abel and let Abel take to wife Lebhudha who was brought forth with Cain." And Cain said unto his mother, "Eve, I will take to my wife my twin sister Lebhudha and let Abel take to wife his twin sister Kelimath. Now Lebhudha was beautiful. When Adam heard these words, which were exceedingly displeasing unto him, he said, "It will be a transgression of the commandment for thee to take to take to wife thy sister, who was born with thee. Nevertheless, take ye to yourselves fruits of trees, and the young of sheep, and get ye to the top of this holy mountain. Then go ye into, and offer ye up your offerings, and make your prayers, and then ye shall consort with your wives."

After Cain killed his brother, he took his twin sister and went to Nod (11) where he is believed to have built a city. There are no authentic numbers of Adam's children.

Genesis 5:4: says that Adam and Eve begat sons and daughters (12).

By name, there are three sons, namely, Cain, Abel, and Seth, and their twins (not named in the Bible).

In Qur'an, it only mentions two brothers in connection with the murder of one of them (13). There is no mention of the marriages of Adam's children. Yet unsubstantiated stories, innuendos and fabrications are abound It is understandable to formulate a scenario that Adam's children had to marry each other as it was believed that there were no other human beings around, and the religious scholars and commentators of the past did not know then, what we know today. Our earliest ancestors (children of Adam and Eve) have been portrayed as subscribing to incest to start human family at its inception. But now we can rewrite the history, so far shrouded in mystery and unwanted accusations of immoral behaviors of our remote ancestors and restore their respected and amicable position as the progenitors of humanity. It can be conclusively shown that there were human beings (genetically identical to us) around Adam's time to continue the propagation of our species in a moral and God sanctioned way. But not denying the fact that some might have committed certain crimes and immoral acts like incest. The fact something should not be done doesn't mean it never happened.

Josephus, the Jewish historian, states that the number of Adam's children, as says the old tradition, was thirty-three sons and twenty-three daughters (14).

It will be unlikely that God permitted a sin to be perpetrated by the beginners of humanity, as incest was prohibited as a sin, as precribed in the later scriptures, the bible and Qur'an. Even Adam's conversation with Cain suggests that marrying one's own sister is against the commandments of God. At least we have fragmentary evidence that marriage between brother and sister was not approved even by Adam. It also suggests Cain had other wives (Adam tells Cain in the above conversation, "Then ye shall consort with your wives" [10]).

This does not mean that something unlawful did not happen. Cain was a deviant son, who killed his own brother and might have taken his own sister to his wife. Even today these things do happen. Even though it is morally repulsive.

Some argue that at the time of Adam and Eve, marriage between brother and sister was permissible as there were no other human beings on earth. This is the issue we need to explore. Were there other human beings at that time? If incest is a sin, then God would not have allowed it to happen when human beings are beginning to multiply and start a civil society imbibed in morality under the direction of the Almighty. Since God created one pair, namely Adam and Eve, He could have created more human couples to avoid such a sinful beginning. Some people say it became sinful only after God declared it is sinful later on, and prior to that command, it was not sinful. They point to the marriage of Abraham to his half sister (15) (Gen. 20) as an example. The Islamic view is that the sister referred to here was Abraham's wife, and he told the deputies of the Egyptian king a false statement that the woman with him was his sister so that the king won't kill him to acquire her. (As the king could not marry someone else's wife unless the husband was dead according to their custom.)

The notion that there were no other human beings at the time of Adam is now totally disproved. The evidence that there were enough human beings for Adam's children to marry outside their family will be described.

References for Life and Death of Adam:

1. Genesis 2:8.
2. Qur'an 2:35.
3. Genesis 2:15.
4. Qur'an 5:27.
5. Genesis 4:3-4.
6. Pseudepigraphal writings. Non canonical religious books. http://en.wikipedia.org/wiki/Pseudepigrapha.retrieved, 3-30-2009
7. Vita Adae et Evae. from the Apocrypha and Pseudepigrapha of the old testament. Translation by R. H. Charles. Oxford. Clarendon Press.1913.
8. Second book of Adam. Pseudepigrapha.http://www.earth-history.com/Pseudepigrapha/FB-Eden/adamandeve-2ohtm.
9. The cave of treasures. Brit.Mus.Ms.Add.25875.A Pseudepigrapha.
10. The Book of the Bees. A Pseudepigrapha.
11. Nod: The land into which Cain went after he killed his brother Abel. Genesis: 4:16.
12. Genesis 5:4.
13. Qur'an 5:27.
14. Titus Flavius Josephus (37-100 CE), the Jewish historian. http://en.wikipedia.org/Josephus.
15. Genesis: 20:11-18.

CHAPTER 3
Adam and Eve: Designed for Heaven or Earth

It is still believed by some in the Judeo-Christian faith, and many in the Islamic faith, that Adam and Eve were created in heaven and later sent down to earth as a punishment for eating from the forbidden tree in the Garden of Eden. In this view, the Garden is believed to have been in heaven. If this is true, then the obvious question will be, if they had not eaten from the forbidden tree, what would have happened to them? Will they forever live in the heavenly garden? Then how could they have children on earth, as we are told both in the Bible and the Qur'an that all human beings are descendents of Adam and Eve?

Since the creation process was un witnessed, the details of the creation were transmitted through the prophets of Judeo-Christian-Islamic religions for us to understand and believe in it.

Is there any evidence in the scriptures for the belief that Adam was designed to be a heavenly creature and became an earthly human being only after he was expelled, along with Eve, from the heavenly garden as a punishment for eating from the forbidden tree? There is no indication as to how long in the heaven, Adam and Eve would have lived, or whether they would have been subjected to death as had happened to them on earth. (Heaven is entered into after death. For those who are in heaven, death is not prescribed according to the scriptures as described below)

Is there any evidence in the scriptures that Adam was to be in heaven? Except in the pseudepigraphal writings, the Book of Jubilees, there is no other credible reference to the notion that Adam was meant to be a heavenly creature.

There are remarks by some Muslim commentators that Adam was in heaven initially, before he was expelled there from.

Are there convincing evidence in the scriptures that Adam and Eve indeed were to dwell on earth from the beginning, just like any other human beings like you and me?

A critical look at the revealed texts, both the Bible and Qur'an will show that Adam was meant to be an earthling and was not meant to be in heaven when he was created.

Genesis 2:7 (1) Then the Lord God took some soil from the *ground* and formed a man out of it; He breathed life-giving breath into his nostrils and the man began to live.

Then how did the thought arise that Adam and Eve were born or created in heaven?

In the Book of Jubilees (2), a pseudepigraphal writings, which have been incorporated in the Ethiopian Orthodox Church, relate a tradition that the angels did not place Adam in the garden for forty days after his creation and Eve only after eighty days. It is believed that during these days, they were kept in heaven.

In Qur'an (3) references to Adam can be found in the chapters al-Baqara 2:30-39, al-Araf 7:11-25, al-Isra 17:61-65, Ta-Ha 20:115-124, and Sad 38:71-85.

The garden is mentioned in 2:35 and 7:19 (4). There is no indication that this garden is the heavenly garden spoken of in the scriptures which is reserved for the devout and the faithful after their death, resurrection, and judgment. This heavenly garden is meant for the perpetual residence for the God-fearing after their death, and those who attain perfection in their life on earth. Only the God fearing persons will enter this garden (heaven), and once entered, they will never have to leave it. With regard to the garden of paradise (heaven), Qur'an 15:48 (5) states, "Toil afflicts them not therein, nor will they be ejected from it."

The situation with Adam and Eve is different for two reasons. One is that Adam and Eve entered the garden before their death, and second, they were removed from it later. These two situations are not consistent with the conditions established for living in the perpetual heavenly garden described in the scriptures. This is a strong indictment *against* the belief that the garden to which Adam and Eve were assigned to live, before their expulsion (the biblical Garden of Eden) was the heavenly garden (heaven).

As mentioned in chapter 10, (6), the origin of the word Eden may be from the Hebrew word din, which means "abundant and lush." In Hebrew,

Par-des is synonymous with paradise. This has similarities to the Persian word Paridaize, used to describe a "walled orchard garden" or "an enclosed park."

The heavenly paradise is indescribable in its gorgeous enormity and comfort and the spiritual satisfaction it imparts, as we are told. There is no physical description of heaven in the Bible or Qur'an except in an allegorical context. It will be beyond our wildest imagination possible to describe it. One cannot describe the taste of a food item or fruit unless one tastes it. Hadith (sayings of the Prophet) has described the sights and scenes of heaven in unimaginable fashion, and a human being will not be able to comprehend it.

There is no indication in Qur'an that the garden where Adam and Eve were living before their expulsion was in heaven. Qur'an 2:35 (7) says, "We said 'O Adam! Dwell thou and thy wife in the garden; and eat of the beautiful things therein.'" In the commentary (commentary 50, page 25) on the garden, the author indicates that this garden was not on earth on the basis of the statement in verse 2:36 (8) Yusuf Ali. After Satan deceived them (Adam and Eve), God says, "Get ye down, all (ye people) with enmity between yourselves. On earth will be your dwelling place." (Other scholars translate it as "There is for you an abode on earth and provisions for a while," and the word down means "to go away from here" and not to suggest that the word down was to mean "to get down from heaven.") One can argue that God removed Adam from heaven down to earth from the translation of verse 2:36 (7), but it is not uniformly accepted by all.

Additionally some early Muslim commentators had stated that Adam and Eve were in the heavenly paradise called al-Jannathul-Adn and were later cast out of it, into earth. One Muslim exegete Ibn Sa'd, in Kitab al-Tabaqat al-Kabir, volume 1, page 21, "Sharing the Gospels with Muslims, The Man of Dust, The Man from Heaven," (9) states that "Adam was externed from the Paradise between the Zuhr and Asr (the declining of day prayer) prayers. His stay in paradise had been half the day of the next world, and the day there is equal to one thousand years based on calculations made by the people of this world. He was cast down on a mountain in India known as Nawdh and Eve was cast at Juddah." (Saudi Arabia)

Al-Qummi (10), the Shiite scholar, also maintained the idea that the garden was not on earth.

These speculations aside, one needs to look at what the Bible (Genesis) and Qur'an tell us about the creation of Adam and Eve.

Genesis 2:7 (11) "Then the Lord God formed a man (Adam) from the dust of the ground."

Genesis 2:8 "And Lord God planted a garden eastward in Eden and then he placed the man He had formed."

Qur'an:

When God declared to the angels His decision to create a man from clay, He declares in Qur'an 2:30 (12) "'Behold,' thy Lord said to the angels, **'I will create a vicegerent (ruler) on *earth*.'"** So there it is, in the Qur'an, for all to remember that God intended Adam to be on earth as any other human being and not for heaven. Both the Bible and Qur'an unequivocally demonstrate that Adam was a human being to live on earth and was not intended as a resident of heaven at that time. (Adam will be in heaven after death.)

Let us now recall the conversation of Satan (Iblis)—even though satanic words are not routinely sought after by the believers—with God when Adam was presented to the angels and Iblis.

> Qur'an:15:30: (13) So the angels prostrated themselves, all of them together.
>
> 15:31: Not Iblis; he refused to be among those who prostrated themselves.
>
> 15:32: Allah (God) said, "O Iblis (satan)! What is your reason for not being among those who prostrated themselves?"
>
> 15:33: Iblis said, "I am not one to prostrate myself to man whom Thou didst create from sounding clay, from mud molded into shape."
>
> 15:34: "Allah (God) said , "Then get thee out from here; for thou art rejected, accursed.'"
>
> 15:39: (Iblis) said, "O my Lord! Because Thou hast put me in the wrong, I will make (wrong) fair seeming (all that is evil on earth seem goodly to them) to them on *earth*, and I will put them all in the wrong." Remember this conversation took place when Adam was presented to the angels and Iblis long before Adam and Eve were ever placed in the garden of Eden and long before

they were expelled from the garden. The angels and Iblis (a fallen angel) do not have the intelligence to forsee things in to the future as revealed by their own words. Qur'an 2:32:(14) They replied, "Limitless art thou in Thy glory! No knowledge have we save that which Thou hast imparted unto us."

This was in connection with the naming of all things when Adam was presented to the angels long before Adam and Eve were placed in the garden. At the time there was no discussion of expelling Adam and Eve from the garden. That discussion (to expel Adam from the Garden) took place later when they ate from the forbidden tree in the garden. If Adam and Eve were in heaven, how could Iblis know that they will be expelled from heaven to earth, which only God would know? Since Iblis stated that he will deceive Adam and Eve and their progeny "**on earth**". This entire episode must have taken place on earth and not in heaven.

In Qur'an, this paradise (garden) is described as Jannath. What is the meaning of Jannath?

The Arabic-English Lexicon by William Lane (15) gives the following meaning: a garden or walled garden, or with luxurious foliage as though concealing what is beneath them (similitude is to the heavenly paradise the contents of which are hidden or concealed in the present state of our existence). The above description is that of a garden on earth. The heavenly paradise for the permanent abode for the righteous after death is called Jannathu Adnin.

This earthly garden had many amenities that were hidden from the view from outside due to the lush and heavy foliage. God has described the wonderful amenities that were available in the garden. Qur'an 20:118 (16) states, "There are therein enough provisions for thee not to go hungry, nor to go naked. Nor to suffer neither from thirst, nor from the Sun's heat." This testifies to the earthly nature of the garden where Adam and Eve were supposed to live. Scientists have not discovered any other planet which has available food, water, and shades to protect from sun's heat other than our earth. Only in the earth which we inhabit have those features as described above in the Qur'an (see chapter 11). There fore, there should not be any doubt that the paradise (garden) where Adam was to live must be on earth.

As we discussed in the chapter on Cro-Magnons and pre-Adamic people, Adam and Eve were created out of the seeds of other people on earth, which reiterates the fact they were human beings on earth.

Qur'an 6:133 (17) states, He can take you away (destroy you) and make whom He pleases as successors after you, as he has raised you from the progeny of others (seeds of other people). Muhammad Asad's translation of this verse: "If He wills He may put an end to you and thereafter cause whom he wills to succeed you-even as he has brought you into being out of other people's **seed**".

These facts should be sufficient to establish the fact that Adam and Eve were in a garden on earth and not in heaven.

The notion of the creation of Adam in an extraterrestrial location (heaven) and transplanted on to earth is still alive and well, among followers of the Abrahamic religions. Notwithstanding our ignorance about heaven, its location and physical characteristics, the aforementioned belief persists. All the physical phenomena that we observe in the universe that may seem mystical, magical, or unexplainable are based on the laws of nature as decreed by the Creator.

Qur'an 35:11 (18) says:(Ahmed Ali) "It is God who created you from dust then from a sperm then formed you into pairs. Neither does a female conceive nor give birth without His knowledge. Nor do the old grow older or become younger in years but in accordance with the law of nature."

In due course when science advances further, the present-day phenomena that are unexplainable will become clearly understandable.

Was it feasible for the creation of Adam in another planet and then chute him and Eve down to our earth, on the basis of present-day scientific knowledge? God can do anything and everything that He wishes. We may not be able to understand it from our limited scientific information. But there are references in the Qur'an to the ascendence of angels and spirits to heaven. How do they ascend or descend? It seems beyond our comprehension.

Qur'an (19) 70:4: "To Him ascends the angels and the spirit in a day the measure of which is fifty thousand years (50,000 years)."

32:5: (20) "He orders the affair from the heaven to earth; then it will ascend to Him in a day the measure of which is a thousand years as you count."

34:2: (21) "He knows all that goes into the earth, and all that comes thereof, all that comes down from the sky and all that ascends thereto."

15:14: (22) "Even if we opened out to them a gate from heaven and they were to continue all day ascending therein."

15:15: "They would only say 'Our eyes have been intoxicated.' Possibly there could be Passageways or tracks in space and the universe , to undertake these journeys by nonhuman creatures (angels and spirits), And the methods of these travels by angelic forces are beyond our comprehension. From a scientific standpoint, one such hypothetical passageway is discussed below.

The Wormholes in the Universe

Albert Einstein and Nathan Rosen (23) proposed this concept relating to the theory of relativity in 1935. They realized that general relativity allows the existence of bridges later called wormholes in space-time. These space-time tubes act as shortcuts connecting distant regions of the space. A wormhole has at least two mouths which are connected to a single throat or tube. If the wormhole is traversable, matter can travel from one mouth to the other through the throat or tube faster than light. Even though no one has observed the wormhole, space-time containing wormholes are known to be valid conclusions.

Wormhole

Worm Holes

The speed of light in the vacuum is 186,000 miles per second. The sun's light takes eight minutes to reach the earth.

Wormhole is similar to a tunnel burrowed by a worm to get through the fruit as a shortcut instead of going around the fruit.

Wormhole is a hypothetical topological feature of space-time. The intra universe wormhole connects distant spots in the same universe acting as a shortcut through space-time. There are wormholes called inter universe wormholes that connect between universes.

The wormholes are also described as gateways as revealed in Qur'an:15:14.

Initially dismissed as a scientific fiction, scientists now believe that by using what the physicists call exotic matter, which has a negative energy, that can prevent the collapse of the wormhole, it is possible to utilize the wormhole for travel in space-time faster than light. Recent calculation believes that a future civilization might be able to make wormhole work.

At present scientists do not know where these wormholes are. But the Almighty creator knows.

In Qur'an there is reference to Prophet Muhammad (pbuh) (24) having had a journey from Mecca to Jerusalem during one night. Muslims call this the night journey. There is also a widely held reference to another journey, that the Prophet took, to go to heaven called Miraj (25) (ascension to heaven), which is not mentioned in Qur'an but is attributed to certain Hadith (26) (sayings of the Prophet). Many firmly believe in it as a physical journey due to the fact that some scholars and commentators had come to that conclusion, that the so-called ascension to the heaven (Miraj) had taken place. Some believe that the Prophet traveled physically, and others contend that it is a spiritual (soul) journey. In this instance on the possible physical ascension to heaven, Aisha (RA)(27), the wife of the Prophet, reported that the Prophet never left the house physically; and it was a spiritual experience. With these differing opinions about the ascension to heaven, whether spiritual or physical, or even the Journey from Mecca to Jerusalem overnight fifteen hundred years ago, could there be a scientific explanation for this? Is there a possibility for the physical ascension to heaven by a human being? (Of course we do not know where heaven is located, but we somehow believe it is outside the earth or extraterrestrial, and hence a physical ascension is considered impossible.). But God has the power and authority to do whatever and whenever he wants.

Science has immense potential. Fifty years ago, no one thought that landing on the moon is possible, but it did happen. With advanced science, one may be able to travel faster than light to the corners of the universe or even beyond.

The story of the ascension to heaven by the Prophet (Miraj) is not mentioned in the Qur'an. All the information is coming from Hadith (or the sayings of the Prophet). Nevertheless, we cannot discard the concept of such a travel as there are pathways (wormholes) in the universe. As the Prophet's companion Khalifa Abubacker (RA)(28) is reported to have said after hearing the controversy, "If the Prophet said it, I believe it." So do us.

In this context, the abovementioned verses (pertaining to the ascent of angels and spirits and opening of gates) probably illustrate the presence of these wormholes for such ascensions and descensions in space. As mentioned before, the duration of this ascension could be fifty thousand years of our reckoning. Are the angels taking these passages to reach corners of the universe instantaneously? We can only speculate. Some believe future scientists may be able to travel through these wormholes or the "gates" (verse 15:14, as mentioned above) faster than light.

It is worth noting that in the story of the ascension to heaven by the Prophet, as reported in Hadith, it was not the angel Gabriel (29) who carried the Prophet. Angel Gabriel only accompanied the Prophet. It was a creature with wings that had enormous speed called the Baraq (Buraq) who carried the Prophet during this ascension (30). This could be some contraption unknown to humans at the present time, to shield the Prophet's physical body during the ascent to heaven, like space vehicles that we use today, if indeed the ascension was a physical one. Since God's actions are always based upon the laws of nature laid down by the Almighty Himself, whether it is an earthquake, a lightning, or a cyclone, we must come with a rational scientific explanation for this travel, if indeed it was a physical ascension. The creature called the Baraq may be the answer and the wormhole may be the passageway. It is pertinent to ponder why Angel Gabriel himself did not transport the Prophet. It must be due to the fact that the human body of the Prophet won't be able to withstand such a journey through space unless protected by this Baraq. The angelic ascension is of a different dimension as the angels are made of light and their body composition, if they have any, must be different from ours and as such may be protected from any harm from space travel. As we are made out of clay with carbon-based chemicals, we need a protective shield for space travel.

In this context, Adam, being created and then chuted down through these gates or wormholes, would be a subject of interest for those who believe that Adam was created in the heavenly paradise and was thrown down to the earth when Adam transgressed the commands of God. But as we have shown that Adam was created to be an earthly human being, one need not entertain his extraterrestrial origin or travel through these wormholes.

From these revelations in the Bible and Qur'an, one can conclude that the Garden of Eden was on earth, and there is no indication that the garden was in a paradise outside of earth. In addition, Adam being a human being, he had to have an earthly planet to survive. Scientists have discovered several solar systems outside ours but so far have been unable to discover a planet like earth or any that has liquid water on it. (see chapter 11.Giant earths). The recent Mars exploration suggests that water might have been present on that planet in the past. As such, there is no other place in the universe, that we know of, other than our earth where human beings can survive without an artificial protective environment. Adam must have been an earth dwelling human being.

References for Adam and Eve: Designed for Heaven or Earth:

1. Genesis 2:7.
2. The Book of Jubilees. Pseudepigrapha. Ethiopic Orthodox Church. http:// en.wikipedia.org/wiki/Jubilees.
3. Qur'an 2:30-39; 7:11-25; 17:61-65; 20:115-124; and 38:71-85.
4. Ibid., 2:35; 7:19.
5. Ibid., 15:48.
6. Garden of Eden, Etymology.
7. Qur'an 2:36. Yusuf Ali. The meaning of The Holy Qur'an.
8. Ibid., 2:36.
9. Ibn Said, Muslim commentator. Kitab al-Tabaqat al-Kabir. vol.1, p. 21.
10. Al Qammi, Shiite scholar.
11. Genesis 2:7; 2:8.
12. Qur'an 2:30.
13. Ibid., 15:30, 31, 32, 33, 34, and 39.
14. Ibid., 2:32.
15. Arabic-English Lexicon. Edward William Lane. p. 463.
16. Qur'an 20:118.
17. Ibid., 6:133.
18. Ibid., 35:11.Ahmed Ali.Al-Qur'an.
19. Ibid., 70:4.
20. Ibid., 32:5.
21. Ibid., 34:2.
22. Ibid., 15:14; 15:15.
23. Albert Einstein and Nathan Rosen. Theory of relativity. 1935.
24. Prophet Muhammad (pbuh)
25. Miraj. The journey to heaven by Prophet Muhammad (pbuh).Qur'an:17:1.
26. Hadith. Sayings of the Prophet.
27. Aisha Beebi (RA), wife of Prophet Muhammad (pbuh).
28. Aboobacker (RA), a companion of the Prophet.
29. Gabriel, Archangel.
30. Baraq (Buraq), the winged creature that transported Prophet Muhammad (pbuh) to heaven.

CHAPTER 4

When Did Adam and Eve Live? *

Based on Hebrew text genealogy, it is generally believed that Adam lived about 4000 BC. However, there are many authorities who contend that the genealogical calculation of this time line may not be accurate. They believe that many names might have been left out and only names of important figures must have been recorded and cannot be used as a time line to ascertain the time when Adam was living.

It is important to remember that the genealogical records were passed down orally for generations before it was written down. Some believe that the missing chronologies may be 10 to 80 percent, and considering this assumption, Adam will be placed between seven thousand and sixty thousand years ago. Therefore, it is not an easy task to clearly state the time when Adam was living on the basis of genealogical calculations.

We need to look at other corroborative evidences to examine the most probable time of Adam's life.

The beginning of farming and agriculture:

Early Homo sapiens: Neanderthals and Cro-Magnons were hunter-gatherers (early hominid species). They usually were cave dwellers. The Neanderthals were considered a separate species who lived from two hundred thousand years before the present till thirty thousand years before the present and went extinct. From thirty-five thousand years before the present, the most modern humans appeared in the fossil record called the Cro-Magnons. They were much advanced compared to the Neanderthals in hunting and fishing techniques and are believed to have had a social and cultural life. They began to live in caves and later in huts and other man-made dwellings. But still they were largely hunter-gatherers. For unclear reasons, they also died out by ten to fifteen thousand years ago. The Neanderthals were shorter but robust in build. Their hunting techniques were different from those of the later arrivals called the Cro-Magnons. The Neanderthals had to attack the prey at close quarters including jumping on the prey to subdue them. They used stone tools or spears to kill and at times wrestled them down. The Cro-Magnons were much more advanced with new technologies in hunting equipment and fishing techniques and usage of antlers for throwing spears to farther distance.

Because of their advanced technology, the Cro-Magnons could attack the prey from a distance instead of at close quarters and that had a survival advantage for the Cro-Magnons over the Neanderthals, as the Cro-Magnon did not have to come closer to the prey to kill.

During the late Paleolithic or early Neolithic period (twelve thousand to ten thousand years ago), we see archaeological evidence for farming and domestication of animals (1) (2) (3). In addition, archeology has discovered the evidence for settlements of people of varying numbers suggesting community life. People started to settle down and cultivate food and domesticate animals and changed the previous need for hunter-gatherer lifestyle. This period is believed to be about ten thousand to thirteen thousand years ago.

Genesis:2:15.(good news Bible): then the Lord God placed the man (Adam) in the Garden of Eden to cultivate it and guard it.

Genesis 4:2(4) says that "Abel became a shepherd but Cain was a farmer," which puts Adam and Eve in this time period of establishment of farming and domestication of animals. The hunter-gatherers began rye cultivation in the Near East by thirteen thousand years ago (5).

Fossil evidence:

Fossils are remnants of previously lived plants and animals including Hominids and ancient modern human beings. Archaic Homo sapiens fossils demonstrate physical similarities to apes, with brain volumes of 300 cc. Then we see in the fossil record gradual but clear morphological changes, in that the skeletal features becoming closer and closer to that of modern human skeleton. The brain volume also increased gradually to that of the modern human brain size of 1,300 to 1,500 cc. The most modern human beings, the Cro-Magnons, appear in the fossil record around thirty-five thousand years ago; and they remained till about ten thousand years ago. The Cro-Magnons, belonging to our own species, but considered a separate race, disappeared by about ten thousand to fifteen thousand years ago.(the Cro-Magnons can be called the first generation of mankind, the pre-Adamic people.) The ancestors of our generation (Adam and Eve) can be called the progenitors of the second generation of mankind. The Adamic people appeared at the tail end of the life time of the Cro-Magnons. From the Bible and the Qur'an, we are told that the beginning of the present-day humans started from Adam and Eve (or from a single pair. Bible:Acts:17:26 and Qur'an 49:13)(6). In other words, all living human beings on earth today are the descendents of Adam and Eve (or the single pair). The appearance of Adam and Eve must be at the tail end of the generation of Cro-Magnon race. There is no fossil evidence for any other human species between the Cro-Magnons and the present-day humans. This also puts Adam and Eve living around ten thousand to twelve thousand years before the present. As mentioned earlier, the Cro-Magnons became extinct by ten thousand years before the present.

To date, archaeologists have not unearthed any fossils, after the disappearance of the Cro-Magnon and the appearance of the ancestors of the present-day human beings (Adam and Eve), that are different from the fossil characteristics of Cro-Magnons or the skeletons of modern man. This suggests that Adam and Eve (our ancestors) must have appeared toward the tail end of the existence of Cro-Magnons, placing the time of life of Adam and Eve around ten thousand to twelve thousand years ago.

Geneticists (7) have shown that there is very little variation in the stock human DNA compared to the variations seen in other species and that in the late Pleistocene, there was a severe bottleneck in which human population was reduced to probably one thousand to ten thousand people worldwide. Several theories are proposed for this bottleneck, the most popular being the Toba volcano, which spewed tremendous amount of volcanic ash into the atmosphere and blocked the sun, and many species perished including humans except for a few thousand souls. This occurred probably around seventy thousand years ago (8).As mentioned earlier the Cro-Magnons disappeared ten to fifteen thousand years ago for unknown reasons. Whether it was another bottleneck event is not known.

Recent DNA analysis shows that the Cro-Magnons and the present day humans are genetically identical. (see chapter 6).

Mitochondrial Eve:

This early hominid is not to be confused with the biblical Eve. The name Mitochondrial eve is a nickname, who is believed to have lived about one hundred forty thousand years ago while the biblical Eve is believed to be about ten to twelve thousand years ago. The Mitochondrial Eve is believed to be the most recent common matrilineal ancestor, but not the most recent common ancestor (MRCA) of all humans. The MRCA's (most recent common ancestor) off springs have resulted in all the present day living human beings via their sons and daughters. Mitochondrial Eve can be traced only through female lineages. Therefore, she is estimated to have lived much earlier than the MRCA. The Mitochondrial Eve is estimated to have been alive around one hundred forty thousand years ago. This discovery is based on the mutation frequency of the mitochondrial DNA and creation of a molecular clock.

Who and what is the Mitochondrial Eve?

In order to understand this, we need to look at the human cell.

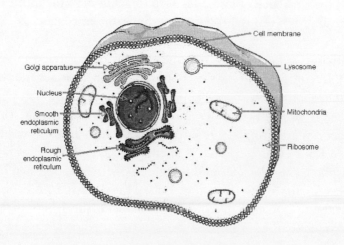

The Human Cell
Figure was produced using Servier Medical Art, www.servier.com.

It contains briefly a cell wall; inside the cell, there is a nucleus, cytoplasm, and mitochondria. The nucleus contains the genetic material DNA. The mitochondria are organelles which provide energy to the cell. Scientists believe that the mitochondrion is a viral DNA that got inside the proto cell for symbiosis and for its own survival billions of years ago. Our DNA is a mixture of DNA from the mother and father, and in turn, our parents' DNA will be a mixture of our grandparents, and so on. In this mixing process, some alteration and mistakes can take place (mutations). But the mitochondrial DNA (MDNA) is unique in that the children get the MDNA only from the mother, through the ovum, during fertilization. The MDNA in the male sperm does not get inside the zygote. In the male sperm, the MDNA is in the flagellum of the sperm, and that is discarded at the time of fertilization, as the sperm enters the ovum. Therefore all MDNA in the human species are from the mothers. Because there is no mixing with the father's MDNA, the MDNA will not show any change except for some spontaneous mutation. (Remember the DNA is a fifty-fifty mixture of mother's and father's DNA.) This spontaneous mutation in the mitochondria occurs at a predictable rate, and from this mutation rate, a clock can be constructed that will enable scientists to decide when did the different races diverge and thereby can trace the migration pattern and the origin of our remote ancestors. This is called the molecular clock (MC). By this molecular clock (mutation rate), they can decide when the mutation crept in to the MDNA and locate the time of the life of the female ancestor of all living human beings.

Scientists studied the MDNA from people all over the world and found certain similarities in these various nationalities and concluded that all the human beings (all six billion of them) had originated from a single woman in Africa who lived between one hundred forty and two hundred thousand years ago. This person is given the nickname the Mitochondrial Eve to emulate the theological concept that all human beings are originated from the biblical Adam and Eve. It is to be understood that these two Eves lived one hundred thousand years apart. To reiterate, these two Eves are not the same, and the biblical Eve came much later about ten thousand to twelve thousand years ago.

Another milestone in our history is the most recent common ancestor or MRCA. Based on a series of computer models, it is calculated that our most recent common ancestor may have lived between two thousand and five thousand years ago. This is 1/10 to 1/100 the length of time to our most common ancestors, along solely male or solely female lines, which have been the target of recent interest. The point beyond which everyone alive today shares the same set of ancestors is somewhat harder to predict. But it most likely falls between five thousand and fifteen thousand years ago.

This time period is consistent with the lifetime of Adam and Eve around ten thousand to twelve thousand years ago. (9)

The Y-chromosome Adam

Even though the word Adam is here, this is in no way related to the Adam referred to in the Bible or Qur'an. This is a genetically determined person from whom all the Y chromosome of all living men today are descended, and he is called the patrilineal most recent common ancestor (Y-MRCA), the Y-chromosome Adam; the name Adam is just a metaphor.

Spencer Wells, a geneticist, by analyzing DNA from people from all the regions of the world, concluded that all humans alive today descended from a single man (Y-chromosome Adam) who lived in Africa around ninety thousand years ago (10). This was done like in the case of the Mitochondrial Eve by analyzing molecular clock and genetic markers. The Y-chromosome Adam and Mitochondrial Eve were not contemporaries. They were separated by at least thirty thousand years or possibly a thousand generations. This difference is believed to be due to differences in male and female reproductive strategies.

The more recent age of the Y-chromosome Adam compared to the Mitochondrial Eve corresponds to a larger statistical dispersion of the probability distribution for a Paleolithic man (Y-MRCA) to have living descendents compared to a Paleolithic woman. While fertile women had more or less equally distributed chances of giving birth to a certain number of off springs, chances for fertile men varied more widely, with some fathering no children and others fathering many, with multiple women.

Y-chromosomal Adam is not the same individual at all points in human history. The Y-MRCA of all humans alive today is different from the one for humans alive at some point in the remote past, or future, as male lines die out. A more recent individual becomes the new Y-MRCA. During population bottlenecks, there are more chances for patrilineal lines to die out than in periods of population growth.

Y-chromosomal Adam was not the only male living at his time.

The Identical Ancestors point:

Starting with the MRCA, one can trace all ancestors of MRCA backward in time. At every ancestral generation, more and more ancestors (via both paternal and maternal lines) of MRCA are found. These ancestors are also, by definition, common ancestors of all living people. Eventually there will be a point in the past where all human beings can be divided into two groups: those who left no descendents today and those who are common ancestors of all living humans today. This point in time **is called the identical ancestors point and** is estimated to be between five thousand and fifteen thousand years ago (11).

This again points to the fact that the identical ancestors (common ancestors of all living humans) could be the biblical Adam and Eve and points to a time line of about ten thousand years before the present (between five thousand and fifteen thousand years ago), which is consistent with the life time of Adam and Eve, who is believed to have lived around ten thousand to twelve thousand years ago, and to be the common ancestors of all humans as stated in the Bible and Qur'an.

Genesis 3:20 (12) Adam named his wife Eve because she was the mother of all human beings.

Genesis 5:2 (13) He created them male and female, blessed them, and named them "mankind."

This implies the beginning of all mankind is from Adam and Eve.

In Acts 17:26 (14) Paul states, "From one man He created all races of mankind and made them live throughout the whole earth. He himself fixed beforehand the exact times and the limits of the places where they would live."

Qur'an 49:13 (6) Mankind, We created you from a single pair of a male and a female (Adam and Eve) and made you into Nations and tribes, that you may know each other.

Qur'an: 4:1 (15)Muhammad Asad. O people keep your duty to your Lord who created you from *a single entity (one living entity) [in Arabic nafs]* and created its mate of the same kind *[nafs may mean soul, kins, humankind, species]*. Many commentators believe it refers to species].

Qur'an:7:189 (16). It is He who created you all out of one living entity, and out of it brought into being its mate.

The Arabic term used for single, living entity (nafs) means among other things soul, spirit, animated being, species, and mankind.

In the explanation of this paragraph, the author refers to the learned opinion of another Muslim exegete (17). He is of the opinion that nafs means humankind. Many commentators now favor the term humankind or species.

This explanation fits very well with the scientific theory of human evolution. *In that Adam and Eve were originated from the pre-Adamic race* (hominids) of Homo sapiens (human kind or human species) by mutation and evolution. It is important to keep in mind that Adam and Eve did not suddenly get evolved from the then existing ape species. But from the existing human race—the Cro-Magnons (see chapter 6).

Qur'an:7:189 (16): "out of one living entity" also could mean, out of the primordial unicellular organism (one living entity) that appeared on earth 3.5 billion years ago, and from which all living forms including man evolved both male and female (the mates).

Qur'an mentions that human beings were raised from the progeny or seeds of other people (18). Translations by three different authors are given below.

6:133: a. He can take you away if He pleases and make him who He will succeed you, as He had raised you from the progeny of others.
   b. He may remove you, and make whom He pleases successors after you, even as He raised you up from the "**Seeds**" of other people.
   c. If He so wills, He may put an end to you and thereafter cause whom He wills to succeed you, even as He has brought you in to being out of **other people's seeds**".

This confirms the evolutionary pathway by which human beings were born out of previous humanoids through their seeds (ova and sperm).

In this context, let us examine the verse in Qur'an 76:1 (19)m, which says, "Has there not been an endless span of time before man (appeared—a time) when he was not yet a thing to be thought of." Here the author translates it as "appeared" (not created) as opposed to created, and also it emphasizes the long period of time before man appeared. In this we can see the endless span of time before man appeared on earth. God could have introduced man at anytime of His choosing. But evidently He let an endless span of time to pass, before the appearance of man on earth, pointing to the long span of a gradual evolutionary process as prescribed by God himself. Here we need to recall the conversation of Zachariah with the angels with respect to the prayer of Zachariah to have an offspring.

Qur'an:19:2-9: When he called out to God in the secrecy of his heart. "Thus it is; God says "This is easy for Me even as I have created *thee* aforetime out of nothing." This statement about man's origin from nothing points to our origin having started back from the big bang which also came out of nothing (from an infinitesimally small spot) and from the big bang everything in the universe came about, including the ingredients for the origin of man. Qur'an further states:19:67: "Does not man call to mind that We created him before out of nothing"

This also implies our origin started at the big bang (the ingredients for the origin [creation] of life) were originated from the big bang.

The divine scriptures all tell us that we have descended from one pair, namely, Adam and Eve.

Genetics and molecular biology also points to a Mitochondrial Eve (not the biblical Eve) as a matrilineal common ancestor who had lived one hundred forty thousand years ago. Similarly Y chromosome analysis points to a common male ancestor who had lived much later than the Mitochondrial Eve. These two hominids are not to be confused with the biblical Adam and Eve who were fully modern humans while the aforementioned Eve (mitochondrial) and Adam (Y chromosomal) were early hominids and not fully developed human beings. Nevertheless, we all are descendents from them who had lived in the remote past. This fact is reiterated in the above mentioned passages in Qur'an as we are descendants from progeny (children-[seeds]) of previous humanoids.

As mentioned above, a more recent person could become the most recent common ancestor (Y-MRCA); in our case it must be Adam as discussed above.

It is believed that the last ice age ended ten to fifteen thousand years ago (20). This coincides with agricultural development in the Near East and led to the settled life of humanity. This also falls into the lifetime of Adam and Eve, as Adam's sons were engaged in farming and raising animals.

As described earlier, all relevant factors established by paleoanthropologists, geneticists, and molecular scientists place the lifetime of Adam and Eve around ten to twelve thousand years ago. The fact that all human beings originated from this pair has been revealed both in the Bible and Qur'an, and the scientific facts all put together favor the theological belief that this pair to be the biblical Adam and Eve.

References for When Did Adam Live:

1. Bar-Yosef O. and A. Balfer Cohen. From Foraging to Farming. 1992.
2. Anne Brigitte and T. Douglas Price. From Foraging to Farming. 1992.
3. Lev-Yadun, Gopher and Abbo. 2000. Transition to Agriculture in Prehistory. Monographs in World History. 4:1992. 21-48.
4. Genesis 4:2.
5. Slow Birth of Agriculture. Heather Pringle. Science 282 (1998): 1446.
6. Bible:Acts:17:26.Qur'an: 49:13.
7. Lynn Jorde and Henry Harpending. Geneticist. University of Utah.
8. Toba Volcano. Wikipedia. http://en.wikipedia.org/wiki/Toba-catastrophe. Retrieved,3-30-2009.
9. Most Recent Common Ancestor. Douglas L. T. Rhode. Massachusetts Institute of Technology. Nov. 11, 2003. On the common ancestor of all living humans. (http://ted lab.mit.edu/~dr/papers/Rhode-MRCA-two.Pdf (2005). Dawkins, Richard. The Ancestors Tale; A Pilgrimage to the Dawn of Life (2004)
10. Spencer Wells. The Journey of Man: A Genetic Odyssey. Random House. ISBN.0-8129-7146-9.
11. Human. Wikipedia. http://en.wikipedia.org/wiki/Human.3-30-2009.
12. Genesis 3:20.
13. Ibid., 5:2.
14. Ibid., Acts: 17:26.
15. Qur'an 4:1.Muhammad Asad. The Message of The Qur'an.
16. Ibid., 7:189.
17. Muhammad Asad. The Message of The Qur'an verse 4:1. Reference, Muhammad Abduh. page 100.
18. Ibid., 6:133. Translations by: (a).Ahmed Ali,(b.)Maulana Muhammad Ali, (c).Muhammad Asad (Asad as one name)
19. Ibid., 76:1. Muhammad Asad's translation.
20. Wikipedia.http://en.wikipedia.org/wiki/Ice-age.

CHAPTER 5

The Genetics of Human Brain Evolution

Molecular biologists have some ideas as to the genetic changes that may underlie human brain evolution. Researchers at the University of Chicago (1), Harvard Medical School (2), and University of Leeds, UK (3) theorize whether the genes that cause microcephaly, an inherited human disorder in which the brain size is decreased, might include genes involved in human brain evolution. In 2002, mutation in the genes ASPM (abnormal spindle-like microcephaly associated) and microcephalin were identified as two causes of microcephaly. These researchers have since reported that both genes have been under selective pressure during primate evolution. ASPM encodes a protein involved in spindle formation. Therefore, changes in its sequence might cause increase in brain size, but some scientists caution that we do not know enough about the involvement of ASPM in this. Researchers have shown that deletion of a gene called Nde 1 in mice produces small brains and are investigating if variation in Nde l have been positively selected in human evolution (4).

Genetic researchers at the University of California (5) have found a gene HAR1 (human accelerated region) which is present in the brain of all animals. For most animals, this gene underwent little change over hundreds of millions of years, suggesting it is performing a vital function. Approximately 10 percent of human HAR1 gene is different from that of the chimpanzee. This change might have been the cause for the human brain to be three times larger than that of the chimpanzee. HAR1 is a new type of gene made of RNA instead of DNA. The HAR1 gene is very active early in the embryonic stage when certain neurons produce a protein called reelin that help guide the growth of brain cells and their connections. After this period of rapid neuron development, HAR1 is turned off. The HAR1 gene does not produce a protein unlike other genes. It is believed to be capable of regulating the activity of other genes according to geneticists (6).

Human Brain is still Evolving

The human brain may still be evolving. The evolution of large complex brain is the hallmark of human beings even though the size itself has not changed in the last two hundred thousand years. Researchers (1) analyzed sequences of two genes active in the brain, microcephalin and ASPM. Both regulate brain size. First, they sequenced microcephalin gene found in eighty-nine clinically diverse groups. They found dozens of variation (alleles) of the gene but one particular set stood out. These alleles all carry a specific mutation that changes the protein, the genes code for.

This distinctive mutation is now found in 70 percent of humans and half of this group carries completely identical variation of the gene. These suggest that the mutation arose recently and spread quickly through human species due to selection pressures rather than accumulation of random changes through neutral genetic drift. The new mutation is much more common in people from Europe, Middle East, and the Americas than those from sub-Saharan Africa. They estimate that this new variant of ASPM gene first appeared in humans somewhere between fourteen and fifteen thousand years ago. Their best estimate is five thousand eight hundred years ago.

They found that this variant also is more common in people from Europe and Middle East. The evidence for selection is compelling according to geneticists at the University of Copenhagen (7).

Many researchers doubt that there is any mechanism by which nature could be selecting for greater intelligence today as they believe culture has blocked the action that natural selection might have on our brains.

Scientists are now studying if these variants provide any cognitive advantage. Natural selection could have favored bigger brains, faster thinking, different personalities, or lower susceptibility to infections (8).

What relevance these new mutations have for Adam and Eve? It was about thirty-five thousand years ago when a brand of hominids, the most modern human beings, appeared in Europe migrated from Africa. Analysis of variations in the microcephalin gene suggest that one variant of microcephalin gene arose between sixty thousand and fourteen thousand years ago with thirty-seven thousand years ago being the best estimate. Microcephalin 1 is related to microcephaly. A derived form of microcephalin, microcephalin 5 appeared about thirty-seven thousand years ago (between fourteen thousand and sixty thousand years ago) which is associated with larger brain.(9). This time line corresponds to the appearance of the anatomically modern man with larger brains than that of ours, the pre-Adamic generation of hominids called the Cro-Magnons. They had better tools, early music instruments, painting capabilities, and social structure than their contemporaries, the Neanderthals (considered a different hominid species).

The new variant of ASPM gene first appeared in human species between fourteen thousand and five thousand years ago, with best estimate being five thousand eight hundred years ago. The variant ASPM gene is considered to be the driving force for the development of language and writing in human history.

Paleoanthropologists have evidence that agriculture first appeared in the fertile crescent (which is located in the Near East and includes parts of present-day Turkey, Iran, Syria and Iraq), about ten to twelve thousand years ago, pointing out an association of the time frame of the appearance of the mutant ASPM gene, settled lifestyle of humans, appearance of agriculture, domestication of animals and a little later, the invention of letters and writing. Even though these developments in human history might not fall into an exact and strict time line in terms of dates, month, or even hundreds of years, the confluence of these significant events into a relatively comparable time line in our past history also is commensurate with the beginning of the civilized society with the arrival of the first "human couple" Adam and Eve.

We have genetic evidence as described above (when compared with millions of years of hominid evolution) that two mutant genes in the brain appeared between thirty-seven thousand and five thousand eight hundred years ago, and during that time line we see the appearance of modern man, the Cro-Magnons and later the appearance of Adam and Eve.

As discussed earlier, Adam exhibited many extraordinary features, most notable being his longevity of 930 years at his death (Gen. 5:4, 5) (10). This long life cannot be corroborated by scientific means but we have to believe it as a biblical evidence. In addition, God had determined that Adam is the fully developed human being probably on the basis of a well-developed brain, to have God consciousness. Also the subservience to and understanding and conceptualization of the Supreme Being, God, and the faculty to carry out the commandments of God might have been the result of the brain development. According to Qur'an, Adam was fully developed. Verse 15:29; 38:72 (11) Muhammad Asad. "And when I have *formed him fully* and breathed in to him **of my spirit**, fall down in prostration". From this, one can assume that Adam had a fully developed physical morphology and more importantly that he had a fully develop brain. This is the first time that God mentioned that His spirit has been infused to the human being to suggest the special brain area where spirituality and God consciousness are nurtured and had been imparted to Adam and that Adam was the first person to acquire it. (Genesis:2:7: he breathed life giving breath in to his nostrils and he became alive. Qur'an:38:72:When I have fashioned hih fully and breathed in to him of My spirit,fall ye down in obeisance unto him).

References for The Genetics of Human Brain Evolution

1. Bruce Lahn. Geneticist. University of Chicago.
2. Christopher Walsh. Harvard Medical School. Boston. Massachusetts.
3. Geoffrey Woods. University of Leeds. U.K.
4. Yanyi Feng; Christopher Walsh. Neuron. vol.44.aoct.2004.
5. David Haussler. University of California, Santa Cruz.
6. Sofie Salama. Howard Hughes Medical Institute. Nature (April 2006).
7. Rasmus Nielson. University of Copenhagen. Denmark
8. Wikipedia. Journal Science 309:1717.
9. Wikipedia.http://en.wikipedia.org/wiki/Brain-size-and-evolutio; http://en.wikipedia.org/wiki/Microcephalin.
10. Genesis 5:4, 5.
11. Qur'an 15:29; 38:72.Muhammad Asad.The Message of The Qur'an.

CHAPTER 6

The Pre-Adamic People: the Cro-Magnons.

The First Generation of Mankind

The traditional theological belief, that there were no other human beings at the time of Adam is now totally disproved and the fact there were enough human beings for Adam's children to marry outside their family will be described.

Hominid evolution has gone through several stages (Qur'an (1) (2)).

In Europe, up until thirty thousand years ago, a hominid species lived called Neanderthals (3) belonging to the species Homo neanderthalensis. The Neanderthals died out by about thirty thousand years ago; the reason for their extinction is not clear. The name Neanderthal was given to this species because the first skeletal remains of these hominids were found in the valley of the river Dussel in Germany, which was called the Neander valley. The name Neander was given to this valley to honor a theologian named Joachim Neander who lived nearby in the seventeenth century. There are many speculations regarding the reasons for their extinction namely their inability to survive due to competition with more advanced Cro-Magnons (homo sapiens sapiens) for available resources, or war with the newcomers (the Cro-Magnons). Another reason might have been the introduction of new diseases by the Cro-Magnons, against which the Neanderthals had no immunity. The Cro-Magnons had better tools and hunting techniques than the Neanderthals which had given the former a survival advantage. The extinction may also be due to extreme climatic changes in the form of glaciations.

In March 1868, Lois Lartet, a geologist, discovered the first five skeletons in a Cro-Magnon cave shelter. These were the remains of what is called the Cro-Magnons (most modern men) (4) who lived thirty-five thousand years ago. The name Cro-Magnon is not the name of a species, but it is the name of the place where the first skeletons of this race were found. In paleontology, the various names given to each species are the names of the places where their fossils were found. The Cro-Magnons belong to the Homo sapiens sapiens otherwise called the most modern human beings like us.

Cro-Magnon is the name of a rock shelter near Les Eyzies-de-Tayac, Dordogne, France, where several prehistoric skeletons were found in 1868. Geologists and archaeologists dated these skeletons to be belonging to the upper Paleolithic age (thirty-five thousand to ten thousand years ago) (5). Most likely twenty-five thousand years ago. At Cro-Magnon site, there were remains of more than ten individuals. One specimen was the cranium and mandible of a fifty-year-old male. This is known as the Old man of Cro-Magnon and has been regarded as the prototype of Cro-Magnon people. Subsequently many more specimens from different regions have been recovered.

The Cro-Magnons were people like us in all respects. Some consider them a separate race of human beings. Physically indistinguishable except some changes in the skull and long bones, From the present day living human beings, the homo sapiens sapiens. The DNA analysis shows that they were identical to us genetically.

Physical characteristics of the Cro-Magnons:

Early investigators were impressed with their stature. The reconstruction of the old Cro-Magnon suggested that he is about six feet and three to five inches tall. Other site discoveries also suggest that the Cro-Magnons were very tall. The skull is long (dolichocephalic). The parietal bones on the sides of the skull were outward bulging. The forehead is straight with minimal brow ridge. The occipital bone (the back of the skull) projects backward. The cranial capacity (volume inside the skull) is very large, 1,600 cc. The average present-day human's brain is relatively smaller, about 1,500 cc. The face is wide. The maxilla (upper jaw) projects forward. This combination of skull features is considered a common feature of the Cro-Magnons. The eye sockets are square and low set. The nose is narrow and projecting. The mandible is robust with a massive ramus (the upward going portion of the mandible) showing points of muscular attachments. The chin was prominent. The dentition of Cro-Magnons and the present day human beings are identical. The rest of the skeletal parts that were recovered from other sites reveal that the forearm and the thigh were long. The thighbone has a prominent ridge on the back and the tibia is flattened from back to front. The hand is large with short fingers. The foot has a prominent heel.

The skeletal finds of the Cro-Magnons established their range of existence from Europe to Asia and North Africa. Two French pre historians, A. de Quatrefages and Ernst Hamy in 1882 took the Cro-Magnon fossils to be prototype of a Cro-Magnon race (5) as opposed to the Neanderthal race, the first remains of which were found about twenty-five years earlier. The Cro-Magnons were considered to be the most ancient form of Homo sapiens sapiens.

The physical characteristics based on the skeletal remains suggest that these Cro-Magnon people were of the size of giants compared with the earlier species, the Neanderthals and ourselves.

Dwellings:

The Cro-Magnons lived in caves and rock shelters made by overhanging rocks. Also archaeologists have evidence of foundation stones laid in the shape of houses or huts suggesting that they were living in man-made dwellings. The Cro-Magnons had a fairly settled life as these shelters were occupied continuously except when hunting or the weather made them move. They might have had several huts or so in one camp. They carried the prey after hunting to the camp and shared it with others as evidenced by an archaeological find in France where the bony parts of the same animal was found in different campfire sites separated by hundreds of feet, presumably occupied by different families (6).

During winter, large huts were made to hold the entire tribe with many entrances and places to make fire. During summer, easily movable huts were used. The remains of these encampments were found at a Ukrainian site (7).

Burial:

After studying the burial sites, it is speculated that these people believed in some sort of an afterlife. Most of the skeletons were buried with carved pendants, bracelets, and other grave goods. Some were buried outstretched, others were flexed. Some graves were covered with rock slabs. Experts believe, after examining the burial characteristics and the grave goods, that the Cro-Magnons exhibited for the first time the existence of religious experience in human history.

Cave paintings:

Cro-Magnons are well known for their cave paintings. Over two hundred caves with Cro-Magnon artwork have been discovered and more are being uncovered. Most of the paintings consisted of animals they hunted, others were of panthers, bears, and wooly rhinos. They used brushes and oral spray painting techniques. These colors were made of iron oxide, black manganese, and other mineral pigments.

Cognitive thinking:

They created a type of lunar calendar in order to understand the seasons of herd movement. Bone and stone plaques with regular markings have been unearthed from a Cro-Magnon site in France and has been interpreted as representing to keep hunting tallies or other forms of record keeping. These may be some highly complex symbolic systems, we will never know (Ian Tattersall. Becoming Human) (6).

They developed a method of curing and preserving meat throughout the cold winters by digging holes in the permafrost. Hot stones were used to heat water in skin-lined pits. They were baking clay statuettes in kilns that heated up to 800 degree Fahrenheit.

Tool making:

The Cro-Magnons made retouched blade tools and scrapers, bruins (chisel-like tools) bone tools, and tools for smoothing and scraping leather, bars of antler or bone with holes in them.

Hunting techniques:

Very little is known about their techniques but must have been better than that of Neanderthals. They have used traps, bow and arrow, and poisons. Boats and rafts were used for fishing. Fishnets were made of vines and hooks from animal bones.

They were considered to have some histrionic talents as evidenced by the finding of possibly a Stone Age equivalent of a xylophone (litho phone) (6).

It is in these Cro-Magnons that we see for the first time the beginnings of the testimonials befitting to the modern humans. Their social life, collective hunting and fishing, distributing the spoils of foraging among the neighbor dwellers, arts, music, and signs of belief in the afterlife. But yet from God's standpoint, they were not fully developed to carry the baton of humanity until Adam appeared on earth with significant beneficial mutations out of the existing human race the Cro-Magnons (the nafs, human kind), whom God considered the fully developed human being mentally and physically (8).

Genetics:

A team of scientists have succeeded in retrieving DNA from Cro-Magnons who are believed to be the ancestors of humans living today (9). From the rib and leg bones of two individuals found from the Paglicci cave, a Paleolithic site in southern Italy, they analyzed segments of mitochondrial DNA. The sequences fall "well within" the range of variation of modern humans and "differ sharply" from findings on three Neanderthals that have been published so far. Even though Neanderthals died out about thirty thousand years ago, they were contemporaries of Cro-Magnons, and there is no evidence for Neanderthal blood in present-day humans or Cro-Magnons. One of the Cro-Magnons fossils dates back to twenty five thousand years ago and another to twenty-three thousand years ago. Neanderthal fossils that have yielded mitochondrial DNA range from twenty-nine thousand years to forty-two thousand years ago. There was no evidence for contamination from either the animals unearthed from the cave or from people who had handled the specimen, according to the scientists.

In conclusion, the Cro-Magnons, a separate species of Homo sapiens sapiens, that is us, have exhibited identical characteristics including a belief in the afterlife. We cannot ascertain their concept of God as we conceptualize Him, but their cave paintings showed probably worshipping female symbols of God and earth as it is the females who give birth to the off springs and new life, and the earth, since it is the earth that gives sustenance.

Unfortunately, they disappeared about ten to fifteen thousand years ago. How and why the Cro-Magnons went extinct is unclear.

But it is worthwhile to recall the passages from Qur'an, pertaining to the destruction of previous generations, "How many generations we have destroyed before you" (10). Those destroyed generations were, by far, from the descendents of Adam and Eve; and apparently, they were warned before their destruction through prophets or warners. Whether these destroyed generations also include the generations of previous hominids from

Australopithecus including the recent ones like the Neanderthals and the Cro-Magnons is certainly possible. However, these generations did not have any prophets or warners as they were not fully developed human beings, and there was no need to send a prophet to them. Some verses specifically mention people or town destroyed after warning was given to them (11). There are other verses that mention about the destruction of previous generations. It is also mentioned that a term was appointed to various populations or generations. Does this suggest that the previous species that were destroyed or went extinct was due to various calamities brought on by God for their extinction? The span of existence (the duration of existence of the species on earth) of the previous species before going extinct shows a declining pattern from the Australopithecus through the Neanderthals to the Cro-Magnons. But the life span of individuals (longevity of individuals) in the Neanderthals (average of 55 years) and Cro-Magnons (average of 65 years) shows significant improvement. It was very noticeable in Adam and Eve.(the biblical account of the Age of Adam was 930 years.)

The earliest hominid species, the Australopithecus, lived from four million years ago till one million years ago; the recent ones, the Neanderthals, lived from six hundred thousand years ago till thirty thousand years ago; and our immediate predecessors, the Cro-Magnons, lived from thirty-five thousand years ago till ten to fifteen thousand years ago. In that order, the span of existence of our species might be even shorter.

Genesis 1:26 (12) states, "Then God said, 'And now we will make human beings: They will be like Us and resemble Us. They will have power over the fishes, the birds, and all animals, domestic and wild." (The King James Version does not mention domestic animals, but instead says cattle.)

Genesis 1:28 says, "I am putting you in charge of the fish, the birds, and all the wild animals." Genesis 1:29 says, "I have provided all kinds of grain and all kinds of fruits for you to eat." (Here it is worth noting that there is no mention of cultivation and agriculture, and suggests those beings were hunter gatherers who were the pre-Adamic people.) This statement in the Bible comes before the creation of Adam, Gen :2:7 and Adam was specifically ordered to cultivate in the garden., suggesting the end to hunter gathering and the beginning of agriculture.

Genesis: 2:7 (13) states, "Then the Lord God took some soil from the ground and formed a man out of it." (Adam)

Genesis 2:15 (Good News Bible), "Then the Lord God placed the man in the Garden of Eden to cultivate it and guard it."

Genesis 4:2, "Later she (Eve) gave birth to another son, Abel. Abel became a shepherd, but Cain was a farmer."

Those people, before Adam was created, were obviously the hunter-gatherers. As mentioned with reference to Adam's creation, he was to cultivate the land, and Abel was a shepherd and Cain was a farmer. Here we have the beginning of agriculture and domestication of animals. There is no inference whether this settled life started with Adam and Eve or before them, except that the information in the bible and Qur'an says they were leading a settled life with farming and domesticated animals, unlike hunter gatherers. (Adam and Eve were put in the garden to live and cultivate there and were not intended to be hunter gatherers). There is indication that some settled life was seen among the pre-Adamic people, the Cro-Magnons.

Therefore, we have biblical evidence, in addition to the fossil evidence, to say that there were people on earth before Adam. As will be discussed, there are evidences in Qur'an that suggest that there were humanlike species on earth before Adam.

References for Cro-Magnons:

1. Qur'an 71:14.
2. "Human Evolution." Encyclopedia Britannica. 2004. Encyclopedia Britannica Premium Service. http://w.w.w.britannica.com/eb/article?eu127622.
3. Wikipedia, retrieved 5-4-2008.http://en.wikipedia.org/wiki/Neanderthals.
4. Wikipedia. Ibid.http://en.wikipedia.org/wiki/Cro-Magnons.
5. A. de Quatrefage and Ernst Hamy. "Human Evolution." Encyclopedia Britannica. 2004.
6. Ian Tattersall. Becoming a Human (1998) Chap. 1.
7. Andrea E. http://cas.bellarmine.edu/tietjen/human%2os%201999/andrea-e-htm.
8. Qur'an 38:72.
9. Caramelli, D. and G.Bartorelle. 2003. "Evidence for Genetic Discontinuity between Neanderthals and 24000 years old anatomically modern Europeans." Proc. National Academy of Sciences 23 (May 2003). vol. 300, no. 5623: 1231.
10. Qur'an 19:98; 36:31; 32:26.
11. Qur'an 26:184; 32:26; 19:98; 36:31; 32:26.
12. Genesis 1:26, 28, 29.
13. 2:7,15; 4:2.

CHAPTER 7

Second Generation of Mankind.

The Adamic People

Adam and Eve: The Beginning of the Second Generation:

The Adamic People

Adam: Age: 930 years.
Lived: ten to twelve thousand years ago.
Eve: Probably same age. Eve died soon after Adam's death.

This time line of Adam's lifetime can be reasonably presumed as discussed earlier (chapter 4) on the basis of the following land marks:

Evidence for new brain evolution about ten to thirty-seven thousand years ago. This suggests that Adam and Eve probably were the earliest ones to acquire this mutant brain tissue.

Development of agriculture about ten to twelve thousand years ago. Adam was to cultivate in the garden of Eden,and Cain was a farmer and Abel a shepherd

Domestication of animals ten to twelve thousand years ago.

End of last glaciation, twelve thousand years ago.

Return of warm climate that facilitated farming and agriculture.

The identical ancestral point.

The disappearance of the pre-Adamic race called the Cro-Magnons by 10,000 years ago. There are no other fossils after the disappearence of the Cro-Magnons other than that of the Adamic race. Adam and Eve appeared towards the end of the existence of the Cro-Magnon race.

From these circumstantial evidences, one can conclude that Adam and Eve lived around ten thousand to twelve thousand years before the present, a couple of thousand years overlapping on either side.

On the basis of the longevity of Adam and Eve (930 years), and the appearance of certain mutant genes in the brain (ASPH, Microcephalin 5, HAR 1 [Human accelerated region] during the time period of their life time, it can be concluded that Adam and Eve were of a different type (race) of human beings due to the above mentioned mutations, compared to the pre-Adamic race, the Cro-Magnons.

This fact is echoed in Qur'an in that Adam is described as a fully developed human being: 15:29: "when I have formed (fashioned, made complete) him fully and breathed into him of my spirit, fall down before him in prostration. This is the first time God breathed His spirit in to the human species, as an indication that Adam and his progeny are fully developed human beings capable of being fully God conscious. It is worth recalling the statements in the Qur'an that we may be replaced by another kind (race) of people as Adam and Eve came about from the pre-Adamic race (the Cro-Magnons) by evolutionary changes and replaced them completely by their (Adam's) progeny. Qur'an: 76:26: "Bu when We will We can substitute the like of them by a complete change." Or it may be to another species unlike us. Qur'an: 47:38: "If you turn back He will substitute in your stead another people, then they would not be like you."

Let us briefly look at the scenario by which humanity spread from these two persons without the need to have marriage between their children, which we call incest. The human beings from Adam and Eve onwards will be referred to as the second generation of mankind or the Adamic people.

As we have seen, the first generation of modern humans, the pre—Adamic race, the Cro-Magnons, were living ten thousand to fifteen thousand years before the present and went extinct (lived from thirty five thousand years to ten thousand years before present). The biblical Adam and Eve were also living at that time. They must have been contemporaries for a while from the accumulated evidence as presented before. Adam and Eve had several children. Qur'an only refers to two sons. But various biblical sources indicate that Adam and Eve had several children.

Genesis 5:3-5 (1) "When Adam was 130 years old he had a son who was like him, and he named him Seth." Further it says, "After that Adam lived another 800 years. He had other children and Adam died at the age of 930." There is no mention of how many children Adam and Eve had. The Jewish historian Flavius Josephus (AD 37-100) (2) mentions that Adam had thirty-two sons and twenty-three daughters.

Adam's children and their contemporary human beings, the Cro-Magnons' children, could marry each other. They will have healthy off springs as they were of the same genetic stock. But there is one big difference that would not be discernible to the naked eye. That is the mutation that must have occurred in the longevity gene of Adam and probably in Eve and other beneficial mutations likely in the brain, like ASPM gene (chapter 5). We do not have any evidence whether physical, molecular, or other evidence to prove that Adam and Eve lived as long as they did as described in the Bible. Adam lived 930 years, And Eve of the same age or a little longer as she died later than Adam.

This certainly is an astonishing long period of lifetime. And it is certainly possible with mutation in the longevity gene. Realizing the fact that the life span of the previous hominids, the Neanderthals was less than fifty years and that of the later hominids, the homo sapiens sapiens (the Cro-Magnons) life span was much better around sixty to sixty five years. This shows that in hominid evolution, each new species have been noted to have better longevity. Their brain size also increased. Therefore, it is quite possible that the biblical life span of Adam and Eve is a result of genetic mutation in the longevity gene, in addition to other possible genetic alterations giving them certain survival advantage.

People have doubts about the age of Adam and Eve as recorded in the Bible. How did the people then know about a person's lifetime as they were not clever enough to keep time? And their lack of knowledge in numerals and calculations. All we need is to look at the first generation of us, the Cro-Magnons, who indeed had a lunar calendar and had the knowledge of timekeeping (3) (Ian Tattersall). Therefore, the Adamic people (Adam's generation) would have had the same or even better means of timekeeping.

As we know, the Cro-Magnons had longevity of around sixty to sixty five years. Adam and Eve lived for 930 years or so as described in the bible. What is the reason for this unusual longevity? This has to be based on several reasons, which are unclear to us including most importantly the mutation on the longevity gene. Scientists have located the longevity gene on chromosome 4 and probably on chromosome 11 and 16 (chapter 9).

We cannot prove whether Adam and Eve had a beneficial mutation on their longevity gene. In this case, we can only go by historical evidence for Adam's longevity. It is also worth noting that even present-day humans live much longer than that of the Cro-Magnons. Many of the descendents of Adam, as described in the religious relics, tell us about the very long life span of many prophets including Abraham who lived 175 years. Scientists have noted allelic changes in the DNA of a family with long life span (chapter 9). From these, we can speculate that those ancestors of humanity (Adam and Eve) must have had a beneficial mutation on their longevity genes.

On the basis of this, we can surmise that the recipients of this longevity gene of Adam, among the offsprings from wedlock between the children of Cro-Magnons and that of Adam and Eve, will propagate in larger numbers due to their longer life span and other survival advantages due to mutation in the brain and will proliferate like a wildfire, while the possessors of the Cro-Magnon genes which did not have the longevity factor or other survival advantage and with shorter life span will die out.

Just like what we have seen in the cases of previous hominid species, when the newer species came about with certain survival advantage due to a better brain [due to mutation],and resultant improved faculties will survive, and the previous species will die out.

We are unable to explain the cause or causes for the disappearance of our own ancestors (the Cro-Magnons) about ten thousand to fifteen thousand years before the present. One can speculate (not proven) that the disappearance of the Cro-Magnons was due to the arrival of the longer living pair of humans (Adam and Eve) with their longevity gene mutation positively benefiting their descendents into living longer and having more off springs and causing the disappearance of the short lived Cro-Magnons.

It is believed that the dinosaurs became extinct 65 million years ago due to a meteorite fall, causing huge amounts of dust spewing into the atmosphere, causing the destruction of all vegetations.

It is also claimed that the Toba volcano (4), about seventy thousand years ago, caused near extinction of human species, leading to a bottleneck (probably the number of human species were down to a few thousand persons in the world at that time).

We cannot find any other reasons for the extinction of the Cro-Magnons. It may not be due to food shortage as agriculture was developed by ten to twelve thousand years ago when the Cro-Magnons were believed to have gone extinct, at a time, when food supply should have been adequate for the population. Nor do we have any evidence for a natural catastrophe or a meteorite impact for their extinction.

The abovementioned genetic mechanism will be enough to explain the disappearance of the Cro-Magnons (mating between short lived Cro-Magnons and longer living Adam's children with their probable mutant brain and survival advantage).

This will explain the Biblical and the Qur'anic statements that we the present day human beings are the off springs (descendants) of Adam and Eve (the single pair). Even though we have the Cro-Magnon genes in us, from a genetic stand point we can say that we are descendants of Adam and Eve as described above. Human genome contains genetic material identical to chimpanzee, mouse and cattle and others, but we are not called the descendants of these species.(From an evolutionary stand point we are evolved from these lower specie, though)

This will explain the statements in the Bible and Qur'an about us (the present-day human beings). It is said in the Bible Acts : 17:26 (5) that all human beings are descendents from Adam. "From one man He created all races of mankind and made them live throughout the whole earth". And the Qur'an states that all human beings are made out of a single pair (Adam and Eve) 49:13(6). In this scenario as described above, the oft-repeated assertion that the sons and daughters of Adam and Eve had to marry each other (committing incest) becomes invalid and the thought sacrilegious. Please remember those incestuous theories are only speculations on the basis of the then prevalent view that Adam and Eve were the only two human beings on earth at that time, and consequently they had no choice but to commit incest.

I believe the theory of incest was also based on the statement in the Genesis and in the Qur'an as described above, that the present day human beings on earth are created out of this one pair (Adam and Eve). A literal belief in those passages namely that all human beings are created out of one pair can only lead us to the path of incest by Adam's children for the propagation of humanity, even if there were other people around. How could anyone say that we are the descendants of only Adam and Eve, if their children married from other community?

The religious scholars who subscribed to the theory of incest, did not have the information revealed by the fossils, nor the intricate mechanisms of the DNA and genetics and therefore had no other way to explain the scriptural statements that all human beings are descendants of this one pair

(Adam and Eve), other than by invoking incest being committed by Adam's children. We know now that the Cro-Magnons, who were there before Adam came, were genetically identical to us, but has gone extinct. They are not here to lay claim on us to say that they were our fore fathers. Only the Adamic race is left behind. The beneficial mutation present in Adam and Eve will enable their progeny to populate the world solely, by replacing others There fore genetically and naturally we are the descendants of Adam and Eve without having to commit incest by their children.

We now have ample evidence, on the basis of fossils, anthropology, and genetics, that there were perfectly modern humans (the Cro-Magnon race) before Adam and they were genetically similar to us so that marriage between Cro-Magnons' and Adam's children will have fertile off springs for the propagation of mankind. There is no compelling reason to believe that the children of Adam and Eve had to commit incest.

References for Adam and Eve: the Second Generation:

1. Genesis 5:3-5.
2. Flavius Josephus (AD 30-100). William Whitson, translator. The Complete Work of Josephus. Kregel Publications. 1981. p. 27. Grand Rapids, Michigan.
3. Ian Tattersall. Becoming Human.
4. Wikipedia. Toba Volcano. http://en.wikipedia.org/wiki/lake-Tobo.
5. The Bible: Acts :17:26
6. Qur'an 49:13.

CHAPTER 8

The Giants in the Bible and Qur'an

The Giants Who Lived in Ancient Times

Biblical history: Genesis 6:1 (1)

"When mankind spread all over the world and girls were being born some of the supernatural beings saw that these girls were beautiful so they took the ones they liked." In those days and even later, there were giants on earth who were descendents of human females and supernatural beings (men). They were heroes and famous men of long ago.

Numbers 13: 33 (2) "And we have seen giants there, the descendents of Anak."

Deuteronomy 1:28 (3) "People there are stronger and taller than we are and that they live in cities with walls that reach the skies, They saw giants there." [?sons of Anak]

Deuteronomy 2:10 "A mighty race of giants called Emim used to live in Ar. They were tall as the Anakim, another race of giants."

Deuteronomy 2:21 "They were as tall as Anakim. There were many of them and they were a mighty race. But the Lord destroyed them, so that the ammonites took over their land and settled there."

References in Qur'an:

There are several references in Qur'an about a people called Ad (Qur'an:89: 6-8 [Asad]) (6), "Art thou not aware of how thy sustainer has dealt with the Ad people, the people of Iram the many pillared, the like of whom have never been reared in all the land."

Asad's commentary notes (page 213) that Hud, prophet of Ad people, is the Arabic name for Judah (Yahuda in Hebrew). He is believed to be the first Arabian prophet and may be identical to the biblical Eber, the ancestor of the Hebrews. The commentary further notes that this tribe might have crossed over from Arabia to Mesopotamia in pre-Abrahamic times. The tribe of Ad lived in the vast desert territory known as Al-Ahqaf, between Uman and Hadramawt. They had great power and influence. The Ad people disappeared centuries before the arrival of Islam.

Qur'an 7:65; 89:8 (commentary Yusuf Ali) (7) states "The Ad people were fourth in generation to Noah. They occupied a large territory in Southern Arabia extending from Persian Gulf to Yemen to Red Sea. The people were tall in stature and were great builders. But their disobedience to God caused a three-year famine and later a terrible blast of wind storm destroyed them perhaps leaving some remnants called 'later Ads.' This land was very prosperous and contained ruins and inscriptions. In the time of Muawiya, some precious stones were found among the ruins of this locality. A bronze lion's head and a bronze piece of gutter with Sabian inscriptions were found recently in Najran and have been described in the British Museum Quarterly 11, no. 4, September 1937(8).

The tomb of the prophet Hud is believed to be in a place ninety miles north of Mukalla. There are ruins and inscriptions in the neighborhood. See Hadramut: Some of its Mysteries Unveiled by D. van der Muelen and H. von Wissmann, Leyden, 1932 (9).

Their great stature refers to their tall nature or their great power and influence. Hud was the prophet of Ad people, and Hud was known to be very tall and, it can be assumed that the Ad people were very tall and can be described as giants. It is claimed that the tomb of the prophet Hud is unusually long, whether this is due to his height or something else is not clear.

Muslim exegetes maintain that there were giants among original Arab peoples and their prophets like Hud and Salih. (The tombs of these prophets are larger than normal.) There were giants in Moses's time belonging to the Amalekites tribe.

2:251 "By Allah's (God's) will, they routed them. And David slew Goliath and Allah (God) gave him power and wisdom. The giant Goliath according to Muslim exegetes may be from the tribe of Amalekites."

5:22 "O Moses in this land are people of exceeding strength. Never shall we enter it until they leave. If they leave then shall we enter."

18:94 "O Dhu al Qarnayn, the Gog and Magog people do great mischief on earth.

Some believe Gog (Awj) also called Ibn Aneq was a son of Adam's daughter." (Mecca and Eden by Brannan Wheeler) (10).

These tall and mighty people as described in the Bible and Qur'an may be the ones referred to as giants in the Bible and Qur'an

My own interpretation is that the giants mentioned both in the Bible and Qur'an may well be the tall, muscular, and gracile pre-Adamic people called the Cro-Magnons, whose remnants might have survived a little longer after Adam appeared. But one needs to consider the fact that the Ad people were living after Adam and may also be the remnants of the pre-Adamic race called the Cro-Magnons. Nevertheless, there were giants on earth before, and by the time Qur'an was revealed, they all have disappeared. And any vestiges of the Cro-Magnons were all wiped out and only the descendents of Adam and Eve remains as of today as mentioned in the Bible and Qur'an.

Qur'an says that God had destroyed several previous generations. Qur'an also says that he will not destroy a nation before a warner had been sent (26:208) (11). Many of the pre-Adamic races might have been destroyed without a messenger being sent because they were not fully developed human beings to understand any kind of instructions or restrictions, given by God and there was no reason to send a messenger to them. Just like apes that will not benefit from a warner or messenger. Then what was the reason for God to destroy those pre-Adamic people? Did they go extinct due to natural catastrophes or was it a divine predetermined plan to eliminate them. It must be for the fully developed human beings like Adam and Eve to appear by way of evolution and prosper without having to share the resources with them. It is also possible that by eliminating the less developed pre-Adamic people, the Adamic race don't have to live side by side with the lesser hominids.

Archeology: The Giants:

In Australia, excavation noted continuous occupation of human races in Ananka burial site in Murray Basin. Archaeologists found seven feet tall people from 6000 BC to 4000 BC (12).

A Tasmanian devil's (an extinct animal) teeth were found adorned around the neck of one of them, which points to certain ancient burial practices. This was found in the Lake Nitchie burial site and is dated to Adam's time (13).

The Kowe Swamp people had long heads and are considered as pre-Adamic.

In Adam and Adamite by Dominick McCausland, Hebrew Awdam (Adam) means "a rosy fair complexion" and suggests that Adam may be representing a new race (14).

The reason to dwell on these giants of the past is to bring into light the people who were around during Adam's time. In human evolution, we see the earliest hominid species as the Australopithecus, then Homo habilis, Homo erectus, all considered as transitional hominids, and most recent ancestors as Cro-Magnons. We need to examine the relationship of the fossils of this magnanimous species (the Cro-Magnons with their innovations and technological advancements) compared to the previous species and/or their contemporary species, the Neanderthals. In order to make a case that these Cro-Magnons are indeed the same giants described in the scriptures, we need to examine their physical characteristics supported by archaeological evidences as described above and can be surmisde that the Cro-Magnons indeed had the stature of giants.

References for the Giants:

1. Genesis 6:1.
2. Bible: Numbers 13:33.
3. Deuteronomy 1:28.
4. Ibid., 2:10.
5. Ibid., 2:21.
6. Qur'an 89:6. Muhammad Asad's translation.
7. Ibid., 7:65; 89:8. Yusuf Ali's translation.
8. British Museum Quarterly 11, no. 4 (September 1937).
9. D. van der Muelen and H. von Wissman. Leyden.1932.
10. Mecca and Eden :Rituals in, Relics and territory Islam. Brannan Wheeler.
11. Qur'an 26:208.
12. Australia. Murray Basin excavations.
13. Lake Nitchie burial site excavations.http://www.wentworth.rsw.gov.au/heritage/study/appendix5.php?id=112.
14. Adam and Adamite. Dominick McCausland. Richard Bentley & sons. London

CHAPTER 9

The Longevity Gene

Can genetic variation (mutation) influence longevity? Scientists have been experimenting to find out if alteration in genetic material can prolong survival and disease-free life.

In October 2004, Biological research (1) discovered that manipulating just one gene Sir2 in mouse could affect longevity of mouse. In their research, they found that a version of the Sir2 gene releases fat from storage tissues by turning off other genes that help fat storage. The fat moves into bloodstream and travels to other tissues and get burnt, and this keeps the mouse lean and for unknown reasons, young looking and healthy into old age.

In August 2001, researchers (2) (3) reported that a region on chromosome 4 holds the key for longevity. The researchers believe among hundreds of genes in that region on chromosome 4, there is a gene or genes whose modification can prolong life. They studied genes from 308 long-lived people and 139 siblings. They did not have bad gene alleles at the loci involved in age-related diseases. But they had alleles that enabled them to live often twenty years beyond their life expectancy. An allele is an alternate form of a gene. They found that on chromosome 4 there was a little blip of allele sharing, that was greater than would be expected by chance.

It is also known that chromosomes 11 and 16 have loci for longevity.

Such an allele transformation (mutation), in addition to other yet unidentified genetic mechanisms with survival advantage, might have happened in Adam and Eve to account for their extraordinary longevity as recorded in the Bible (930 years) though we do not have any scientific ratification of it. It is to be recalled that the Neanderthals lived to an average age of forty-five years, and the Cro-Magnons lived for an average age of sixty to sixty-five years. Genetic alteration can indeed alter longevity as seen by the abovementioned scientific research. In addition to longevity genes, other genes involved in immunity for prevention of diseases, agricultural advancement, and better intelligence all can help with longer life.

Adam and Eve, from the biblical account, had good longevity (genes) and that alone can cause an explosion of the population of their descendents who carry this advantage (genetic), when intermarriage occurred between the children of Adam and Eve and those of the Cro-Magnons, whose life expectancy was around sixty to sixty-five years. The Cro-Magnon gene(without this survival advantage) carriers will die early, leading to fewer descendents, and eventually all the recipients of the Cro-Magnon genes will die out. But all siblings who have acquired the long-living (longevity) gene from Adam and Eve will survive and prosper. Therefore, as stated in the Bible and the Qur'an, all human beings living today are descendents of Adam and Eve genetically.

We have scientific and other indications that we are descendents of a pair of human beings who lived sometime between ten thousand and fifteen thousand years ago. Even though we do not have direct incontrovertible evidence, the totality of evidence from paleontology, anthropology, the identical ancestor point, fossil record, recent brain mutation, and the longevity factor points to the biblical Adam and Eve as our sole ancestors. We do not have DNA from Adam or Eve for confirmation, but we do have enough corroborative evidence to say so.

It is to be reiterated that even though we are descendents of these two individuals Adam and Eve, they were not the only two persons alive at their life time. This ingenious and divine plan of decimating one race (the Cro-Magnons) with which Adam's children interbred, and propagated another race (the Adamic race—that is us) through gene mutation and genetic variation is beyond our imagination. Qur'an 6:133(4) says, "Appoint whom He will as your successor, even as he raised you up from the posterity (**Seeds**) of other people." Looking into the past, we see the transformation of species from one to the next and the disappearance of previous species, by creating subtle changes in the amino acid sequence in the DNA (in the genes) called mutation and nature's influence on them. This is mind-boggling.

References for Longevity Gene:

1. Leonard Guarente. Massachusetts Institute of Technology.
2. Louis M. Kunkel, and Thomas Perls. Proceedings of the National Academy of Sciences. Aug. 28, 2001.
3. Research from Children's Memorial Hospital, Boston; Harvard Medical School and Beth Israel Medical Center.
4. Qur'an 6:133.

CHAPTER 10

*The Biblical Garden of Eden**

The Garden of Eden (1) is described in the Bible as the place where God accommodated the biblical Adam and Eve after they were created from the soil. Genesis 2:8 (2) "Then the Lord God planted a Garden in Eden, in the East, and there He put the man He created."

What are the real implications of these words, namely, Garden and Eden? Was it a real garden that we are familiar with, in a place called Eden? Where was it located? Was it on earth or in heaven or any other extraterrestrial location? These are some questions being asked by many from time immemorial.

Etymology:

The Sumerians (3) are an ancient civilization and in Sumerian language, there is a word Edin which may be the source of the word Eden. The Sumerian term Edin means "steppe, plain, desert, or wilderness." It is believed that the Sumerians used this term to refer to the arid land west of Euphrates (4). There is an Akkadian (5) word edinu, which may be synonymous with Eden. The Sumerians and Akkadians were ancient civilizations of Mesopotamia. Others maintain that the origin of the word Eden might be from the Hebrew stem, **din** which means abundant and lush.

The word paradise is sometimes used to refer to the Garden of Eden. In Hebrew Par Des is synonymous with paradise. This word has similarities with certain ancient Persian word used to describe a "walled orchard garden" or an "enclosed hunting park."

As mentioned above, the place called Eden must be a larger area as the garden is described as having located in the east of Eden as mentioned in the Bible.

In Qur'an, there is reference to the garden which God had prepared for Adam and Eve to live.

Verse 7:19 (6) "O, Adam dwell thou and thy wife in the Garden."

2:35(7) "O Adam dwell thou and thy wife in this Garden and eat freely thereof both of you whatever you may wish but do not approach this one tree lest you become wrong doers."

The same Garden is referred to in 7:22; 20:121, 123. (8)

Genesis 2:16 (9) He told him, "You may eat the fruit of any tree in the Garden except the tree that gives knowledge of what is good and what is bad."

Qur'an 20:118 (10) "There is therein enough provisions for thee **not to go hungry**, not to go *naked. 20:119*: (11) Not to suffer *from thirst, or Sun's heat.*" This description clearly shows that the garden was a very comfortable place with shades for protection from the sun's heat and the availability of water may be from rivers, lakes, lagoons, or ponds. There were also provisions not to go naked. All necessities for human survival were provided, for it is to be remembered that the time of Adam and Eve was the age of the hunter-gatherers. These hunter-gatherers had to seek food by foraging and hunting. Therefore, a place where food is readily available with other amenities for livelihood would certainly be a unique and heavenly place.

The Hebrew word Pardes is used to denote paradise and is used to refer to the Garden of Eden. The Persian word **Pairidaeza** (paradise), and the Hebrew word **Gan** (garden) both of which mean a "walled garden or park." The word paradise is also mentioned in the Old Testament with reference to places other than the Garden of Eden. In Sanskrit, there is a word **pardesha**, meaning a foreign land. In Arabic, the equivalent word is **firdauz** meaning paradise. In the Song of Solomon (12) 4:12, there is mention of a walled garden. "My sweet heart, my bride," is a secret garden, a walled garden, a private spring; 4:13 "There the plants flourish, they grow like an orchard of pomegranate trees and bear the finest fruits."

In the Pauline Christian New Testament, paradise is referred to as a heavenly place for the blessed after their death (13).

In Qur'an, there is mention of paradise, a heavenly place for the righteous after their death, resurrection, and judgment 18:107; 23:8-10 (14).

Many among the Muslims and among the Judeo-Christian faith regard the garden as a heavenly place somewhere outside the earth. And wherefrom Adam and Eve were expelled to the earth below when they ate from the forbidden tree. There is no credible evidence for this assumption in the Qur'an or the Bible except the statement in the Pseudepigrapha, "The jubilees" (15), which have been incorporated in the Ethiopian Orthodox Church. It states that the angels did not place Adam in the Garden for forty days after his creation, and Eve only after eighty days, it is believed that during these days, they were kept in heaven. But there is some implication in Qur'an that Adam might have been in the heaven, wherefrom he was ordered to go down. According to one scholar, Qur'an 2:36 (16), "We said, get ye down all (ye people) with enmity between yourselves. On earth will be your dwelling place and your means of livelihood for a time." From this verse, people might have concluded that Adam was expelled from the garden (paradise) above and thrown down to the earth for the rest of his life.

But the translation of the same verse by another scholar says (17): but the devil made them slip from it, and caused them to depart from the state in which they were. "And We said, go forth, some of you are the enemies of others, and there is for you in the earth an abode and provision for a time." In this translation we do not see the scenario that Adam and Eve were ordered down from a heavenly location into another, namely the earth. This only states that there will be an abode for Adam and Eve on earth for a time.(In the commentary, the author writes that the word "habt" sometimes means "descending from a high place to a lower one," but more frequently used in the literature to imply removing from one place to another as in "ihbitu-misr-an" (Qur'an 2:61)(18) which means, "go to or enter into a city." It also signifies simply change in condition.

According to the Arabic lexicon (William Lane)(19)" habata" means "he came forth from it" and also "he became lowered or degraded." And "habt" further means "falling into evil," or "becoming low or suffering loss or diminution."

The translation of the same verse by another scholar (Al-Qur'an, A contemporary Translation) (2:36 [20]) says, "And we said go, one the antagonist of the other, and live on earth for a time ordained and fend for yourselves."

The totality of the information contained in the revealed texts suggests that Adam was moved out of the garden to another place on earth in diminished stature due to his transgression of God's command, "*not to eat from the forbidden tree*", and does not suggest that the garden was in heaven and wherefrom was thrown down to earth. It appears that the part of earth to which Adam was transferred was different from the garden as to the availability of food. God said to Adam to tend for himself after expelling from the garden while in the garden, food was available in plenty.

Earthly Location of the Garden of Eden

In Genesis 2:10 (21), God gives some information as to the location of the Garden of Eden, thereby indicating that the Garden of Eden was an earthly place. A stream flowed in Eden and watered the garden, beyond Eden it divided into four rivers. The first river is the Pishon: it flows around the country of Havilah. (Pure gold is found there and also rare perfumes and precious stones.) The second river is the Gihon; it flows around the country of Cush. The third river is the Tigris, which flows east of Assyria, and the fourth river is the Euphrates. Among these names, the location of Cush and Havilah are not clearly identifiable in the present-day topography of the Near East. But many believe it might have been somewhere in the ancient Mesopotamian territory.

Among the four rivers mentioned, two are clearly identified, namely, the Tigris and Euphrates. They are running in the territory consisting of Turkey, Iran, and Iraq.

Topographical map of the lands called the Cush and Havilah are not clearly identified on the current topography of the region wherein the present-day Tigris and Euphrates are located.

Reference to the two identified rivers indicates that the Garden of Eden was located on earth in the Near East.

The Garden of Eden is believed to be the pristine dwelling place of Adam and Eve, (22) who were designated as the first pair of fully developed human beings by God and became the progenitors of all human beings alive today. This has been described in the Genesis and Qur'an. Genesis 2:7; 2:22 and Acts:17;26 (23) describe the creation of Adam and Eve believed to be the first human pair and it is believed that subsequent generations of human beings originated from this pair.

In Qur'an, there is specific reference to this effect. Chapter 49:13 (24) "O, mankind, we created you from a single pair of a male and female and made you into nations and tribes."

The present locations of at least two of the four rivers mentioned in the Genesis, and the following discussion will make it clear that the so-called Garden of Eden was an earthly place.

Genesis 2:15 (25) (Good News Bible) "Then the Lord God placed the man in the Garden of Eden to cultivate it and guard it."

Genesis 4:1 (26), "She (Eve) bore a son and she said, 'By the Lord's help I have gotten a son.'" So she named him Cain. Later, she gave birth to another son Abel. Abel became a shepherd, but Cain was a farmer. Both of these professions are earthly occupations.

After Cain killed his brother Abel, God banished Cain from the Garden and Eden. Genesis 4:16 (27) And Cain went away from the Lord's presence and lived in the land called Nod (wandering), which is East of Eden.

Genesis 4:17 (28) "Later Cain built a city there and named after his son Enoch."

From these descriptions, one has to conclude that the Garden of Eden was an earthly place.

References to the Garden can be found in Qur'an:

Qur'an 7:19 (29) "O Adam, dwell thou and thy wife in the Garden."

20:117(30) "O Adam, this is an enemy to thee and to thy wife; so let not drive you both out of the Garden."

In addition to the above verses, Qur'an states in 2:35 (31), "O Adam dwell thou and thy wife in this garden and eat freely thereof both of you whatever you may wish but do not approach this one tree lest you become wrongdoers." Also reference to the same garden can be found in 7:22; 20:121, 123(32). But there is no indication as to its location.

Several verses in Qur'an mention about the heavenly garden with rivers flowing beneath with trees and fruits in it. (3:15; 15:45; 22:14; 85:11) (33). But as mentioned before, these gardens are entered only after death.

Additionally once a person enters the heavenly paradise, he will not be expelled from it. Qur'an: 15:48 (34) says, "Toil afflicts them not therein nor will they be ejected there from."

References pertaining to the terrain of Eden and the garden can be found in the Pseudepigrapha and Apocrypha (35). The Pseudepigrapha and Apocrypha are books written by Jewish and Christian writers and considered not to be canonical to be included in the Bible. But the Ethiopian Bible considered them canonical to be included in it.

In the Book of Adam and Eve (36) a Pseudepigrapha , in 2:6 it says, "As for Cain when the mourning for his brother was over (after Cain killed his brother Abel) he took his sister and married her, without leave from his mother and father. For they could not keep him from her by reason of their heavy heart. He then went down to the bottom of the mountain away from the garden."

In another Pseudepigrapha, "The Cave of Treasures (37)," under Adam's expulsion from the paradise, note 11 says, "So Adam and Eve went down from the holy mountain (of Eden): To the slopes which were below it. Further Adam tells Cain, 'Nevertheless take ye to yourselves fruits of trees and the young of sheep and get ye to the top of this holy mountain.' And when they came down to the plain, Cain killed Abel."

In all these documents, the reference to the garden is that of an earthly location with respect to the hill and its valleys. It also indicates that the garden might have been on an elevated territory, like a hill or mountain, from where they had to get down to the bottom into the valley or the plain.

This location and the events that are described in the Pseudepigrapha has some bearing to the translation of the verse in Qur'an 2:36 (16) (Yusuf Ali) which says, "We said, get tee down all (ye people) with enmity," (this may mean getting down from the hill top where the garden was located). These references will contribute to our understanding that getting down only means getting down from an elevated place in the garden (or the garden itself being in an elevated place) and not to be confused with getting down from heaven.

The shelter mentioned in the Qur'an could be the cave shelters which were the traditional dwelling places of the pre-Adamic hominids like the Neanderthals and the Cro-Magnons.

These descriptions about the garden in Qur'an are those of a garden on earth with water source like a lake, lagoon, pond, or river and lush with foliage or trees to give shelter from the sun and possibly caves and rock shelters. It is worth pointing out that the previous generation of hominids were cave dwellers

Information contained in Genesis 2:7-8 (2) which refers to the creation of a man out of the soil of the ground and then planting a garden in the east eastern part of Eden, after He completed the creation of earth and the evidences presented above from the Qur'an, there can be no doubt that the biblical garden of Eden was situated on earth and not in heaven.

References for Garden of Eden and its earthly location:

1. The Biblical Garden of Eden.
2. Genesis 2:8.
3. Sumerians. Ancient Civilization. Lived in Mesopotamia in 3500 BC.
4. Wikipedia. http://en.wikipedia.org/wiki/Sumer.retrieved,3-30-2009.
5. Akkadians. Ancient Civilization in Mesopotamia 2350 BC. http://en.wikipedia.org/wiki/Sumerian-civilization. Retrieved, 3-30-2009
6. Qur'an 7:19.
7. Ibid., 2:35.
8. Ibid., 7:22; 20:121, 123.
9. Genesis 2:16.
10. Qur'an 20:118.
11. Ibid., 20:119.
12. The Bible. The Song of Solomon 4:12-13.
13. Gourt;http://artides.gourt.com/en/garden%20of%20Eden.http://en.wikipedia.org/wiki/Garden of eden.Retrieved,3-30-2009
14. Qur'an 18:107; 23:8-10.
15. The Book of Jubilees. Pseudepigrapha. Ancient Jewish religious Book.http://en.wikipedia.org/wiki/Jubilees. retrieved, 3-30-2009
16. Qur'an 2:36. Translation by Yusuf Ali.
17. Ibid., Translation by Muhammad Ali.
18. Ibid., 2:61. Translation by Muhammad Ali.
19. William Lane. The Arabic-English Lexicon.
20. Qur'an 2:36. Translation by Ahmed Ali. Al-Qur'an: A contemporary translation.
21. Genesis 2:10.
22. The Biblical Adam and Eve.
23. Genesis 2:7; 2:22; Acts;17;26.
24. Qur'an 49:13.
25. Genesis 2:15.
26. Ibid., 4:1.
27. Ibid., 4:16.
28. Ibid., 4:17.
29. Qur'an 7:19.
30. Ibid., 20:117.

31. Ibid., 2:35.
32. Ibid., 7:22; 20:121-123; 22:14; 85:17.
33. Ibid., 3:15; 15:45.22:14; 85:11.
34. Ibid., 15:48.
35. Pseudepigrapha. http://en.wikipedia.org/wiki/Pseudepigrapha,retrieved, 3-30-2009
36. The Book of Adam and Eve. A Pseudepigrapha.
37. The Cave of Treasures. A Pseudepigrapha. Translation. Brit.Mus.MS. Add.25875.

CHAPTER 11

The Location of the Garden of Eden

A Place on Earth

Many scientists and archaeologists have been trying to locate this piece of real estate described as the Garden of Eden in the Bible, on our planet for a long time.

Folklore has it that the garden might be in China, Mongolia, and Missouri (USA), the Middle East, or even Sri Lanka. There is a place called Adam's Peak in Sri Lanka (Ceylon) where a human foot print is preserved on top of a mountain believed to be left by Adam. Many believe that the garden is a heavenly place; and after Adam transgressed the commands of God by eating from the forbidden tree, Adam and Eve (1) were expelled to the earth. Some say during that process, Adam fell in Sri Lanka and Eve fell into Saudi Arabia and the snake fell into the present-day Iran. There is even mention of the existence of a grave in eastern Saudi Arabia, which is believed to contain the remains of Eve.

Luke:23:43 refers to paradise possibly being a place after death. Jesus said to him "I promise you that today you will be in paradise with me"(5)

The origin of the word Eden in Hebrew means "delight." This may be derived from the Sumerian word Edin, which means "steppe, plain, desert, or wilderness." This word is believed to have been used by the Sumerians to refer to the arid lands west of the Euphrates (6). There is an Akkadian (7) word edinu, which may be synonymous with Eden. [The Sumerians and Akkadians were ancient civilizations.]

Many in the Muslim faith regard the garden as a heavenly place somewhere outside the earth as discussed below.

But the available information in the Bible, Qur'an, archeological observations, and relevant scriptural details points to an earthly location for the Garden of Eden.

The only relevant description of the geographical and topographical location of the Garden of Eden is seen in Genesis 2:8-14 (8).

Then the Lord God planted a Garden in Eden, in the east and there He put the man He had formed. He made all kinds of beautiful trees grow there and produce good fruit. In the middle of the garden stood the tree that gives life and the tree that gives knowledge of what is good and what is bad,

> A stream flowed in Eden and watered the Garden, Beyond Eden
> it divided into four rivers
> The first river is the Pishon; it flows around the country of Havilah.
> Pure gold is found there also rare perfumes and precious stones.
> The second river is the Goon; it flows around the country of Cush.
> The third river is the Tigris which flows east of Assyria and the fourth river is the Euphrates.

From this we can infer that the Eden is a place on earth as He planted a garden in it, and there were four rivers, two of which are still identified with the biblical names—the Tigris and Euphrates. There were trees and fruits in the garden.

Genesis 2:15(9) says, "Then the Lord God placed the man in the Garden of Eden to cultivate it and guard it." Again suggesting an earthly place as cultivation and growing fruit-bearing trees are traditionally considered as earthly occupation.

Genesis 4:16 (10) says. "And Cain went away from the Lord's presence and lived in a land called 'wandering' (Nod) which is east of Eden."

Genesis 4:17(11) says, "Cain and his wife had a son and named him Enoch. Then Cain built a city and named after his son." These verses describe the Garden of Eden being on earth as there was a land called Nod to the east of the garden and having built a city there by Cain.

In Qur'an, the garden is also mentioned (12) 7:19, "O Adam dwell thou in the Garden and enjoy its good things as you wish, but approach not this tree or ye run into harm and transgression."

20:117 (13) so let him not get you both out of the Garden, so that thou art landed in misery.

20:118 (14) there is therein enough provisions for thee *not to go hungry*, not to go naked.

20:119 (15) not to suffer *from thirst or from the Sun's heat.*

This reference to the protection from sun's heat tells us that indeed the garden is on our earth and not somewhere else as we have no information yet about another planet like our earth in the universe. Similarly, not to suffer from thirst suggests the presence of water. There are no planets at the present time, in the universe, other than earth which have liquid water on it. Scientists believe there was water on Mars millions of years ago but have since dried out. But no one can deny with certainty the existence of another solar system and earth somewhere in the universe, but so far, scientists have been unable to detect one. They have discovered the existence of other solar systems, which contain super earth-size planets, but they are different from our earth. Scientists believe that even though there are other solar systems, our solar system is peculiar in that the planets in other solar systems are unsteady unlike in ours, which have been steady for billions of years.

Qur'an also describes a garden of bliss reserved for those who attain perfection in this world with good deeds and being faithful. This garden is also described as having trees and fruits and has rivers flowing beneath it.

Because of the fact that the garden had water, trees, and rivers does not make it certain that the garden is on earth. Several verses in Qur'an mention gardens with river flowing beneath it reserved for the righteous to be entered after their death (16) 3:15; 15:45; 22:14; 85:11. However, entrance to those gardens can be possible only after death, resurrection, and judgment. In the case of the Garden of Eden, Adam entered it before his death, and certainly it means that it is not the heavenly garden as mentioned in Qur'an as stated above.

These references in the Bible and Qur'an with regard to the garden certainly tell us that the garden in question indeed was an earthly place.

The protection from sun's heat also points to some sort of shade, most probably a cave or overhanging rock-shelter for Adam and Eve to take shelter, or shades of trees. The reference to protection from sun's heat also indicates that the garden was an earthly abode. A garden with sun's heat must be on our earth as we have no knowledge about another solar system with a sun and earth outside of ours. However, scientists have discovered what is described as "Super Earth planets," but it is entirely different from ours (17). The protection may also relate to provisions to make a hut or dwelling made available in the garden. It has been discovered by archeologists that the Cro-Magnons who were in that general locality (in the Near East) before Adam and Eve appeared, were able to build their dwellings with locally available resources and were also living in cave shelters.

When God decided to create Adam, he tells the angels about his intention. Qur'an 2:30 (18) states, "Behold, thy Lord said to the angels, 'I will create a vicegerent (a ruler) **on *earth*'**". This clearly indicates that Adam was meant to be a human being to live on earth and not in heaven.

In the pseudepigrapha,as described above, Cain takes Lebhudha and "goes down the mountain away from the Garden." Cain obviously came down from the mountain in the paradise and went away from the garden, suggesting that there was a mountain in the larger area of Eden, and the garden was on it or nearby it.

In the book, The Cave of Treasures, a pseudepigrapha as mentioned before, it is stated that Adam and Eve went down from the holy mountain (of Eden) to its slopes that were below it, again suggests the presence of a mountain in Eden and on it the garden was situated. Therefore, the statement in the Qur'an: "get you down from here" clearly alludes to getting down from the garden situated on a mountain from which they were ordered to get down to the valley below.

It is not conceivable that the garden was in an extraterrestrial location (outside the earth) like in heaven wherefrom they were thrown down to the earth. Human beings cannot travel without a "space suit" through space nor can they enter the earth's atmosphere from outside the earth without a shield (spacecraft) lest they die and burn into ashes. Of course God is capable of any miracles and anything is possible. Leaving aside that argument, it is impossible to endure such a sojourn by man from an extraterrestrial location to the earth without a space shield.

The Book of Jubilees (19) as described above relates a tradition that the angels did not place Adam in the garden for forty days after his creation, and Eve only after eighty days. It is believed that during these days, they were kept in heaven. This is in keeping with the belief of some followers of Islam that originally Adam and Eve were in heaven and later were ordered to go down to the earth when they ate the fruit from the forbidden tree. With this in mind, can we entertain a believable science-based scenario for the possible ascent or descent by a human being through space during Adam's time, about ten to twelve thousand years ago?

The Wormholes

Scientists describe wormholes (20) as a hypothetical topological phenomenon in space-time. This is a shortcut through the space-time and can act like space-time tubes, connecting one end of the universe to the other and through which, one could theoretically traverse faster than light. In 1935, Albert Einstein and Nathan Rosen (21) realized that general relativity theory allows the existence of "bridges" in space originally called Einstein Rosen bridges, which are now known as wormholes. This theory opens up the possibility of traveling through space faster than light. Initially thought of as a fiction, scientists now entertain the feasibility of such a journey by using what is called exotic matter, which has a negative energy. No one as of yet seen this space tubes, but in general relativity theory, wormholes are known to be valid. Wormholes could be either intra universe or inter universe for possible passage through and in between universes. Are these the routes taken by angels? Or was this the route that Prophet Muhammad, accompanied by Gabriel, might have taken, if the incident described in Qur'an 17:1 (22) was a journey with his physical body? The answers to these statements in Qur'an are beyond our comprehension for now. In Qur'an 70:4 (23) it says, "To Him ascend the angels and the spirits in a day the measure of which is fifty thousand years." Certainly these are passages which are at present a scientific curiosity but may indeed become a reality in the future. Certainly the speed of travel through these wormholes, which is faster than light, is beyond our comprehension at present.

The thought that Adam was created elsewhere and chuted down through one of these space tubes is not readily acceptable but feasible. But as discussed above, in the Genesis and the Qur'an, God's intention was to create a man on earth, out of mud or clay, which is present on our earth (Mars also has clay on it) and the information described earlier establishes that the Garden of Eden was on earth and nowhere else. Therefore, traveling through a wormhole is not worth mentioning. Some in Judeo-Christian and Islamic faiths believe that the garden was a heavenly place outside of earth (similar to the paradise or heaven that is promised after death and resurrection for those who follow the commands of God.) Qur'an 2:36 (24) (Yusuf Ali), states, "We said 'get ye down, all ye people, with enmity between yourselves. On earth will be your dwelling place and your means of livelihood for a time." This suggests to some that Adam was originally in some place other than earth, and after Adam violated the prohibitions imposed on him by God, he was thrown down to the earth.

After Satan misled Adam and Eve into eating from the forbidden tree, they were expelled from the garden; and because of the above verse in Qur'an, many Muslims harbor the feeling that they were ordered to get down to earth from possibly a heavenly residence.

But as seen from the description of the garden in the Bible and Qur'an, there should not be any doubt that the garden indeed was an earthly place.

As described in the Pseudepigrapha, there is an elevated region in the garden on the top of which is the place of worship into which Adam tells Cain to go up to for the purpose of giving offerings to God. This suggests an elevated area or a hilly place and from which they have to get down to reach the plains below. When Adam and Eve were expelled from the garden, God said, "Get ye down." To get down from the sacred surroundings of the hill's top, the place of worship, as indicated in the Pseudepigrapha and possibly the garden itself might have been on an elevation as it was surrounded by four rivers according to the Bible. In order to have lush vegetations and fruits without getting damaged by the flooding from the rivers mentioned in the Bible, this area must be on a higher elevation from which Adam and Eve had to get down to reach the plains. Therefore, "getting down" does not mean getting down from a heavenly garden outside of the earth.

Genesis 4:16 (9) states, "And Cain went away from the Lord's presence and lived in a land called wandering (Nod) which is east of the Garden. Where Cain later built a city." This description of Cain's exile clearly describes an earthly place.

When God expressed His plan to create a human being, He said to the angels as mentioned before.

Qur'an: 2:30 (25) it says, "Behold thy Lord said to the angels 'I will create a **vicegerent on earth**'".

This should dispel all doubts about the earthliness of the garden and also of Adam and Eve, its residents.

After having established that the garden was on earth, we will explore the possibility of locating the site of the garden in the present topography of the Near East in the next chapter.

Genesis: 2:15 (10) says, "Then the Lord God placed the man [Adam] in the Garden of Eden to cultivate it and guard it.

Genesis 4:2 (26) says, "Later she (Eve) gave birth to another son, Abel. Abel became a shepherd, but Cain (the first son) was a farmer."

These words tell us that the garden was in a locality where agriculture and domestication of animals have already been started by humans. Archaeologists have evidence to show that the agriculture and domestication of animals first started in the Near East in the general location of the Fertile Crescent (27), this includes part of Turkey, Iran, Armenia, Iraq (specifically Mesopotamia) extending up to Egypt.

Paradise (Hebrew, Pardes) has been used to refer to the Garden of Eden. In the ancient Persian language, paradise means "a walled garden or an enclosed hunting park."

I believe that this discussion will prove that the biblical Garden of Eden was on earth.

References for Location on Earth:

1. Biblical Adam and Eve.
2. Genesis: Song of Solomon 4:12-13.
3. Wikipedia. Gourt.http;//artides.gourt.com/en/Garden%20 of%20Eden. Retrieved.3-30-2009
4. Qur'an 18:107; 23:8
5. Bible:Luke:23:43.
6. Wikipedia. http:// en. Wikipedia.org/wiki/ Sumer. Retrieved.3-30-2009
7. Akkadian. Ancient Civilization. http://en.wikipedia.org/wiki/Sumer. Retrieved.3-30-2009
8. Genesis 2:8-14.
9. Genesis 2:15.
10. Ibid., 4:16.
11. Ibid., 4:17.
12. Qur'an 7:19.
13. Ibid., 29:117.
14. Ibid., 20:118.
15. Ibid., 20:119.

16. Ibid., 3:15; 15:45; 22:14; 85:11.
17. Super-Earths.http://en.wikipedia.org/wiki/Super-Earth. Retrived.3-30-2009
18. Qur'an: 2:30.
19. The Book of Jubilees. A Pseudepigrapha.http://en.wikipedia.org/wiki/Jubilees. Retrieved.3-30-2009
20. Wormholes. Space-time tubes in space.http://en.wikipedia.org/wiki/ Wormhole.
21. Albert Einstein and Nathan Rose. General theory of relativity.
22. Qur'an 17:1.
23. Ibid., 70:4.
24. Ibid., 2:36.Yusuf Ali. The Meaning of the Holy Quran.
25. Ibid., 2:30.
26. Genesis 4:2.
27. Wikipedia. http:// en. Wikipedia. com/ wiki/Fertile-Crescent. Retrieved.3-30-2009

CHAPTER 12

Where Is the Topographic Location of the Garden of Eden?

Since we have established that the garden was on earth, We will try to identify its Biblical location. As mentioned above, the Bible gives reference to two known rivers, namely, the Tigris and Euphrates, which are located in the territory now consisting of Eastern Turkey, Iran, and Iraq. In addition, there is a mention of the land of Nod in the Bible, to the east of Eden, and this may have been recognized now as Nodqui according to Archaeologist David Rohl (1), who has traveled extensively in the region. From the Genesis, we understand that God had ordered Adam to cultivate the land. Cain was a farmer, and Abel was a shepherd. From this we can assume that the territory must have been in the Fertile Crescent (2). This area was a crescent-shaped region where agriculture and domestication of animals were started. Specifically the region of the Zagros (3) mountain range is believed to be the area where rye was first cultivated and domestication of animals began. Topography will indicate that the rivers mentioned in the Bible have origins in the foot hills of the Zagros mountain range (the North Western range). Therefore, this general area in the foothills of the Zagros Mountains will be the most likely location for the Garden of Eden.

The following are some of the suspected location, with some credible evidence, and all are located in the general area of the Fertile Crescent in relation to the scenic mountain range of Zagros.

Michael Sanders (4) believes that the Garden of Eden was in Eastern Turkey. The rivers Tigris and Euphrates take their source there. The four rivers mentioned in the Bible according to Sanders are the Murat River (5), the Tigris, the Euphrates, and the north fork of the Euphrates. Sanders refers to a satellite photo showing that "a river rises out of Eden and divides into four." (6).

In Assyrian records, there is mention of a Beth Eden (house of Eden), a small Aramaean state located on the bend of the Euphrates river just south of Carchemish, in the vicinity of Urfa and Harran (7).

Archaeologist Juris Zarins (8), after extensive study, believes that the Garden of Eden is at the head of the Persian Gulf where the Tigris and Euphrates rivers run into the sea. From Landsat images, (9) Zarins identifies the river Karun in Iran and suggests that Karun River corresponds to the biblical Gihon River. A fossil riverbed is identified in eastern Saudi Arabia that once flowed in to the Persian Gulf, which corresponds to the Wadi Batin river system (10). The Wadi Batin River drained the once fertile central part of Saudi Arabia. In the past, before Christ, this region of present-day Saudi Arabia was a fertile land with vegetations and animal life. At that time, the Wadi Batin River was draining water from the entire region but has since been dried out, leaving a fossil river that could be seen by Landsat. This will represent the river Pishon according to Zarins.

This theory is also supported by C. A. Salabach (11).

Some historians believe that Dilmun (present-day Bahrain) (12) as the Garden of Eden. In ancient times, Dilmun was a reputed trading center and later described as a long lost garden of exotic perfections.

It is to be remembered that the present-day Persian Gulf area may have been a raised and fertile land during the last glaciations about fifteen thousand years ago. During ice ages, water level in the sea can fall four hundred feet or more and at that time the present day Persian Gulf area might have been above the surrounding sea. And also the geography that we see today may not have been existing at that time due to the devastation brought on by Noah's flood (13) and the topography of the erstwhile garden might have been lost.

Archaeologist David Rohl (1), after a tedious expedition, locates the "Garden of Eden" in Northwest Iran. He believes that the garden was located in a vast plain referred to in ancient Sumerian texts as Edin (meaning "plain" or "steppe") east of the Sahand Mountain near Tabriz, Iran. He finds several geological similarities with biblical descriptions. He also cites several linguistic parallels. In Sumerian texts, there is mention of an emissary being sent through "Seven Gates" also known as mountain passes in ancient times.

Hebrew lore makes reference to "seven layers of heaven, the seventh being the Garden of Eden or paradise. Just beyond the seventh gate, or pass, was the kingdom of Aratta. The region today is bound by a large mountain range to the north, east, and south and marsh lands to the west. The eastern mountain region has a pass leading in and out of the Edin region. This is consistent with the description of the biblical geography of Eden, namely, marsh land to the west and the Land of Nod to the east outside the garden. Geographically speaking, it would form a wall "around the garden consistent with the definition of the Persian word pairidaeza (paradise) and the Hebrew word Gan (garden) both of which mean a 'walled garden' or park."

Additionally, this location would be bound by the four rivers mentioned in the Bible, to the west, southwest, east, and southeast.

The biblical word Gan (as in Eden) means "walled garden," and the valley according to Rohl is walled by towering mountains.

David Rohl read about this location from ancient Sumerian cuneiform clay tablets held by the Museum of the Orient in Istanbul, Turkey. The tablet describes a five-thousand-year-old route to Eden.

Rohl followed a route documented in the Sumerian cuneiform epic, "Enmerkar and the Lord of Arrata" supposedly traveled by an emissary of the Sumerian priest-king of Uruk. The emissary had been dispatched to Arrata on the plain of Edin. This place was known to Sumerians as the land of "happiness and plenty" to obtain gold and lapis lazuli to decorate a temple that Emerkar was building in Uruk.

Rohl believes the ancient Sumerians, Babylonians, and Assyrians all knew of an earthly paradise that had once lay beyond what they called the seven heavens. For them, Eden was still an earthly place.

Rohl identifies the river Uizhun as the biblical river of Pishon.

Rohl got this idea from an amateur historian, Reginald Walker (1917-1989) (14) who proposed the location of the Garden of Eden might be in northwestern Iran. He had also suggested that all the four rivers mentioned in the Bible would be found in that region. All four rivers had their sources (biblical "heads") in the two lakes, Van and Urmia. The location of the two rivers, namely, Gihon and Pishon has been a mystery. According to Walker, the present River Arras, originating from Lake Urmia and flows to the Caspian Sea was previously called Gaihun. Rohl, by checking the recording of Islamic geographers during Arab invasion of Iran, could confirm this information. Additionally Rohl sees that the Victorian Atlases refer to the river as Gaihun-Aras and concludes that the river Gaihun is the biblical Gihon.

Reginald Walker believes, according to Rohl, that the word Pishon was derived from an old Iranian word Uishum where the Iranian vowel U had been converted to Semitic consonant P, and Uizhum became Pishon. The modern Qezel Uzun (the river Uizhum) identified as the biblical Pishon flows from the mountain of Kurdistan to the Caspian Sea. Therefore, Rohl concludes that all the four rivers mentioned in the Bible can be found in the highlands between the present-day Iran and Turkey.

In these highlands, Rohl identifies a large plain surrounded by mountains similar to the walled garden as in Gan Eden. The highest of the mountains is Mt. Sahand. The Sumerian word for plain is edin, and the scholars believe that that is the source of the word Eden. This edin (plain), according to Rohl, is very lush with orchards and vineyards and rivers, and believes the Garden of Eden was located here.

Rohl also states that he has found the biblical "Land of Nod" which is known as Noqdi today (15).

He further states that south of the "Nod or Noqdi lies a town called Helabad formerly it was known as Kheruabad," which means "settlement of the Kheru" people. He believes that Kheru is a permutation of the Hebrew word keruvim that is translated as "cherubs." These people were fearsome warriors.

The cherubs are described in Genesis 3:24 (16) and are believed to be supernatural creatures.

In the Bible, there is reference to certain creatures to protect anyone entering the garden after Adam and Eve were expelled from it.

Genesis 3:23-24 (17) says, "So the lord God sent him [Adam] out of the Garden and made him cultivate the soil from which he has been formed. Then at east side of the Garden he put living creatures and a flaming sword which turned in all directions. This was to keep anyone from coming near the Tree of life." These creatures are believed to be the cherubs (16). (If cherubs are really the Kheru people as David Rohl postulates, then there is again evidence for humans other than Adam and Eve at that time, if the biblical cherubs and the cherubs described by Rohl are the same. And these may well be the remnants of the Cro-Magnons [author's opinion])

Furthermore, Rohl has discovered the biblical "Land of Cush." Many had speculated that the Cush may be Ethiopia, but some biblical scholars believe that Cush was also a country east of Babylon in ancient times. But now Rohl says it is north of the Adji Chay River valley and over the Kusheh

Daugh (the mountain of Kush). One of the four rivers mentioned in the Bible with reference to the garden winds through it.

From all these archaeological expeditions and biblical information, the locality of the garden of Eden can be narrowed down to places in the "fertile crescent" area. (A crescent shaped area in the Middle east consisting of present day Kuwait, north and western part of Iran, Eastern part of Iraq, South of Armenia, Eastern Turkey, eastern Syria, Lebanon, Israel and north eastern Egypt, where agriculture and domestication of animals were believed to have originated. The name fertile crescent was coined by the University of Chicago archaeologist James Henry Breasted around 1900.) one is at the northern tip of the Persian Gulf, which is believed to have been above the sea level, during the last glaciation. The other two locations are in Eastern Turkey and in Northwest Iran, both in the northern aspect of the Zagros mountain range and its valleys. We can conclude that the Garden of Eden was an earthly place where Adam and Eve were sent by God to stay, and that the Garden of Eden was in the Near East along the Fertile Crescent and can be further narrowed down to the region between the present-day Iran, Iraq, and Turkey, or possibly in the region of the present day Persian gulf. Based on the biblical reference to the garden of Eden and the archeological evidence for the beginning of agriculture in the Fertile Crescent, one can locate the biblical Garden of Eden in the area between North eastern Iraq, South eastern Turkey, North western Iran and to the south of present day Armenia.

Why God selected this garden for Adam and Eve over all other places is unknown to us. But one can speculate some earthly reasons:

1. Before Adam appeared on the scene, we know there were the hunter-gatherers called the Cro-Magnons. Agriculture and settled life was believed to have originated in that region (the Fertile Crescent).
2. The so-called garden from the description in the Bible was watered by a river, which then became four rivers.
3. This topography clearly tells us that the region was surrounded by these rivers with a great likelihood of frequent flooding.
4. Because of this, the hunter-gatherers might have moved into remote areas which are not prone to flooding and presumably would have better chance of getting food to survive.
5. The hunter-gatherers, by definition, need hunting for their livelihood. (Recall when Adam was expelled from the garden, he did not find food for several days outside the garden, according to

some pseudepigrapha [Vita Adae et Evae] either plant or animal food.) This lends support to the theory that this area must have been deserted by the hunter-gatherers for lack of food.

6. Because of the abandonment of the garden and its vicinity by the hunter gatherers, the garden becomes lush with vegetations, with all kinds of fruit trees and fruits as there were no one to consume it. Thus it becomes a pristine land as described in the Bible and Qur'an with enough provisions for the couple to live.

7. As seen by archaeology, it is in this area that agriculture and domestication of animals started.

8. As indicated by David Rohl, there were rocks in the higher mountains of the region that contains the holes or caves of those cave dwellers of the hunter-gatherer population. This will provide shelter for Adam and Eve. It also means that Adam and Eve may have some distant neighbors and will not be the only human beings in that territory (even though most of the hunter-gatherers might have deserted the immediate vicinity and moved out to surrounding plains to live).

It is also possible that the area of the garden being surrounded by four rivers, the island like locale might be subjected to frequent flooding. This also might have caused the local hunter-gatherers to move out into higher grounds to avoid flooding, and therefore this area of the garden must have been devoid of inhabitants; and consequently the garden became a fruit paradise as there were none to consume it.

Though Abel was a shepherd, the tending for domesticated animals would be much later when he became a young adult. That was several years after the expulsion of Adam and Eve from the garden and not at the time when Adam and Eve entered the garden for the first time as there were no children when they entered the garden. The shepherding must have started outside the garden and after their expulsion.

As noted in the Bible, Cain went to the land of Nod (15) and built a city there, suggesting there were humans far removed from the garden itself (to build a city needs lots of people, not just Cain and his family); and Abel could get domesticated animals from them to be a shepherd. It is hard to imagine that Abel could domesticate animals for the first time in his youth as domestication takes decades or centuries. This suggests that there were domesticated animals raised by others being available in that territory for Abel to acquire them.

Or it is possible that the garden was considered a sacred place by the people living around (see Rohl's account above) that it was left undisturbed, and as a result, there was plenty of food remaining in the garden. Definitely, there was significant difference in the availability of food inside the garden compared to the surrounding area outside the garden as Adam could not find food for several days after he was expelled from the garden according to the pseudepigraphal accounts.

Qur'an 2:35(18) "O Adam, dwell thou and thy wife in the garden, and eat from it a plenteous food, wherever you wish and approach not this tree."

From this, we understand there was plentiful food readily available in the garden without having to cultivate and raise the food.

Now look at the next paragraph 2:36 (19) (Ahmed Ali) "But Satan tempted them and had them banished from the (happy) state they were in. And We said, "Go one the antagonist of the other, and live on the earth for a time ordained, and fend for yourselves.'"

What a contrast between these two verses. In the garden, food being plentiful and made available without having to labor and cultivate, and outside the garden, Adam and Eve had to tend for themselves.

Reference for Topographic Location:

1. David Rohl. British Archaeologist. Book the "Legend: Genesis of Civilization." Scholar. University College, London.
2. The Fertile Crescent. Ch. 30.
3. The mountain range, running through western Iran.
4. Michael Sanders. Director of expeditions for the Mysteries of the Bible Research Foundation. Irvine, California.
5. Believed to be the river Pishon. The Murat River.
6. Wikipedia. http:// en.wikipedia. org/ wiki/ Garden-of-eden.
7. Answer. com: http:// www. answer. com/topic/eden.
8. Juris Zarins. Archaeologist. Worked in Saudi Arabia and Kuwait.
9. Landsat takes images of various earth locations from space.
10. Wadi-Batin River. Now dried out, leaving a fossil river shadow in the northwestern territory of Saudi Arabia. http://en.wikipedia.org/wiki/garden-of-eden.wikipedia.
11. Wikipedia. C. A. Salabach. http://en.wikipedia.org/wiki/garden-of-eden.
12. Bahrain in the Middle East
13. Noah's Flood. http://en.wikipedia.org/wiki/Noah's-Ark
14. Reginald Walker (1917-1989). Historian.

92

15. Nod, the biblical land in to which Cain got banished by God.
16. Genesis 3:24. The biblical cheruvim (cherubs), winged creatures deputed to watch the gate to the garden. Fierce fighters
17. Genesis 3:23-24.
18. Qur'an:2:35.
19. Ibid., 2:36. Ahmed Ali.

CHAPTER 13

God Puts Mark (Tattoos) on Cain.
The First Son of Adam and Eve

Were there other people (human beings) at the time of Adam?

There are passages in the Genesis and the Qur'an that indicate there were other people on the earth before Adam appeared

In the chronological order of the Genesis, it appears that there were human beings on earth before Adam was created.

Genesis 1:26 (1) "Then God said, 'And now we will make human beings; they will be like us. They will have power over the fish, the birds and all animals, domestic and wild, large and small."

Genesis 1:27 (2) "So God created human beings, making them to be like himself. He created them male and female."

Genesis 1:28 (3) (King James Version) "And God blessed them and said unto them, be fruitful and multiply and replenish the earth and subdue it."

Many scholars believe there was a gap of millions or billions of years between Genesis 1:1 and Genesis 1:2 (4).During that period, a catastrophe might have destroyed all living beings and resulted in the different fossils that we see today of ancient creatures and early humans. Therefore, the word replenishes in Genesis 1:28 (3) refers to the existence of previous human species who were destroyed by God by his worldwide judgment and as a result, God wants to "replenish" the earth with a new set of human beings. This is called the "gap" theory.

The Urantia Book;(5)

This book was published between 1924 and 1955.The authorship is unclear. It is a spiritual and philosophic book dealing with origin of life and its meaning. The word Urantia refers to earth. In this book there is reference to Adam and Eve.

> 74:24; as news of Adam's arrival spread abroad, thousands of the nearby tribesmen accepted the teachings of Von and Adamon while for months and months pilgrims continued to pour into Eden to welcome Adam and Eve to do homage to their unseen Father.

God Puts a Mark on Cain

In the conversation with Cain after he murdered his brother Abel, God tells Cain, Gen:4:11: "You are placed under a curse and can no longer farm the soil. It has soaked up your brother's blood as if it had opened its mouth to receive it when you killed him. If you try to grow crops, the soil will not produce any thing; you will be a homeless wanderer on earth."

Genesis 4:13-14 (6) "And Cain said to the Lord, 'This punishment is too hard for me to bear. You are driving me off the land and away from your presence. I will be a homeless wanderer on the earth and anyone who finds me will kill me.'"

In Qur'an, there is not much information as to what happened to Cain (Kabeel) after he murdered his brother Abel (Habeel). But in Genesis, there are some details of Cain's exile into a nearby land called Nod.

Genesis 4:15 (7) "But the Lord answered, 'No, if anyone kills you, seven lives will be taken in revenge.' So the Lord put a mark on Cain to warn anyone who met him, not to kill him. And Cain went away from the Lord's presence and lived in a land called Nod [wandering] (8) which is east of Eden. Then Cain built a city there and named it after his son Enoch."

Who were those people that Cain was afraid of, to be protected from? There must have been people around that place called Eden (Cain was in the area called Eden outside the Garden when he murdered Abel) who might kill him if they knew of this murder. Adam lived for 930 years according to the Bible, and consequently there could have been a huge family of Adam and Eve themselves, who can be angry at Cain and could kill him. But Cain was only seventeen years old and Abel was fifteen when this murder occurred according to traditional belief and also mentioned in some psedepigrapha. And all the rest of the children of Adam and Eve were born after Cain and Abel. Therefore, it certainly is not Adam's progeny that Cain was afraid of when he left Eden where the Garden was located. There must have been other people around Eden from whom God had to protect Cain. Even today the aborigines of the Amazon rain forest wear a mark on their body for identification among tribes. In fact tribesmen in any corner of the world wear marks of varying colors for identification of one tribe from the other.

This is a strong evidence for the presence of other human beings on earth when Adam and Eve were alive.

God had placed a mark on Cain so that he may not be killed by other human beings around. What is the significance of this mark? In order to recognize and respect this mark and to prevent a revenge killing of Cain, there must be people living there beforehand, to see similar marks and give due respect for this mark as either a traditional mark of divine manifestation or as a symbol of a tribe so that the tribesmen would not kill him. The aborigines used marks or emblems to identify their clan or tribe, as the modern-day gang members do. In either case, there must have been people who lived before Adam and Eve and was around the vicinity of the valley to which Cain was banished at that time.

After Adam and Eve were expelled from the garden, the subsequent events are described in the bible as follows: Genesis 3:24 (9) "Then at the east side of the Garden He put living creatures and a flaming Sword which turned in all directions. This was to keep anyone from coming near the tree of life". These guards were called the cherubims or cherubs. Who were these creatures (people) whom the cherubs were preventing, from entering the garden? This further solidifies our belief that there were other people around the territory of Eden at the time of Adam and Eve. These living creatures who were deputed to guard the Garden were called the cherubims (cherubs) (10). Judeo-Christian theologians believe that these were some kind of winged creatures in the class of angels.

Archaeologist David Rohl (11) in his book, Legend: The Genesis of Civilization notes that he has found a small town called Helabad during his search for the biblical Garden of Eden near the biblical land of Nod which is now called Nodqi according to Mr. Rohl. This town was formerly called Kheruabad, meaning "settlement of the Kheru people." Rohl believes the word kheru is a permutation of the Hebrew word Keruvim that is translated as "cherubs." The cherubs were deputed, according to the Bible, by God to guard the Garden of Eden after Adam and Eve were expelled from the garden. The Cherubs that were identified by Rohl were a tribe of fearsome warriors.

It is conceivable that these warrior tribes may be the cherubs mentioned in the Bible and were human beings , unlike the belief of many that they were angels.

These observations confirm the theory that there were other human beings during Adam's time and before.

In the British India, there was a special unit of the army called the Gurkha Regiment.(12) They are an ethnic Nepalese tribe who lives in a locality similar to the Zagros Mountains (13) between Iran and Turkey where it is presumed that the biblical Garden of Eden was located. They are well known to be exceptionally brave and fierce fighters as a tribe. The British Army still maintains a Gurkha Regiment in their armed services. Even today many Indian institutions and private establishments use these Gurkhas for security purposes. The cherubs could be a human tribe of fearsome fighters with great courage as the Nepalese Gurkhas.

Does Qur'an mention about "human creatures" (people) before Adam?

There are several verses in Qur'an that refers to the existence of humanoid species before Adam:

> 7:11 (14) (The Meaning of Holy Qur'an) Yusuf Ali "Indeed we created you and gave you shape AND THEN We bade the angels 'bow down to Adam.'" This verse suggests that there were people (pre-Adamic) who were being shaped (created) in the form of human beings and after fully formed in the form of Adam, the angels were ordered to bow before Adam.

> 7:11 (15) (The Message of The Qur'an) Asad "Indeed We created you and then formed you and THEN We said unto the angels, 'Prostrate yourselves before Adam.'"

> In these verses, it appears that human beings were created and reached a certain form and shape, and when fully developed in terms of mental faculties and physical perfection, he was called Adam, and when Adam arrived, God asked the angels to prostrate before him.

6:133 (16) (Asad) "If He so wills, he may put an end to you and thereafter cause whom he wills to succeed you—even as he brought you into being '**Out of Other Peoples' Seeds**'" .

This verse indicates that the present-day human beings were brought into existence from the seeds—(ova and sperms) of previous hominid species. Even though they were not fully developed human beings by themselves, by a process of genetic alteration (mutation-evolution) the off springs of the previous hominid species became fully developed human beings as Adam and Eve.

2:30 (17) "Will thou place there in one who will make mischief there and shed blood?"

The angels were asking God when God mentioned His intention of creating a man on earth. Obviously the angels have witnessed humanlike creatures on earth causing bloodshed.

Angels probably do not have the intellectual capacity to peep into the events ahead or to forecast the behaviors of the vicegerent (human being) to be soon created by God.

The angels therefore can relate to only what they have seen, namely, the bloodshed, probably created by the fighting between the Neanderthals and the Cro-Magnons or the species that existed even before. By their own admission, the angels are ignorant of things that God had not told them about.

Qur'an 2:31 (18) "And He taught Adam the names of all things, then he placed them before the angels, and said, 'Tell Me the names of these if you are right.' 2:32: They said 'Glory to Thee: of knowledge we have none, save what Thou hast taught us: in truth it is Thou who art perfect in knowledge and wisdom.'"

This is to reinforce the fact that the bloodshed that the angels spoke of is what they saw on earth among the hominids and not their prediction of what might the newly created man and the mankind will be doing in the future, and it was the actions of those pre-Adamic hominids that the angels were referring to when they were describing the bloodshed. This angelic statement again points to the fact that there were human species on earth before Adam and Eve appeared.

As we can see from the prostration of angels to Adam, human beings (Adam) must be superior intellectually to the angels, as can be inferred from the above verse (2:32); otherwise, God would not have ordered the angels to bow down to Adam. Therefore the angels have to see the actions of the humanlike creatures on earth, namely, the bloodshed and mischief the angels were speaking of, to remember rather than predict and forecast what the future human being might do, as the angels are not capable of forecasting future events. Angels only carry out the commands of God.

They had to witness the behavior of those pre-Adamic human species for them to remember it and then to mention to God about their behavior on earth. This verse clearly suggests the existence of humanlike creatures on earth before Adam appeared.

Who were these human creatures who were committing these mischief and bloodshed?

From the evolutionary history of human species, we can recognize two species before Adam that might have engaged in fighting and bloodshed, namely, the Neanderthals and the Cro-Magnons. And their physical appearance was like that of the modern humans, and these creatures must be the ones who were shedding blood and created mischief as described by the angels. This again supports the fact there were human beings (not fully developed) before Adam on earth. If these creatures were not existing on earth at all, how could the angels speculate on the mischievous behavior and bloodshed to be committed by the man being created by God? The angels would not have raised the question of bloodshed and mischief to be committed by this new creation in the near future, unless they had witnessed it on earth, being committed by the human species existing on earth at that time (the Neanderthals and the Cro-Magnons) or even the remote ancestral species.

Qur'an 2:30 (19) "Behold thy Lord said to the angels, 'I will create a vicegerent on earth.'"

Here the word "kh-l-f" is used to describe the status of the creation that God is going to introduce. This word khalifa has been interpreted to mean "a successor, vicegerent or inheritor" by various authorities. God has selected from human beings the prophets or warners to every nation or people to give them guidance and the laws of God, from the beginning of humanity including Adam. Adam is considered a prophet by Muslims and some Judeo-Christian denominations. Many will argue the fact that what was the reason for a prophet when there were no other human beings around

Adam's time. It may be agued, for one thing, Adam lived 930 years according to tradition and could have fathered many children and grandchildren and great-grandchildren to have a big clan who need spiritual guidance. It may not be for the pre-Adamic people as they were not fully developed as mentioned in Qur'an (Qur'an 15:29; 7:11(20). It can be considered that Adam was meant to be a vicegerent of God on earth

The other meaning for khalifa is "inheritor on earth," which makes sense in that no previous species of humanoids had the ability or the ingenuity that the present-day human species have to populate any part of the world and subdue it. Most of the previous species were not able to control and adjust to the various climatic and other natural vagaries of the earth. Up until Homo erectus appeared, most of the previous hominid species were limited to certain niches on earth and not worldwide as the present-day human beings have done.

The most commonly accepted meaning for Kh-li-fa is "a successor," and that is the area of interest to us. If God intended it, to mean a successor, one needs to understand the real meaning of the word successor.

According to William Lane's lexicon, khalifa means "one who came after, followed, succeeded, or remained after another, or another that had perished or died."

Lexicographer Ibn-e-Manzoor Ifriqi: "khalifa fulaaman" means when someone becomes successor to some one else. "Wa al-khalifah, alladhi yustu khalafu minimum qablahu" means the one who became successor to his prior (Ibn-Manzur: Lisaen al-Arab.1405-AH 9:82)

Imam Razi: "al-khalifah man yakhlufu ghayarahu wa yaqunnu muqaamahu': Khalifah is the one who comes after another person and takes his place.(Imam Razi.Tefsir-e-Kabir 12:202).

Commenting on Qur'an:2:30: on the word "khaleefathan" Rashid Rada (Tafseer Al Manaar) says that some scholars understood from this verse that there were other species of hominids before Adam, that had disappeared. Referring to the Islamic commentator Muhammad Abduhu, Rashid Rada states "that Adam was not the first rational creature on earth. The new class of social animals has some resemblance with the primitive group or groups in person and nature. But has differences in some ethics and nature" It also suggests that Adam was not the first rational creature on earth.(21)

We need to examine what will be the appropriate interpretation of the word khalifa. Both the interpretations (vicegerent and successor) are very appropriate under two different contexts. The dictionary meaning of vicegerent is "an administrative deputy of a king or magistrate." Under this explanation, Adam is considered as a deputy to establish and administer the laws of the Creator, among the people on earth, as has been the practice of God since Adam was deputed, in the form of prophets and warners that were sent to several communities later on.

The second interpretation is more relevant (successor) to our discussion regarding the presence of human species before Adam. A successor is named or appointed by an existing organization, a political party, a government, or a king when the prevailing authority of the entity either came to an end or by death of the king who is in charge or change at the top level of authority in order to continue its function. In the case of a king or a queen, a child born to him or her becomes the successor. A successor is one who succeeds an entity that either dies or changes. Obviously the reference to a successor is not to God who neither changes nor dies. Therefore, this reference to successor has to be to the human beings, that were there on earth before Adam came into being, and they eventually went extinct. Adam and Eve were the successors to the previous race of human beings, the first generation of mankind, namely, the Cro-Magnons (see chapter 6).

Why did these previous species die out is unclear from Qur'an except those generations who disobeyed God's commands were destroyed.

In Qur'an, there are several references to the destruction of generations in the past.

Generations destroyed: Qur'an (22) 6:6, 10:13, 11:100-101, 116; 13:30; 19:74; 20:51; 28:58; 32:26; 36:31; 38:3; 43:8, 77:16.

Some of the generations were destroyed after they had reached their term, and other people were destroyed after warned of their misdeeds. As we see from paleoanthropology, many early hominid species went extinct and the reason could not be clearly identified except to speculate on their infighting, starvation, diseases or the arrival of a new species with beneficial mutations and resultant survival advantage. It may well be due to the result of a supernatural design. As scientists indicate that the longevity of the Neanderthals was around forty-five to fifty years and that of the next species, the Cro-Magnons' being around sixty-five years. The Qur'an does not indicate the span of existence of the present-day human race on earth or the average life span of an individual. The average life expectancy of human beings on earth is below ninety years. Occasionally we hear about one or two individuals being alive into the hundredth mark. The oldest verified super centenarian was a French national by name Jeanne Louise Calment (1875-1997)who lived 122 years. The oldest living person is an American woman 114 years old (23) But the Bible indicates that God has appointed a term for human beings.

Genesis 6:3 (24) "Then the Lord said, 'I will not allow people to live for ever, they are mortal. From now on they will live no longer than 120 years.'"

Qur'an 26:208 (25) "And withal, never have We destroyed any community unless it had been warned and reminded." This will apply only to the modern humans as the early humanoid species were not developed enough to be warned about. Those hominids were destroyed probably after they reached a term appointed and the next species emerged, and there was no need for the previous species to hang around.

Therefore, Adam became the successor to the last pre-Adamic race, the Cro-Magnons. These Cro-Magnons were genetically and physically identical to us but they disappeared from the fossil record by about ten thousand to fifteen thousand years ago, and that is the most probable time for the appearance of Adam and Eve on earth. This again proves the existence of humans before Adam.

In the case of Adam, all the three interpretations of the word khalifa are very appropriate. He was a vicegerent of God, he was a successor to the immediate previous human race, the first generation of mankind, the Cro-Magnons (chapter 6), and indeed he was an inheritor of earth as the entire earth is populated by his progeny.

From these scriptural statements, genetic and fossil evidences, we can conclude that there were previous hominids, including the Neanderthals, and more recently there were human beings like us, the Cro-Magnons (the first generation of mankind) before Adam and Eve appeared on earth.

References to God Marks Cain:

1. Gen.:1:26, 27, 28.
2. Ibid., 1:27.
3. Ibid., 1:28.
4. Ibid., 1:1, 2.
5. Urantia Book. http://en.wikipedia.org/wiki/The-Urantia-Book
6. Genesis: 4:13-14.
7. Ibid., 4:15.
8. Nod, the Biblical land where Cain was banished.
9. Gen. 3:24.
10. Cherubims (cherubs), the biblical winged creatures. http://en.wikipedia.org/wiki/Cherub.

11. David Rohl. The British archaeologist and historian author The Legend: Genesis of Civilization.
12. Gurkhas. A Nepalese population. Brave fighters.
13. The Zagros mountain range, between Iran and Turkey.
14. Qur'an: 7:11.Meaning of the Holy Qur'an. Yusuf Ali.
15. Ibid., 7:12. Muhammad Asad, trans. Message of the Qur'an.
16. Ibid.Qur'an:6:133.
17. Ibid., 2:30.
18. Ibid., 2:31, 32, 33.
19. Ibid.2:30.
20. Ibid.15:29
21. Science Religion Dialogue. Dr.M. Izharul Haq.http:// *www.hssrd.org/journal. Summer 2002/evolution.htm*. Imam Razi:Fafsir-e-Kabir.12:202.
22. Ibid 6:6; 10:13; 11:100;101;111;116; 13:30; 19:74; 20:51; 28:58; 32:26; 36:31; 38:3; 43:8; 77:16.
23. Wikipedia.http://en.wikipedia.org/wiki/Life-of-oldest-persons. Retrieved.2-26-2009.
24. Gen. 6:3.
25. Qur'an 26:208.

CHAPTER 14

Incest:
Descent of Mankind from Adam and Eve

We are told (Judeo-Christian-Islamic faith) for generations that the entire humanity on earth are descendents of the one pair of human beings called Adam and Eve.

If Adam and Eve were the only two people on earth at that time, one needs to examine the various mechanisms as to how present-day human beings came about from just two individuals. First of all, the evolutionists and biologists say, that if there was only one pair of any species on earth at any time, they will not survive and will die out. (people will argue that this pair namely Adam and Eve were specially created and deputed to earth by God himself, and there is no need to be afraid of their annihilation by any natural forces, or otherwise).

If there were only these two souls, namely, Adam and Eve, on earth and who had children, the only way for the propagation of their progeny is by marriage (sexual relation) between own sisters and brothers. Whether marriage as a social contract as we practice now, existed at Adam's time is unclear, which obviously is committing a despicable act that the present-day society will call incest. One cannot imagine that God himself will cause such an act to be committed in the very beginning of mankind, especially in view of the fact that incest was prohibited and made unlawful as described in the scriptures later on. The Bible: Leviticus: 18:6-20; 22; and 23 and the Qur'an: 4:23.

Obviously during Adam's time, alphabets were not invented nor was writing. There is no evidence of a scripture that might have been given to Adam by God. This does not preclude oral instructions being given to Adam about rules and regulation pertaining to God's requirements (commandments) for the nascent society to be created after Adam and Eve and for themselves. Indeed that seems to be the case as God had instructed Adam not to approach the forbidden tree. Qur'an 2:35(1) "O Adam dwell thou and thy wife in the Garden, and eat of the beautiful things therein as where and when ye will; but approach not this tree, or ye run into harm and transgression."

Qur'an 5:28 "Abel tells Cain 'if thou dost stretch thy hand against me, to slay me it is not for me to stretch my hand against thee to slay thee: for I do fear Allah (God) the cherisher of the worlds".

5:29 "For me I intend to let thee draw on thyself, my sin as well as thine, for thou wilt be among the companions of the Fire, and that is the reward of those who do wrong."

2:37 "Then learnt Adam from his Lord words of inspiration."

2:38 "Surely there will come to you a guidance from Me, then whoever follows my guidance no fear shall come upon them, nor shall they grieve."

2:39 "And to those who disbelieve in and reject Our messages, they are the companions of the fire, in it they will abide."

The Bible also indicates that God had given instructions to Adam.

In Genesis (2) 2:16-17 it says, "You may eat the fruit of any tree in the garden, except the tree that gives knowledge of what is good and what is bad. You must not eat the fruit of that tree. If you do, you will die the same day."

From the above, it is clear that God had given certain commandments to Adam and their children.

It seems from Adam's comment (Pseudepigrapha. Life of Adam and Eve) about Cain's desire to marry his own twin sister Lebhudha, that such a practice was frowned upon.

Incest

Incest means different things to different societies. Uniformly, all societies abhor sexual relation and marriage between siblings, parents, and children. But many societies even preclude such activities among first cousins, uncles, and aunts.

God has the power to have created more than one Adam and Eve and avoid such a scenario of marriage between siblings. But God had a different plan as can be seen later, that without having to have several Adams and Eves and without having to commit incest, human species can be propagated as had happened through Adam and Eve by a morally and spiritually acceptable method sanctioned by God. (Through the seeds of other people. Qur'an: 6:133 (4).

Why incest is prohibited?

There are many kinds of prohibitions in different religions and societies. One cannot explain the reasons for these prohibitions on the basis of science. Whether these prohibitions, if not heeded to, will cause any physical harm is unclear. Examples are beef prohibition in Hinduism, hoofed animals without a cleft and pork in Judaism and Seventh-day Adventists, pork and alcohol in Islam, to mention a few. Alcohol can cause inhibition of thought process and long-term harm on vital organs. But not in small quantities, except it can become an addiction. But even small amounts are prohibited in Islam unless it is contained in a medication or to treat an illness. Similarly, beef and pork has no known harmful effects on our health unless consumed in excessive amounts. These prohibitions are meant to keep our runaway behaviors and activities in check and to remind ourselves to the need to restrict our actions and thoughts, and as limit setting practices which in turn make us God conscious. Within our sphere of present-day knowledge, one cannot explain it otherwise.

The Mosaic Law

Leviticus 18:6-20, 22-23 (5) says, "Do not have sexual relations with any of your relatives. Do not disgrace your father by having sexual acts with your mother. You must not disgrace your own mother. Do not disgrace your father by having sexual relation with any of his other wives. Do not have sexual relation with your sister or your stepsister, whether or not she was brought up in the same house with you. Do not have sexual relation with your granddaughter, which would be a disgrace to you. Do not have sexual relation with a half sister, she is too your sister. Do not have sexual relation with an aunt whether she is your father's sister or mother's sister. Do not have sexual relation with your uncle's wife, she too is your aunt. Do not have intercourse with your daughter in law, or your brother's wife. Do not have sexual relation with the daughter or granddaughter of a woman with whom you have had sexual relation, they may be related to you, and that would be incest. Do not take your wife's sister as one of your wives as long as your wife is living.

"Do not have intercourse with a woman during her monthly period, because she is ritually unclean. Do not have intercourse with another man's wife that will make you ritually unclean. No man is to have sexual relation with another man, God hates that. No man or woman is to have sexual relation with an animal that perversion makes you ritually unclean."

Qur'an

> 4:23 (6) "Prohibited to you (for marriage) are your mother, daughters, sisters, father's sisters, mother's sisters, brother's daughters, sister's daughters, foster mothers [who gave you suck], foster sisters, your wife's mother, your stepdaughters under your guardianship, born of your wives to whom ye have gone in, no prohibition if ye have not gone in [those who have been] wives of your sons, proceeding from your loins. And two sisters in wedlock at one and the same time except for what is past. Also [prohibited are] women already married except those whom your right hand possess.

In the Cave of Treasures: A Pseudepigrapha) (7)

After Adam and Eve were expelled from the paradise, Eve conceived and brought forth Cain and his twin sister Lebhudha. And Eve conceived again and she brought forth Habbil [Abel] and Kelimath, his sister with him. [The book of Bee makes Kelimath the twin sister of Cain and Lebhudha the twin sister of Abel.]

And when they grew up Adam said to Eve, "Let Cain take to wife Kelimath who was brought with Abel and Abel take to wife Lebhudha who was brought with Cain."

And Cain said unto Eve his mother, "I will take to my wife my twin sister Lebhudha and let Abel take to his wife his twin sister Kelimath." Now Lebhudha was beautiful.

When Adam heard these words, which was exceedingly displeasing to him, he said, "It will be a transgression of the commandment of thee to take to [wife] thy sister who was born with thee." Even at this early history of our generation, there is indication that brother-sister marriage was not accepted.

In Islam, sexual relation with a wet mother is also prohibited. The abovementioned scriptural guidelines indicate that incest is not approved by God Almighty. There are guidelines established by God for marriage practices as described above and hence incest will not be accepted as a permissible act even at the beginning of mankind. (The Adamic generation—from Adam and Eve onward.)

Is incest different from other prohibitions in the scriptures?

Does it have a physical and psychological adverse effects on the offspring other than a social taboo?

Indeed it has.

Incest is defined as sexual intercourse between closely related persons. Most modern societies have legal or social restrictions on consanguineous marriages. But in ancient Egypt brother-sister, father-daughter, mother-son relations were practiced (8).

In some lower species, inbreeding between close relatives including parents and children has been observed. But there is a tendency to discourage it. For example, in some lower species, the male offspring are often driven away by the mother when they reach sexual maturity.

"Full-sibling or parent-child incest results in about 17 percent child mortality and 25 percent child disability for a combined result of about 42 percent nonviable off springs."(9).

This happens not only in humans but in most life-forms especially among mammals and multi cellular organisms.

A study of thirty-eight captive mammalian species found, a cross species, average of around 33 percent offspring mortality, resulting from closely incestuous mating (10).

Even if there are more families to marry from, if they are closely related, off springs will have same degree of defects and that the frequency of defective births will increase if this practice is repeated in generations.

Inbreeding increases the frequency of homozygotes within a population. Depending on the number of generations in which inbreeding occurs has positive and negative effects.

Inbreeding is the scientific term and incest is a social term for procreation among individuals with genetic closeness [close relatives].

The psychology of sexual attraction toward [siblings] is poorly understood. An overwhelming evidence from research shows that evolutionary biology and evolved human psychology played a central role in human aversion to incest.

Inbreeding [incest] leads to increased incidence of homozygosity (the occurrence of the same allele at the same locus on both members of a chromosome pair). Because of this, close relatives are much more likely to share the same allele than unrelated individuals. This is especially important for recessive alleles that happen to be deleterious. It will be harmless and inactive in a heterozygous pairing but when homozygous, it can cause serious developmental defects. Such off springs have a higher chance of death before reaching puberty. This leads to "inbreeding depression," a measurable decrease in fitness due to inbreeding among populations with deleterious recessives. Recessive genes, which can contain various genetic problems, appear more often in the offspring of procreative couplings whose members both have the same gene. If both parents are hemophiliacs, then there is a 100 percent chance that the child will be hemophiliac.

The so-called positive effects of inbreeding are neutralized by the "fitness depression" as described before, which causes selection to discourage it (11).

Because of genetic harm done, animals inbreed only in extremely unusual circumstances like major population bottlenecks and forced selection by animal breeders. Scientists have found evidence that some species possess evolved psychological aversion to inbreeding via kin-recognition heuristics (12) (13).

The Westermark Effect: (14)

When two people live in proximity during the first few years of their life, either one or both are desensitized to later close sexual attraction. He proposed that humans have a mechanism, whose evolved function is to discourage incest. Children who are raised together during the first five to ten years of life have inhibited sexual desire toward one another and is a very strong piece of evidence in favor of human being's psychological aversion to incest. In a cohort study of children raised communally like siblings in the Kiryat Yedidim kibbutz in the 1950s, the anthropologist (15) found practically no intermarriage between his subjects as adults despite pressure from parents and community. These children were genetically unrelated. This further confirms the Westermarck hypothesis described earlier.

The hypothesis is that some undefined psychological mechanisms cause children who grow up together to lack sexual attraction to one another. Fox in 1962 (16) corroborated Spiro's findings in his study of Israeli kibbutzim.

In a study of Taiwanese "child marriages," researchers (17) reported a similar aversion. In these marriages, the future wife was brought into the family and raised with her fiancé. Such marriages were extremely difficult to consummate and led to decreased fertility.

Childhood co residency with an opposite sex sibling (biologically related or not) was correlated with moral repugnance toward third party sibling incest, as reported by Lieberman Et al., 2003 (18).

It is not unusual for biological siblings who did not know each other in childhood to be attracted to each other when meeting as adults.

From the above discussion, we can see that even lower species shunned incest due to the deleterious effect on their progeny that will affect adversely on the propagation of their respective species. As the species progressed through evolution, incest became a cultural and social stigma. It is believed that the Cro-Magnons probably were monogamous, and there is no evidence for or against incest. Because they were a more advanced human species and were similar to us, we can conceptualize that they were not incestuous even though we cannot prove this hypothesis.

In the pseudepigrapha, we read that Adam was upset with Cain for his advances toward his sister Luella and commented that was against God's commands. This suggests that God had given Adam certain divine instructions, which may include prohibition of brother-sister marriage [Pseudepigrapha is not considered canonical. But Ethiopian bible considers it canonical].

The Cave of Treasures (19), a noncanonical book, pseudepigrapha, relates the story of Cain's birth and the dispute of the brothers. "When Adam wished to know Eve (his wife), he took from the skirts of paradise gold, myrrh, and frankincense and put them in a cave, and he blessed it and sanctified it that it might be the house of prayer for himself and of his sons, and he called tit the 'cave of treasures.'" And Adam and Eve came down from that holy mountain to its outskirts below, and there Adam knew his wife (knew in this context means sexual relation). Some say that Adam knew Eve thirty years after they had gone forth from the paradise. And she conceived and bore Cain and Lebhudha, his sister, with him, and again she conceived and bore Abel and Kelimath, his sister, with him' When youths had grown up, Adam said to Eve, "Let Cain take to wife Kelimath who was born with Abel and let Abel take Lebhudha who was born with Cain." But Cain said to Eve his mother, "I will take to wife my own sister and let Abel take his for Lebhudha was beautiful." When Adam heard these words, he was very grieved and said, "It is a transgression of the law that thou shouldst take to wife thy sister who was born with thee. But take ye of the fruit of the trees and the young of the flocks, and go ye up to the top of this holy mountain, and enter into the cave of treasures, and offer up your offerings there and pray before God and then be united unto your wives."

From all these we can conclude that brother-sister marriage was not sanctioned by Adam and there was no need for it either. This cannot be taken as if incest did not ever take place. Whether Cain married his sister or not is unclear. Probably not, as he went on to the neighboring land of Nod after he killed his brother Abel, and there he erected a city and knew his wife there.

Genesis 4:16-17 (20) says, "Cain went to the land of Nod and found his wife [knew his wife] and built a city and named after his son Enoch."

With this information, how then the family of Adam and Eve propagated the human species in the form of multitudes of human beings on earth, including us without committing incest.

Let us examine this scenario:

As indicated above, we have established that the most modern human race, the Cro-Magnons, was living before the appearance of Adam and Eve. The Cro-Magnon race and the Adamic race (Adam's children), that is us, are genetically identical (vide supra), and they can successfully interbreed with each other resulting in fertile off springs unlike between the Neanderthals and the Cro-Magnons, where, if they had interbreeding, the offspring will not survive as they are considered different species of hominids. The Cro-Magnons were very gracile and tall people, and the Cro-Magnon males, the pre-Adamic people, were very big and strong to attract the Adamic (Adam's descendents) girls, and the Cro-Magnon girls were very gracile to be attracted by the sons of Adam and Eve and vice versa. And marriage between these groups (sexual relations [whether marriage as a social contract as we practice today , was existing at that time is not clear]) Can result in viable off springs as they were genetically identical without any problem for their children.

This discussion will suffice to discard the prevailing theory that Adam's children had to marry between themselves as there was no choice for them, since there were no other human beings around at that time.

As shown here, there were fully developed, and genetically identical, human beings around, during the life time of Adam and Eve and that their children could marry from the children of this race, the Cro-Magnons, without the need for incest.

It was a sad event that our ancestral race (pre-Adamic), the Cro-Magnons, disappeared from the fossil record about ten to fifteen thousand years ago. How and why is not clear. Some explanation can be found in chapter 6 (Cro-Magnons). They were the first generation of mankind. Were they victims of an epidemic, deprivation of food, or due to the new arrivals, the Adamic people with superior intelligence and mutation related survival advantage or due to a short climatic aftermath, all are points of contention as reasons for their extinction. It is the same pattern with earlier hominids that when a new species appeared with some advanced technology or tools or bigger brains and consequently having some survival advantage, the previous species died out. This is generally attributed to competition for food and probably fighting each other for survival or death from newly introduced infections and others. But why did the Cro-Magnons, the pre-Adamic people, disappear? They looked like us, genetically similarto us and very gracile people with technological advancement and even having had a culture?

In order to explain this, one needs to review the qualities and attributes of the next generation of mankind (the second generation. Chapter 7), starting from Adam and Eve. (first generation of mankind being the Cro-Magnons).

References for Incest:

1. Qur'an 2:35; 5:28, 29, 37, and 39.
2. Gen. 2:16-17.
3. Pseudepigrapha: The Life of Adam and Eve. http://en.wikipedia.org/wiki/Life-of-Adam-and Eve.
4. Qur'an 4:23.
5. Leviticus 18:6.
6. Qur'an:4:23.
7. Cave of Treasures. A Pseudepigrapha. http://en.wikipedia.org/wiki/Cave-of-Treasures.
8. Maurice Godelier. Meta Morphoses. De la Puente. 2004 and New left Review. Jack Goody, "The Labrynth of Kinship." http/:newleftreview=2592.retrieved 2007-7-24.
9. Donald Brown. Human Universal, 113.
10. Ibid., 124.
11. Fitness: depression. Inbreeding, Moore 1992; Uhlman 1992. Wikipedia.
12. Pusey A, Wolf M.Trend.Ecol.Evol.1996.11:201-206
13. Penn D, W. K. Potts. American naturalist. 153:145-164.
14. Edward Westermarck. Sociologist and anthropologist The history of human marriage, 5th ed. (Macmillon: London, 1921). Wikipedia.
15. Melford E. Spiro, anthropologist. Kiryat Yedidim. Wikipedia.
16. Fox N. A. 1992. Wikipedia.
17. Wolf and Huang. Taiwanese Child Marriage.
18. 18. Debra Lieberman. Did Morality have a biological origin. Center for Evolutionary Psychology, University of California. Wikipedia.
19. Cave of Treasures.
20. Genesis 4:16, 17.

CHAPTER 15
Evolution (general)

In the following chapters we will explore the ongoing evolution(transformation)of the universe, the earth, the atmosphere and the life forms since the big bang.

The word evolution is derived from the Latin word evolutio (unrolling). Evolution is a change over time and is applied to changes in society, religion, culture, economics, science, and political systems including biological. Here, we are solely dealing with our origin on earth whether by creation or evolution (biological) and to reconcile these two opposing arguments.

From the big bang onwards, everything has evolved or transformed to become what we are today (as human beings) and what wee see around us. The big bang brought about the immense energy and matter in to being. From the early gaseous state came about the interstellar matter and from it, the galaxies were formed. Then the sun, planets, stars, moon, and earth were gradually formed over a period of billions of years.

The earth itself had to go through a period of cooling, formation of the crust, a mantle, and volcanic activity in the center and later an atmosphere, originally devoid of oxygen, then oxygen came about so that animals can survive. This is earth's evolution (Chapter 20). Everything has changed over time.

Biological evolution is a theory that explains the origin of all the diverse forms of life on earth (origin of species). Evolution is a change in inherited traits of a population from generation to generation. These traits are expression of genes that are copied and passed on to off springs during reproduction. The different kinds of living organisms that we see today have evolved from a common ancestor or an organic pool over billions of years according to science. Changes in an individual is not evolution. Only population evolves. Random mutation and genetic re combinations are factors that create changes in population. Mutation is due to the change in the base sequences of the DNA. Those with beneficial mutation will survive and those with harmful mutation will die. The mechanism that weeds out the beneficial and positive changes from negative changes is called natural selection.

Biological evolution is believed to have been the process by which the unicellular organism, which appeared on earth about 3.5 billion years ago through a process of random mutation or mutation due to impact of environmental factors, influenced by natural selection, evolved into plants and animals that are present on earth today and finally to man. Mutations are either neutral, beneficial, or harmful. Harmful mutants will not survive.

When we talk about evolution, the first name that comes to anyone's mind is that of Charles Darwin (1). But there were several scientists proposing evolution centuries before Darwin. However, Darwin and Wallace (2) were the first to give a credible theory of evolution by what is called natural selection and descent with modification.

In 400 BC, Greek atomists were teaching that the sun, earth, life, humans, civilizations, and society emerged over eons from the eternal atoms colliding and vibrating in the void.

In the epic poem "On the Nature of Things" the Roman atomist Lucretius (99-55 BC) described the stages of living earth coming to be what it is. "The earth and sun formed from swirls of dust congregated from the atoms colliding and vibrating in the void. Early plants and animals sprang from the early earth's own substance because of the insistence of the atoms that formed the earth. The aging earth gave birth to a succession of animals including a series of progressively less brutish humans that made a succession of improved tools, laws, and civilization with increasing complexity. Finally arriving at the current earth and life-forms as they are (3). These ideas were forgotten in the West for over 1400 years but continued to be discussed in the Islamic world." (4)

In the fourth century BC, there were proto evolutionists and evolutionary concepts being expressed in Indian and Chinese philosophy. In the Vedas of Hinduism, there are passages that indicate that more complex phenomena rose out of simpler phenomena (5). Also it is seen in the writings of Patanjali.

The Incarnations of Vishnu (the Desavataras), reflect theory of evolution (6).

In Buddhism, emphasis is seen on people's and creature's rise and fall over vast periods of time, suggesting an evolutionary nature.

The earliest logically proposed evolutionary theory is generally agreed to have come from Anaximandros (Anaximander) of Miletus in Greece (610-547 BC), about a century before the writing of Genesis. His writings are not readily available, but some teachings of Anaximander are preserved by later writers who disagreed with him as described below, by Plutarch, Hippolytus and Cesnorinus. He believed that life started in water, and from this, other life-forms including man came (7).

"Wherefore they (Syrians) reference the fish as of the same origin and the same family as man, holding a more reasonable philosophy than that of Anaximander, for he declares not that fishes and men were generated at the same time, but that at first, men were generated in the form of fishes and that growing up as sharks do, till they were able to help themselves, they then came forth on the dry ground". (Plutarch, first century CE) (8).

Further he says that at the beginning, man was generated from all sorts of animals, but man alone requires careful feeding for a long time. Such things at the beginning could not have preserved his existence. Such is the teaching of Anaximandros (Hippolytus, third century CE) (9).

"Animals came into being through vapors raised by the sun. Man, however, came into being from another animal, namely, the fish for at first he was like a fish". (Hippolytus, third century CE)(10).

Anaximander speculated about the origin of animal life. Observing fossils, he claimed that animals sprang out of the sea long ago. As early humidity evaporated, dry land emerged, and in time humans, that had to adapt.

The third century Roman writer Cesnorinus reported, "Anaximander of Miletus considered that from warmed up water and earth emerged either fish or entirely fishlike animals. Inside the animal, man took form and embryos were held prisoners until puberty. Only then, after these animals burst open, could men and women come out. Now able to feed themselves." This theory of an aquatic descent of man was received later as aquatic ape hypothesis. Many consider him evolution's most ancient proponent (11).

Xenophanes of Kolopbon (570 BC[12]) was the first person on record to have understood the implication of fossils. Shells are found inland and in the mountains, and in the quarries of Syracuse, an impression of a fish and a sea weed has been found, and impressions of fish were found in the depth of the rock and impressions of many marine creatures. These, he (Xenophanes) says, were produced when everything was, long ago, covered with mud; and the impressions were dried in the mud. He rejected the then prevalent Greek belief in the pantheon of Gods and believed in one God.

Hippolytus (discussing the teachings of Xenophanes) notes that he believed that the earth must have gone through many cycles of life during which different forms of animals existed and were then wiped out.

The Greeks, along with other ancient cultures, came into frequent contact with fossils. The word fossil came from Greek and means "dug up item." The Greeks quarried massive amounts of rocks and came across fossils.

In China, according to Joseph Needham, (13) "The Taoists elaborated what comes near to a statement of a theory of evolution. At least, they firmly denied the fixity of biological species."

There are two theories of evolution (a) punctuated equilibrium (14), which states that evolution consists of occasional spurts of rapid change and (b) gradualism (15) that states that evolution is slow and gradual. In this view, evolution is seen as smooth and continuous. This also postulates that there is no clear demarcation between old species and new species. Evolution occurs at a constant rate. (Evolution by creeps as opposed to punctuated spurts.)

It is claimed that after dinosaurs went extinct, there was a sudden and rapid evolution of mammals over forty-five million years, suggesting punctuated equilibrium. While fossil evidence of plants and animals show a very slow process of change, suggesting gradualism.

G. Ledyard Stebbins (16) proposed that evolution is without direction, and it is not an evolutionary tree. Rather it is like a bush and each branch grows randomly (17).

In the Judeo-Christian-Islamic theology, there is considerable debate and disagreement as to whether evolution is compatible with faith, to outright rejection of evolutionary thought. Many believe that God created every species individually without any need for evolution. In that argument, no one, nowhere has ever hinted at the sources or materials from which such An array of creatures (presumably unrelated) were created, unlike as in the case of human beings (Adam), it was from mud or clay as mentioned in the Bible and Qur'an. Unless alteration and re composition are made, there are not many different materials for creating millions of different creatures from.

Many believe that human beings (Adam) were created from mud or clay literally. In that concept, God took some soil or clay and made (sculptured) an image or model of a man from it, and then breathed His life-giving spirit into it, and it became alive; and Eve (wife of Adam) was made out of Adam's rib. Then all human beings originated from this pair. This is the creationists' view. This can be called the "**sculptured creation concept**".

Man's origin (the origin of all living things) from clay by the process of abiogenesis will be described later.

This religious belief (the creationist belief) has been conveyed from generation to generation by word of mouth and through the preaching of religious scholars. The belief that Adam, the first human being, was created from mud or clay must have been rooted in our society from time immemorial. Mud, specifically clay, has been used to make a variety of objects like pottery, figurines, and images of different gods and goddesses. On the basis of this, it is befitting to conclude that human being was made out of mud or clay as a human model and then made him alive by God's command. As it is mentioned in the Bible and Qur'an (vide infra) that God made human being from clay or mud, many believers have taken upon themselves to believe in that statement literally on the basis of the scriptures. There are no statements in the scriptures whether it is Genesis, Qur'an, or the Vedas of Hinduism that negates the theory of biological evolution. The clay was only an intermediary in the creation of life and man (see chapter 28).

What are the Scriptures saying?

Genesis 1:26 (17) "Then God said, 'And now we will make human beings; they will be like Us, and resemble Us.'" In this statement, there is no mention from where these human beings were created.

Genesis 2:7 "Then the Lord God took some soil from the ground and formed a man out of it."

Genesis 2:22 "He formed a woman out of the rib of Adam (the man God made) and brought her to him."

There are several references to man's creation from mud or clay in Qur'an (18): 6:2; 15:26; 22:5; 55:14. And additionally Qur'an (19) refers to the creation of man from earth, dust, and water (Qur'an 15:28; 25:54).

The information that scientists have acquired over the past 150 years in terms of geo paleontology, fossil evidence, and molecular biology were not available to our ancestors, and hence, the creationist belief (the sculptured creation concept) remained unchallenged. In some of the translations of the Qur'an, one can detect the permeation of the creationist view as far as the origin of man is concerned.

As newer and newer evidences are being acquired in terms of human origin, this creationist view is changing, and the scientific concept of evolution (abiogenesis of life from nonliving and later becoming a proto cell changing next to a multi cellular organism, plants, mammals, and finally to man) is being accepted by most.

It is to be re affirmed that there are no grounds to exclude God in this concept of evolution, as it is the result of the grand design of the creator, subservient to His laws, that everything in the universe started out from singularity out of the big bang, including human beings.

As mentioned above, both in the Genesis and Qur'an, clay has been mentioned as the source of the creation of human beings. If we reject the notion of the "Sculptured Creation concept" of the creation of Adam in that God took some clay in his hand and made a human model and then inspired His spirit into it and made him alive, then what would be the reason that God repeatedly reminds us that human beings are made from mud and specifically the clay? Many commentators contend that the reason is to remind us of our low origin, and our return to earth after death. Certainly that is the only way out for us.

If it was not the "Sculptured Creation concept" what is the alternative scenario for our origin from clay? Evolutionary scientists believe in the abiogenic origin of life from nonliving molecules (origin of life from non life) that were present on the pre biotic earth. From organic compounds to proto cell, to unicellular organisms and then into multi cellular organisms and through evolutionary process into the present biota that includes human beings. In their pursuit of the origin of life, scientists are experimenting with a variety of chemicals. They are astonished by the fact that clay is playing a very important part in creating the building blocks that are essential for the creation of artificial life, namely, the cell contents and the cell wall. The well-known chemist Graham Cairn-Smith (chapter 26) maintains that clay was the primal source for the origin of life on earth.

In spite of many other substances on earth, God mentions clay more often as the source of our creation. There must lay the essential truth of the basis of our origin (clay), and indeed the scientists are beginning to confirm the idea what the scriptures are proclaiming. This is the result of scientific exploration over the past 150 or so years. In keeping with the available scientific evidence and more recently the genetic and molecular biological evidence, we have to take a new look at how human species appeared on earth including Adam and Eve.

Many of the verses in Qur'an are clear and many are left ambiguous as per the intention of God. When these ambiguous statements are interpreted by the scholars, they have to rely on their own understanding of the matter in question coupled with the available scientific information. If there is no established scientific information, they interpreted it according to what they thought about it at the time of their interpretation, which may not be the correct one later when new scientific information becomes available.

We are fortunate to have the vast amount of information from scientific research and the philosophical discussions and "tafseers" of the eminent scholars of Islam. Due to the paucity of scientific information available during their times, some apparent errors might have happened in their explanation of some verses in the Qur'an.

The errors in the translations and interpretations should never be misunderstood as errors in the Holy Book. Only in the translations may have errors in it.

For example:

Qur'an: 38:75(20) "Allah (God) said, "O Iblis! What prevents thee from prostrating thyself to one whom I have created with my hands". (Yusuf Ali)

"O Iblis! What has kept thee from prostrating thyself before the being which I have created with my hands" (Muhammad Asad) (21). In the commentary, it is explained as the handiwork of God.

"O Iblis what hindered you from adoring what I created by my own authority."(Ahmed Ali) ((22)

In this instance the translation of the verse: 38:75 (22) by Ahamed Ali and the rendering in the commentary of the author (21) are more consistent with the overall understanding of the creation of man from an evolutionary standpoint. As we understand, God is all powerful and does not need to take clay in His hands, to create a clay human model and then to make it alive. All God has to do is to give the command and it is done. Qur'an 2:117 "When he wills a thing to be, He but says unto it, "Be" and it is. Qur'an:3:59: "The likeness of Jesus with Allah (God) is truly as the likeness of Adam. He created him from dust, then said to him, "Be" and he was". (23). The assumption that

God has hands is like humanizing the Almighty, whose shape, nature, and form are all unknown to mankind and are beyond human perception.

Qur'an 6:103 "No vision can grasp Him. But His grasp is over all vision. He is above all comprehension." Verse 112:4 "And none comparable to him." In the commentary for verse 6:103, page 324 explains the meaning of Latif—fine, subtle, so fine and subtle as to be invisible to the physical eye; so fine as to be imperceptible to the senses; so pure as to be above the mental or spiritual visions of man. It may also mean "one who understands the finest mysteries."

Qur'an: 42:11 "There is nothing like unto him."

6:100, The Meaning of the Holy Qur'an, "Limitless is He, is his glory, and sublimely exalted above anything that man may describe by way of definition." (24)

The shapelessness of God is also mentioned in the Vedas and Bhagavad—Gita (Hinduism) (25). Arjuna asks Krishna, "O, Supreme Lord, you are as you describe yourself to be; I do not doubt that. Nevertheless I long to behold your divine form. If you find me worthy of that vision, then reveal to me, O master of yogis your changeless Atman."

Krishna says, "Behold O Prince, my divine forms, hundreds up on thousands, various in kind, various in color and in shape.

Behold the Adityas, and the vasus, and the Rudras, and the aswins, and the Maruts. Behold many wonders, O descendent of Bharata, that no man has seen before. O conqueror of sloth, this very day you shall behold the whole universe with all things animate and inert made one within this body of mine. And whatever you desire to see, that you shall see also. But you cannot see me with those human eyes. There fore I give you divine sight."

The reference to God's hands reinforces the belief that God took some clay/mud literally in His hands to make the effigy of the man (Adam) like a sculptor and then made it alive by blowing His spirit into it (The creationist view). God has no need to take the clay in His hands to create the human being. God only needs to say "Be" and it will be done.

As revealed in the Qur'an and the evidence obtained from paleoanthropology, science, and molecular biology, the origin of man through evolution is very convincing.

So far, our discussions have been solely on the clay/mud substrate for the creation (origin) of man. Further, believers are fiercely debating whether God took some clay and made a human model and made it alive by blowing His spirit into it, or our origin was from clay as a result of evolution. In this debate, only the mechanism of our origin is in question and not the source of the origin itself (clay). But the evolutionary theory makes more probable when we read the verse in Qur'an that throws our origin back to fifteen billion years ago and not to ten thousand to twelve thousand years ago when Adam was created.

Qur'an 19:67(26) "But does not man call to mind that We created him before, **out of nothing**." This suggests that our creation started with the big bang when the universe began out of nothing (or an infinitesimally small dense hot spot (singularity)) and implies that everything started then, fifteen billion years ago and later clay came along. (The universe and everything in it including the primordial ingredients for the origin (creation) of life and eventually of man, all started at the big bang.

With respect to the glad tidings conferred on Zachariyah (prophet) about his future son Yahya (John the Baptist) Qur'an mentions human origin out of nothing as did the big bang. Verse: 19:9 "I did indeed create thee before **when thou hadst been nothing**". It has to be mentioned that life and eventually man, whether created out of clay, or if scientists could prove that life started from abiogenesis (life from non living) with clay as the most important causative ingredient and by evolution man finally arrived, the ingredients for forming the clay and for the primordial organic compounds, from which life is believed to have originated and for the formation of the cell and its contents, all started at the big bang.

There is no instance to date that a scientific discovery has been inconsistent with the revealed information contained in Qur'an. Rational thinking is a pre-eminent requirement for the followers of Islam. Qur'an :7:179: (27) Asad: And most certainly have destined for hell many of the invisible things and men who have hearts with which they fail to grasp the truth, and eyes with which they fail to see, and ears with which they fail to hear. They are like cattle-nay, they are even less conscious of the right way ;it is they, they who are the truly heedless!

Qur'an:12:2;Asad; Behold We have bestowed it from high as a discourse in the Arabic tongue, so that you might encompass it with your reason.

Qur'an:13:4:Asad; and there are on earth many tracks of land close by one another (and yet widely different from one another)and there are on it vineyards, and field of grain, and date palms growing in clusters from one root or standing alone, all watered with the same water; and yet some of them have We favored above others by way of the food.

Verily, in all this there are messages, indeed for people who use their reason.

Qur'an:16:12:Asad: and He has made the night and the day and the sun and the moon subservient to His laws, so that they may be of use to you; and all the stars are subservient to His commands; in this, behold, there are messages indeed for people who use their reason.

The Qur'an stresses the need to use reason by human beings repeatedly. Asad: Qur'an:2:164;16:67;30:24;45:5;43:3
Qur'an 10:36 (28) "For, most of them following nothing but conjecture and behold conjecture can never be a substitute for truth."

In the Qur'an, we see more detailed insight into the creation of man. It mentions that man was created in stages, and there was a wide span of time before man appeared on earth. Further, Qur'an refers to the physical changes made in our body to be a human and to walk upright. These statements are entirely consistent with biological evolution and not with that of a Sculptured Creation concept (chapter 15) on the basis of rational analysis. This view is echoed by the statement that "God's greatest gift to man is reason" by Prophet Muhammad.

In the Middle Ages, Islamic biologists and philosophers proposed theories of evolution and natural selection prior to Charles Darwin. It was taught in Islamic schools. John William Draper (30), a contemporary of Darwin, considered the Mohammedan theory of evolution "to be developed much farther than we are disposed to do, extending them even to inorganic or mineral things."
According to al-Khazini, ideas on evolution were widespread among common people in the Islamic world by the twelfth century (31). The first scientist was al-Jahiz in the ninth century who developed the theory of natural selection (32, 33). Ibn-al Haytham wrote a book arguing for evolution. So did Ibn Mskawayh, al-Biruni, Nasir al-Din Tusi, and Ibn Khaldun, whose works translated into Latin appeared in the West and had an impact on western science.
Ibn Miskawayh's al-Fawaz-al Asghar and the Brethren of Purity's Encyclopedia of the Brethren of Purity [the Epistles of Ikhwan al Safa] expressed evolutionary ideas on how species evolved from matter into plants and then into animals, then apes and then to humans (34, 35). This has

gone far beyond evolution and into the origin of life from inorganic matter, much more profound than evolution itself as propounded by Darwin.

English translation of the Encyclopedia of the Brethren of Purity was available from 1812 (36) while Arabic manuscripts of the al-Fawaz al Asghar were also available in European universities by the nineteenth century. These works likely had an influence on Charles Darwin who was a student of Arabic. (34, 35)

The debate about creation versus evolution has a long history. The creationists believe in the literal meaning of the statements in the Bible and Qur'an. More specifically when it comes to the origin of man. The creationists believe that God created human being (Adam) by physically taking mud or clay and formed a model of man and then blew into it the life-giving spirit and it became alive. They see no reason for the evolutionary process of abiogenesis leading to the first unicellular organism and the gradual transformation through evolution into man as God can create man de novo. The evolutionists believe in abiogenesis and the gradual evolution or transformation into various plants and animals and later human beings. Some invoke that there is no need for a supernatural power for the creation of man, but many believe that regardless of divine intervention or not, once life appeared on earth, it has undergone evolution from a unicellular organism to multi cellular organism, then to plants and animals and eventually to man.

The debate appeared in England and America in the eighteenth century. Jean-Baptiste Lamarck (37) and Robert Chalmers (38) were the early deviants from creationism and popularized the concept of evolution. The discovery of fossils of extinct animals revived the concept of evolution.

Creationism is based on faith while evolution is based on evidence presented by fossils and other scientific facts. The statements in the Bible and the information provided in the Qur'an and the facts established by science clearly points to an evolutionary process in the appearance of man on earth. From a religious standpoint, there is no reason to uproot the tree of evolution, if one takes the debate back to the time of the big bang, fifteen billion years ago when all the energy and matter that we see today, and everything in the universe was "created out of nothing or something (singularity)." From the beginning of the big bang onward, the evolutionist can take over the argument for evolution since everything has changed or evolved from the time of the big bang to the present, and from inanimate material to the unicellular organism and then to man.

Since science is at a loss to explain the cause or origin of the big bang, the creationist view has to be accepted at the beginning of the universe (The big bang) where the "creation" began and afterward everything evolved to the present-day universe and its contents as we see today.

The big bang refers to the expansion of the universe from a primordial super dense ,super hot spot (billions of times smaller than an atom according to some) that exploded about 15 billion years ago and continues to expand. This theory was originally proposed by a Roman catholic priest and physicist named Georges Lamaitre in 1927. Many considered it as a definite moment of "creation" of the universe. And by the process of biological evolution and natural selection, the primitive living cell evolved into the present-day biota including human beings and that the creation of man was not de novo. In this view, both creationism and evolutionism can be reconciled without excluding one view or the other, and there should be no contention between the two camps, the creationists and the evolutionists.

References for Evolution 2008:

1. Charles Darwin (1809-1882). The Origin of Species. 1859. The English geologist and naturalist.
2. Alfred Russel Wallace (1823-1913). Naturalist. Anthropologist. Theory of Natural Selection.
3. Titus Lucretius Cerus (99-55 BC) Philosopher. On The Nature of Things.
4. John William Draper (1878). History of the Conflict between Religion and Science, 237: 153-155. ISBN.1603030964.
5. Vedas: Hinduism.http://en.wikipedia.org/wiki/Sri-Aurobindo;http://en.wikipedia.org/wiki/Evolutionism.
6. The Avatars of Vishnu.http://www.asianartmal.com/AVATARS%20 OF% 20LORD%20 VISHNU. html;http://en. Wikipilpinas. org/index. Php?title=Vishnu.
7. Anaximandros (Anaximander), Greek philosopher. (610-546 BC) Born in Miletus. "Understanding Evolution, History, Theory Evidence and Implications." R. G. Price. March 2005. http://www.Rational Evolution.nt/ article.understandig.evolution.htm
8. Plutarch. Ibid. First century. CE.
9. Hippolytus. Third century CE. Ibid.
10. Hippolytus. Ibid.

11. Cesnorinus. Roman writer (Wikipedia).
12. Xenophanes of Kolpbon 570BC. "Understanding Evolution, History, Theory, Evidence and Implication." R. G. Price. March 2005.
13. Joseph Needham, Alistair Ronan. 1005. "The Shorter Science and Civilization of China," An abridgement of Joseph Needham's Original Text. Vol.1; Cambridge University Press. ISBN:0252783.
14. Niles Eldredge and Stephen Jay Gould. An alternative to phyletic Gradualism. 1972. T. J. M. Schopf. Ed. models in paleontology. San Francisco. Freeman Cooper. p. 82-115. Reported in N. Eldredge "Time Frames." Princeton University Press: Princeton. 1085.
15. Phyletic Gradualism. A pattern of Evolution. Proposed by, Dennet, the philosopher.
16. G. Ledyard Stebbins (1906-2000). American botanist and geologist.
17. Genesis 1:26; 2:7; 2:22.a
18. Qur'an 6:2; 15:26; 22:5; 55:14.
19. Qur'an 15:28; 25:54.
20. Qur'an 38:75. Translation. Yusuf Ali
21. Ibid., Translation Muhammad Asad. The Message of the Qur'an.
22. Ibid., Translation. Ahmed Ali. Al-Qur'an.
23. Qur'an 2:117. Yusuf Ali. The Meaning of the Holy Qur'an.
24. Ibid., 6:103; 112:4; 42:11; (Yusuf Ali), 6:100. (Muhammad Asad).
25. Vedas and Bhagavad-Gita. Sacred Texts of Hinduism.
26. Qur'an 19:67.
27. Ibid: 7:179;12:2; 13:4;16:12;2:164;16:67; 30:24;45:5;43;3.
28. Ibid., 10:36. Muhammad Asad.
29. Ibid., 10:37. Yusuf Ali.
30. John William Draper. The History of the Conflict between Religion and Science, 1874.
31. Al-Khazini: Idea of evolution was widespread in the Islamic World in the twelfth century.
32. Conway Zirkle: 1941. "Natural Selection before 'The Origin of Species'" Proceedings of the American Philosophical Society 84 (1): 71-123.
33. Mehmet Bayarakdar. Third Quarter. 1983. "Al-Jahiz and the rise of biological evolution." The Islamic Quarterly. London.
34. Muhammad Hamidullah and Afzal Iqbal. 1993. The Emergence of Islam. Lectures on the development of Islamic worldview. Intellectual Tradition and Polity. p. 143-144. Islamic Research Institute. Islamabad.
35. Eloise Hart. Pages of Medieval Mid Eastern History (cf. ismaili, yesidi, sufi, the Brethren of Purity). Ismaili Heritage Society.

36. Ikhwan as-safa and their rasail. "A critical review of a century and half research" By A. L. Tibawi, as published in vol.2 of the Islamic Quarterly in 1955. p. 28-46.

37. Jean-Baptiste Lamarck (1744-1824). French naturalist and early evolutionist.

38. Robert Chalmers. Vestiges of Natural History of Creation 1844.

CHAPTER 16
Evolution (biological)

What is evolution?

The word evolution originates from the Latin word "evolutio" (unrolling). Evolution is used to describe the gradual change in any system, be it political, cultural, social, economical, scientific, or biological. All these change gradually. Evolution, according to Webster's Dictionary, is "a process of continuous change from a lower, simpler or worse, to a higher more complex or better state." When we deal with evolution, we have to briefly look at (1) cosmic evolution, (2) planetary evolution, and (3) biological evolution.

What is biological evolution?

One of the evolutionary biologists says, "In the broadest sense, evolution is merely change, and so is all pervasive, galaxies, languages, and political systems, all evolve. Biological evolution is change in the properties of population of organisms that transcend the lifetime of a single individual. The ontogeny of an individual is not considered evolution, individual organisms do not evolve. The changes in population that are considered evolutionary are those that are inherited via the genetic material from one generation to the next. Biological evolution may be slight or substantial, it embraces everything from slight changes in the proportion of different alleles within a population (such as those determining blood groups) to the successive alteration that led from the earliest proto organism to snails, bees, giraffes, and dandelions."(1)
"In fact evolution can be defined precisely as a change in the frequency of alleles within a gene pool from one generation to the next." (2)

Biological evolution is generally described under microevolution and macroevolution. Microevolution is observable, like the development of resistance to antibiotics by the bacteria or the mosquito developing resistance to pesticides. In both cases, there is no change in the species in that the bacteria and the mosquito still remain a bacteria and a mosquito.

On the other hand, macroevolution cannot be observed as it takes millions of years for gradual accumulation of genetic alteration for one species to transform to another. As did the proto organism became a snail, mammal, and lastly the human being.

Here we are dealing with biological evolution. Biological evolution is the concept that the present-day living organisms, plants, and animals started off with a primitive unicellular organism, say, a bacteria which, by evolutionary mechanisms, became a multi cellular creature and gradually branched off to different species going through different life-forms. Most of those earlier species have gone extinct. This transformation over time is called biological evolution. It is believed that the genetic code present in every living organism called the DNA undergo mutation either at random or due to effects of environmental changes or other physical insults, and when sufficient mutations have occurred, the species changes to a new species. Thereafter the new species and the parent species cannot interbreed. This change is also influenced by natural selection in which an organism that have a new characteristic, which will be advantageous for survival, will reproduce and increase in number while that organism which does not have this beneficial characteristic will perish.

When we hear about evolution, the name that often comes to mind is that of Charles Darwin (3). But it has to be kept in mind that evolutionary ideas have been discussed several centuries before Darwin. Charles Darwin was one of the pioneers of explaining the mechanism of evolution by natural selection in a credible fashion.

Before we search for the person or persons who were contemplating the idea of biological evolution, we need to look into the divine scriptures to see what the Creator has to say about the process of evolution. If a student of evolution, who has not been exposed to the time-honored theistic explanation for the creation of Adam and Eve (4) (namely, that God took some mud or clay and formed a statue like human body and blew His spirit into it and it became alive as a human being), which we can call the sculptured creation concept (chapter 15), and happens to read either the Bible (5) or Qur'an (6), he will be surprised to see and ponder that the evolutionary process has already been mentioned in these divine scriptures and will wonder why it has not been discussed in the religious circles. But it has to be pointed out, in the early Islamic culture, the subject of evolution had been taught in the Madrasas or religious schools and was referred to as "the Mohammedan evolution." (7)

John William Draper (7) says, "sometimes, not without surprise, we meet with ideas which we flatter ourselves, have originated in our own times. Thus our modern doctrines of evolution and development were taught in their schools. In fact, they carried them much farther than we are disposed to do, extending them even to inorganic or mineral things. The fundamental principle of alchemy was the natural process of development of metalline bodies."

Let us now open the Bible and see what, if any thing, has been written that points to biological evolution. Genesis (8) is believed to have been written by Moses (9) one thousand four hundred years before Christ (10). Genesis 1:1-2 (11) "In the beginning when God created the universe. The earth was formless and desolate. Genesis:1:11 (12) "Then He commanded, 'Let the earth produce all kinds of plants those that bear grain and those that bear fruit' and it was done. Genesis 1:20 (13) "Then God commanded, 'Let the water be filled with many kinds of living beings and let the air be filled with birds, So God created the sea monsters, all kinds of creatures that live in the water and all kinds of birds." Genesis 1:24 (14) "Then God commanded, 'Let the earth produce all kinds of animal life, domestic and wild, large and small' and it was done."

Genesis 1:26 (15) "Then God said, 'And now we will make human beings they will be like us and resemble Us." Even though the order of the creation is a little deviated form scientific teaching (birds before animals in the Genesis as opposed to animals before birds according to science), one thing is clear that there is a definite gradualism or gap between the introduction of each life-form, and the last being human beings.

This is what exactly we see in the theory of evolution that different species appeared over time, changing from one form to the other gradually. Notwithstanding the power of the Creator in which, if He willed, He could have created all the life-forms simultaneously, but He didn't as described above. It makes sense that God created the plant life before animal kingdom so that the animals will have food for survival. But even then, there is definitely a gradual introduction of various plants and the animal species and the last being man. Some theologians will argue that God was preparing the earth for the arrival of Adam and Eve (16) so that this couple will be well provided for. But if Adam and Eve were the only two people on earth at that time as we are told by theologians, one might ask, why this one couple need all the fishes in the sea, or the myriads of animals on the earth on top of all fruits and vegetables in the entire world? Therefore, these descriptions of the gradual introduction of those different species one after the other clearly indicate an evolutionary process.

Qur'an: We see more elaborate indication for transformation (evolution) in Qur'an. The oft repeated name for God, "Rabb" by the followers of Islam, represents one who transforms things or brings about evolution (17). (Originally signifying the "bringing of a thing to a state of completion by degrees". William Lane). In Islam, just like Judeo-Christian believers, a sizable number of people are of the belief that the creation of Adam and Eve is the beginning of humankind and that they were created by God, taking some clay or mud from the ground and fashioned a human effigy and then blew His spirit into it and he became alive.

The religious scholars of the past who have written commentaries and translation of the Qur'an unfortunately did not have the benefit of the knowledge about paleontology, molecular biology, anthropology, or geology at that time. They had to resort to the practical knowledge and their best imagination in their commentaries. The scientific discoveries that we are now exposed to were not available for the commentators at that time, to reflect the contemporary understanding of science in their commentaries. Therefore, some interpretations could be inadequate or incorrect with respect to contemporary science. This should not be construed as to say that the scriptures are incorrect, but only their interpretations.

Many of our religious scholars have spent most of their lifetime in understanding the Qur'an and have given many of us an opportunity to learn the meaning of the Holy book. Their dedication in the pursuit of knowledge and understanding the meaning of Qur'an, have helped millions of non-Arabic speaking people, Muslims and non Muslims alike, in understanding the meaning of Arabic Qur'an. Some statements in the Qur'an can never be explained by human beings to our satisfaction as their inner meaning will be known only to God (18). Since childhood, we are taught the abovementioned scenario in the creation of Adam and Eve and that the mental picture of God as a sculptor-creator remains in our minds even today, and many even refute the idea of evolution, biological or otherwise.

Let us look at several verses (paragraphs in the Qur'an) that point to an evolutionary scenario in the universe whether it is cosmic, planetary, physical, or biological: "Do not the unbelievers see that the heavens and the earth were joined together, as one unit of creation, before we cloved them asunder? We made from water every living thing. Will they not then believe" Qur'an:21:30.(19). In this, we have the hints of cosmic and planetary evolution and the hallmarks of initiation of abiogenesis (life originating from nonliving) and biological evolution. As the verse (paragraph) says that every living thing were made from water including human beings.

Allah (God) created every animal (out) of water (20) 24:45. This points to the origin of early life-form from water and then evolved into different species. It has to be pointed out that scientists have not yet proven where life began, even though more evidence points to an aquatic beginning. This verse (paragraph) also implies as some commentators note that the human body or any other life-form has large portion of the body mass as water (60 percent). This explanation only touches on the content of life-forms but not on the origin of life.

With regard to the creation of man, the Qur'an says,

> "I will create a vicegerent on earth" (21) 2:30. Vicegerent, meaning an administrative deputy of a king or magistrate or a successor (22). How God is planning to create a man on earth is described as follows: He began the creation of man with nothing more than clay. Qur'an: The Holy Qur'an. (23) 32:7). Thus, he begins the creation of man from clay. Qur'an: 32:7 (The Message of Holy Qur'an) (23).

He began the creation of man from dust. Maulana Muhammad Ali (Holy Qur'an):32:7.(23). (The scientific findings are described elsewhere.) This verse (paragraph) clearly implies that the creation of man was not like making a human figure with clay, which can be accomplished even by a child in a matter of minutes. When God says that He "**began the creation of man with clay**", it implies a long time period for its completion and not an instantaneous event like a sculptor making a human mold from clay. As the word implies, He began creation "with clay" and understandably to end up with something other than clay, the human being with flesh, bone, and other biological structures. This verse has an omnipotent meaning, beyond comprehension. The word, "He began the creation of man with clay" implies beyond any doubt that the creation took an enormous time period through the evolutionary process for man to appear on earth, from an inanimate substance called clay.

God could have instantly ordered a man out of clay but He didn't do that as implied in this verse. "He has created you in successive stages" (24)

71:14. This may imply the gradual growth of the human fetus as some commentators claim, from the womb through childhood, adulthood, and old age. With this explanation, we are talking about the growth of the child. There are no stages in the growth of a child as it is a continuous process. But when we read the next verse, "And God has caused you to grow out of the earth as a growth" (25) 71:17 (The Message of the Qur'an). In his commentary, page 897, he refers to the evolution of man. The author in his commentary (25) (71:17) refers to the evolutionary process starting from a primitive organism through various humanoid species to the level of present stage of man. This reinforces the fact that the creation of man was not consistent with the sculptured creation concept but is indicative of a gradual evolutionary process.

"And when I have formed him fully and breathed into him of my spirit. Fall down before him in prostration." (26) 15:29. Here, God says, "When I have formed him fully," does it mean that God was completing the human effigy by attaching the limbs, ears, nose and eyes to the trunk and complete the figure? On the contrary, this clearly implies the process of human evolution and tells us that prior to Adam, the humanoids were not complete in all the mental faculties even though the physical appearance was that of present-day human beings. They were not mentally fully developed to conceive the existence of a supernatural power and to carry out His commands. God only can determine who is really a fully developed human being not merely by the physical appearance but also by the mental capacity to conceptualize the Creator and the divine existence. This mental faculty cannot be determined by paleoanthropology which can only determine the skeletal features of a creature, and the size of the cranial cavity. It cannot tell us how the intricate structure of brain works, especially human brain's capacity for self-consciousness, planning, control, and thinking of the future as well as introspection. This Qur'anic passage has another significant implication in it. When we discuss Homo sapiens, we are dealing with humanlike species. The most modern human beings are referred to as Homo sapiens sapiens (27). There is great similarity in the gross physical appearance among these different species (human beings and the early hominid species) as seen from the fossil record (unfortunately we do not have a living example of any of our past progenitors as all of them went extinct by the time Adam appeared, ten to fifteen thousand years ago), but paleoanthropologists have determined from excavation of their dwelling sites, their tools, their food gathering techniques, and other artifacts that they were very primitive in their brain function compared to the Cro-Magnons and the Homo sapiens sapiens that is us.

For a casual observer, some of these humanoid fossils look like "humans" even though their brain functions were not as advanced as that of the present-day human beings. In this long chain of humanoid evolution with various species, preceding the most modern humans, for a casual observer, it will be impossible to say, which one species can be called a human and which one is not, based on fossils alone. When we look at the skeletal features of earlier hominids, many look like that of modern man with subtle differences. For example, the skeletons of Homo erectus and Neanderthals, when compared to most modern humans, shows only minor alterations in the shape of the skull, slightly elongated and have prominent bow ridges. The limb bones are thicker and stronger. Nasal passages are wider. These differences are not enough for a casual observer to say, one is that of a most modern human, and the other is not, without the expertise of an anthropologist.

We, the present-day human beings, are trying to establish when and where the so-called most modern human appeared, by sifting through the fossils and examining the sites where the so-called pre humans lived, looking for any evidence of their social life or community living to indicate modernity. We consider the social life and community living of ours as the sine-qua-non of most modern man. May be so. We consider those who do not fit in to this lifestyle to be pre humans, aborigines, or cave men. We have declared that we are the most modern human beings according to our standards. The question to ask is, "are we human enough?" or if there is someone called the perfect human? In the evolutionary process, by chance or by design, if a new race or species come around, in the future, we could be relegated to a lower species?

We call ourselves as the most modern human beings as there is no one else out there to classify us differently. If there was one, we may be named in a different category?

God has determined that Adam and Eve and their progeny are fully developed to be called human beings. The previous human species probably were humanoids but not fully developed, as indicated in this verse, 15:29: "When I have formed him fully and breathed into him my spirit. Fall down before him in prostration." We do not have 'a set of tests to be administered to find out who can make the passing grade to be called a fully developed human! Even though the Cro-Magnons (28) were genetically identical to us, we do not know whether they were mentally as developed as we are? We have to assume they were not, as God did not consider them as fully developed human beings from God's standpoint as it was Adam and Eve who were the first fully developed human beings, according to the Bible and Qur'an, who appeared later than the Cro-Magnons.

It is not the physical appearance or merely the genetic compatibility that makes a fully developed human. It is the mental development and maturity that matters. A case in point is the condition of a child and of a demented individual. Both are genetically human. But they are not functional as a fully developed human as referred to in verse 15:29, because the child's brain has not developed and the dementia has robbed all the mental faculties of the demented. And as such they are not fully functional mentally and cannot be considered fully developed as implied in the verse 15:29. Even though they are perfectly humans from a genetic standpoint. This will explain how and why Adam and Eve were considered the first human beings by God as they were fully developed physically and mentally.

"It is We who created them, and We have made their joints strong" (Holy Qur'an Translation. Yusuf Ali) (29) 76:28. "We created them and fixed their bones and joints" (Translation. Al-Qur'an, Ahmed Ali. (29). I believe this particular verse has some additional significance. Here specifically the bones and particularly the joints are mentioned and no other organs elsewhere in our body. This implies the drastic changes that have occurred in the hip joints, the leg bones, namely, the femur, tibia, and fibula and the redesigning of the structure of human foot compared to the chimps for the singular purpose of bipedalism. In addition to changes in bones and joints, the muscles had to be rearranged and preferential enhancement of the strength of certain muscle groups in our lower limbs must happen for erect posture and bipedalism in humans. The gluteus maximus, the muscle of the hip and the hamstrings, had to be re enforced in strength; and the hamstrings had to be realigned for proper walking. In the evolutionary hierarchy, after the humanoids diverged from the apes, the skeletal structure has undergone gradual and visible changes to make our bony structure ideally suited for bipedalism.

This passage in Qur'an (76:28) specifically refers to the physical alteration and changes that had undergone in our physical structure to enable us to walk erect and walk on two feet (bipedalism), which characterizes and separates us from our ancestral species, and the chimpanzees. This verse (76:28) strengthens the previous passage (15:29) that says, "When I have formed him fully."

This gives us further evidence for an evolutionary pathway that led to the transformation of knuckle walking to bipedalism.

"Has there not been an endless span of time before man (appeared-time) when he was not yet a thing to be thought of (mentioned)" (The Message of the Qur'an) Asad. (30) 76:1.

This indicates that the earth existed for billions of years without human beings. There was no knowledge of paleontology or exploration of fossils during the time of the revelation of the Qur'an. Study of fossils in a credible fashion started in the seventeenth century. George Cuvier (31), the father of paleontology, wrote his book in the eighteenth century on fossils. By studying fossils and applying dating methods, it has been determined that most modern humans (the Cro-Magnons) appeared on earth thirty-five thousand years ago. The earth was formed according to scientists about 4.5 billion years ago, and the life-forms appeared on earth about 3.5 billion years ago.

This clearly confirms the information conveyed in Qur'an (verse 15:29) that the human beings came to earth after a long span of time (billion of years) after the formation of earth during which time there were no human beings on earth. And during this long span of time, evolutionary process continued, and the human beings finally arrived. This information from fossil evidence and dating techniques was not available to man at the time Qur'an was revealed.

"This wide span of time," as mentioned in Qur'an, should mean eons or billions of years from the beginning of the formation of earth, 4.5 billions of years ago, and to the appearance of modern humans about thirty-five thousand years ago and the appearance of Adam and Eve about ten to twelve thousand years ago. This fact is now well established by fossil evidence, dating methods, and paleoanthropology. (we do not have the fossils of Adam and Eve but have the fossils of the Adamic race). The beginning of creation of man from the primordial life-form, 3.5 billion years ago, to the formation of fully developed man as mentioned in verse 15:29 is now established by science and fossil evidence. Therefore, as mentioned in the above verse, after God began the creation of man from clay, it took such a "long span of time" to have a fully formed (15:29) human being.

God let this "long span of time" run its natural course of billions of years for the formation of man from clay via the process of evolution as per the laws of nature, as established by God Himself at the beginning of the big bang fifteen billions years ago. This scenario cannot be explained by any process other than gradual biological evolution. When God says a long span of time, it has to be remembered that a day for God is like a thousand years for us. (Qur'an 32:5) (32).

Now let us review the thoughts and views of evolutionary concept by human beings of the past. In 400 BC, Greek atomists were teaching that the sun, earth, life, human beings, civilization, and society emerged over eons from the eternal atoms colliding and vibrating in the void.

In the epic poem "On the Nature of Things," the Roman atomist Titus Lucretius (99 BC-56 BC) (33) described the stages of living earth. The earth and the sun formed from the swirls of dust congregated from the atoms colliding and vibrating in the void. Early plants and animals sprang from the early earth's own substance because of the insistence of the atoms that formed the earth. The aging earth gave birth to a succession of animals including a series of progressively less brutish humans that made a succession of improved tools, laws, and a civilization with increasing complexity, finally arriving at the current earth and life-forms as they are. These ideas were forgotten for one thousand four hundred years in the West but continued to be discussed in the Islamic world (7).

In fourth century BC, there were proto evolutionists and evolutionary concepts being expressed in Indian and Chinese philosophy (34). In the Vedas of Hinduism there are passages that indicate that more complex phenomena rose out of simple phenomena. Also seen in the writings of Patanjali (35) and Sri Aurabindo (36) are thoughts of evolution of mind and body. Patanjali states" what is the cause of change of the body in to another species. He says this is done by the infilling of nature". Sri Aurobindo states that in relation to our world there are other worlds that follow a different process. There is gradual awakening of consciousness over time an evolution of consciousness. Through its principle of exclusive concentration the One became matter, losing all consciousness in the form of inanimate matter. From this base it is progressively awakened through the life of the plant, the beginning of mind in the animal. The free emergence of mind in humanity and is now stirring to awaken fully through the emergence of greater consciousness than mind the Super mind, in which the fullness of the undivided consciousness and infinite delight of the one will be manifest in earth. This evolution of consciousness from the worm to the God is the central process, aim and significance of our existence.

The incarnations of Vishnu reflect the theory of evolution (37). The Dasavataras, according to J. B. S. Haldane, is a reflection of biological evolution. Incarnation is the English translation of the word Avatar or Avatara (Sanskrit). This means "descent" (avatar) and usually implies the descent of the supreme being to the earth to establish Godliness (dharma) whenever wickedness prevail. It can appear in different forms of living beings. There were several avatars of Vishnu (the supreme being) according to Hindu religious belief, but most authorities agree on ten avatars. The avatars of Vishnu are described below:

The first avatar of Vishnu is Matsya or fish (evolutionary science believes that life first appeared in water leading to fish).

The second avatar of Vishnu is Kurma or tortoise (fish evolved into tortoise, an amphibian).

The third avatar of Vishnu is Varaha or the boar (a land animal).

The fourth avatar is Narasimha, a combination of features of animal and man (animal with humanoid features).

The fifth avatar of Vishnu is Vamana or dwarf (a full human but short).

The sixth avatar is Parashurama (a well-developed, perfect human).

The seventh avatar of Vishnu is Rama (the ideal human, the embodiment of morality and righteousness).

The eighth avatar of Vishnu is Krishna (Niranjan, Hindu Forum, Topix, March 31, 2007). (Some believe the ninth avatar is Buddha and the tenth avatar is Kalki. Kalki has not appeared yet.)

The sequence of the appearance of the avatars of Lord Vishnu is identical to the scientific explanation of the sequence of biological evolution of animals and man. Science tells us that life had an aquatic origin. The first Avatar of Vishnu was the fish. The next step was the appearance of the amphibian (tortoise) next the mammal (boar) then the fourth was narasimha who had features of man and animal which compares to the early hominids, (Homo habilis), varaha the dwarf the fifth avatar was a developed man, Homo sapien but very short. It is interesting to note that early hominids other than Homo erectus were much shorter than the present day humans in the range of 4-5 feet. The sixth Avatar is Parasurama a well developed man who is represented in all the religious descriptions as carrying an axe. This possibly represents the more advanced human species in the line of human evolution, which started to use weapons—the Cro-Magnons. The seventh Avatar is Lord Rama, the perfect human being. The eighth Avatar is Lord Krishna the supreme form of divinity. Many believe that human beings can attain a divine status with constant worship and realization of the omnipotence of God.

Niranjan: excerpts from the code Manu on evolution regarding the progression the spirit (life) through various forms (38).

"The first germ of life was developed by water and heat" (Manu, book 1, sloka 8). "Water ascends toward the sky in vapors, from the sun it descends in rain, from the rain are born the plants and from the plants, animals" (book 11, sloka 76). "Each being acquires the qualities of the one which immediately precedes it, in such a manner that the farther a being gets away from the primal atom of its series, the more he is possessed of qualities and perfections" (book 1, sloka 20). "Man will traverse the universe, gradually ascending, and passing through the rocks, the plants, the worms, the insects, fish, serpents, tortoises, wild animals, cattle, and higher animals—Such is the inferior degree" (ibid.). "These are the transformations declared, from the plant up to Brahma, which have to take place in his world" (ibid.).

Swami Vivekananda while commenting on Patanjali's Yoga Sutra explains the concept of evolution from the Hinduism standpoint in contrast to modern science.

Today the evolution theory of the ancient yogis will be better understood in light of modern research. But the theory of the Yogis is a better explanation. The two causes of evolution advanced by the modern science, viz sexual selection and survival of the fittest are in adequate. But the great ancient evolutionist, Patanjali, declares that the true secret of evolution is in the manifestation of the perfection which is already in every beings, that this perfection has been barred and the infinite tide behind is struggling to express itself. These struggles and competitions are but the results of our ignorance, because we do not know the proper way to unlock the gate and let the water in. This infinite tide behind must express itself, it is the cause of all manifestations. (Complete wisdom of Swami Vivekananda, p. 292).(39)

In Buddhism, emphasis is seen on the rise and fall of people and creatures over vast periods of time, suggesting an evolutionary nature (40).

In China, according to Joseph Needham, the Taoists elaborated what comes near to a statement of the theory of evolution. At least they firmly denied the fixity of biological species (41).

References for Evolution:

1. Douglas J. Futuyama. Evolutionary Biology. Sinauer Associates (1986).
2. Helena Curtis and N. Sue Barnes. Biology 5th ed. (Worth Publishers, 1989), 974.
3. Charles Robert Darwin (1809-1882). The British naturalist. Author, The Origin of Species. 1859.
4. Adam and Eve. Believed to be the first pair of human beings by Judeo-Christian and Islamic faith.
5. Bible: Genesis 2:7, 2:22.
6. Qur'an 6:2.
7. John William Draper. 1878. History of Conflict between Religion and Science. p. 237. ISBN.1603030964.
8. The Bible.
9. Moses is believed to have written the Genesis, one thousand four hundred years before Christ. Moses is revered by Jews, Christians, and Muslims as a prophet of God.
10. Jesus Christ. Originator of Christianity. Muslims believe he is the prophet of God.
11. Genesis 1:1.
12. Ibid., 1:11.
13. Ibid., 1:20.
14. Ibid., 1:24.
15. Ibid., 1:26.
16. Adam and Eve believed to be the first human couple by Judeo-Christian and Islamic faith.
17. (Rabb) Arabic word for God. Edward William Lane. Arabic-English Lexicon; 1003 translation: Rabbi: Originally signifying the "bringing a thing to a state of completion by degrees." Some believe this meaning refers to evolutionary changes.
18. Qur'an 3:7.
19. Ibid., 21:30.
20. Ibid., 24:45.
21. Ibid., 2:30.
22. Webster's Dictionary.

23. 32:7. Yusuf Ali. The Holy Qur'an. Began creation of man with nothing more than clay. Muhammad Asad's Translation in the Message of Qur'an and Maulana Muhammad Ali's translation in Holy Qur'an

24. 71:14. Muhammad Asad. The Message of the Qur'an. Created in successive stages.

25. 71:17. Muhammad Asad. Caused you to grow out of earth in gradual growing. p. 897.

26. Ibid., 15:29. Muhammad Asad. And when I have formed him fully and breathed in to him of My spirit, fall down before him in prostration.

27. Homo sapiens. The species to which all human beings belong. (Latin word meaning "wise men.")

28. The Cro-Magnons. Belong to the most modern human species. Lived from thirty-five thousand years before the present. Went extinct around ten to fifteen thousand years before the present.

29. Qur'an 76:28. Ahmed Ali. We created them and fixed their bones and joints.

30. Ibid., 76:1. Muhammad Asad. Has there (not) been an endless span of time before man appeared—a time when he was not yet a thing to be thought of.

31. Georges Cuvier (1769-1852). Father of paleontology. Book, The Fossil Bones in eighteenth century.

32. Ibid., 32:5. A day for God is like a thousand years for us.

33. Titus Lucretius (99 BC-56 BC), the Roman atomist. "On the Nature of Things."

34. Wikipedia, March 8, 2008. "Indication of Evolutionary Thoughts in Chinese Philosophy." http://en.wikipedia.org/wiki/History-of-evolutionary-thought.

35. Patanjali. http://www.yoga-age.com/Sutras/pata4.html.

36. Wikipedia. Patanjali and Vedas. About evolution. March 8, 2008.http://en.wikipedia.org/wiki/SRI-Aurobindo.

37. Incarnation of Vishnu (Hindu God) reflection of evolution. Niranjan. Hindu Forum. Topix. March 31, 2007.

38. 38. Manu. The laws of manu. A supplementary arm of Vedas. "Manava Dharma Shastra." One of the Sacred Hindu Canons. Believed to be revealed scriptures from Brahma. Sir William Jones ascribed the writings of Manu to about 100-500 BC. "The Institute of Manu." Sir William Jones. 1794.

39. Complete wisdom of Swami Vivekananda. p. 292.

40. Wikipedia.http://en.wikipedia.org/wiki/Bedhism-and-evolution.retrieved 1-16-2009. In Buddhism, emphasis is seen on people and creatures who rose and fell over vast periods of time, suggesting an evolutionary nature.

140

41. Joseph Needham, Alistair Ronan, 1995. "The Shorter Science and Civilizisation of China. An Abridgement of Joseph Needham's Original Text." Vol. 1 (Cambridge University Press). ISBN 052527867.

CHAPTER 17
Evidence for Biological Evolution

Since biological evolution was not witnessed by modern man, in order to understand this phenomenon we have to look at prehistory of plants and animals and the remnants that they have left in the form of fossils and look at comparative anatomy of fossilized animals and all forms of life, geographic distribution of fossils and living organisms, embryological similarities, Homology, chemical composition, molecular biology and genetics.

The Fossil Record (Paleontology):

Fossils are relics or impressions of organisms from the past sealed in rocks. Most of the fossils are in the sedimentary rocks. The sedimentary rocks are formed from sand and mud that settle into the bottom of the seas, lakes, streams, and marshes. New layers cover the older layers. This layered configuration is called strata. When these layers are formed, they will hold the remains of plants and animals that get buried in these strata. The soft parts get decayed, but the skeletons and shells will remain, keeping their original form, and that is called the fossils.

Fossil record shows that earth had a succession of flora (plants) and fauna (animals) of varied shapes and sizes, and most of them are extinct.

French anatomist Georges Cuvier (1) (1769-1832) is regarded as the father of paleontology. He noted that each stratum is characterized by a unique set of fossil species and the deeper (older) the stratum, the more dissimilar the flora and fauna were from that of the modern life-forms. He believed mass extinction has been a common occurrence in the history of life. This concept was controversial at that time. From stratum to stratum, new species appear and others disappear. But Cuvier was an opponent of evolution. He believed that extinction was due to catastrophes like flood or draught that destroyed many species that lived at that time and location. This view was called catastrophism.

Geology : the Study of Earth

Charles Lyell (2) (1797-1875) and William Smith (3), the pioneers of geology, noted the gradual appearance of complex life-forms from older (deeper) strata to newer (top) strata. In 1799, William Smith, an engineer, reported that in undisturbed rocks, fossils occurred in a definite sequential order with more modern-appearing ones closer to the top. William Lonsdale (4) (1830) recognized that fossil remains of organisms from lower strata were more primitive than the ones above. Many thousands of ancient rocks have been found and analyzed, and they show the corresponding succession of fossil organisms. Many fossils show evolutionary transition. Evidence of complex organisms than bacteria, the eukaryotic cells are found in fossils sealed in rocks approximately two billion years ago (5). Multi cellular organisms—fungi, plants, and animals—are found only in younger strata (in the upper strata).

In short, the oldest sedimentary rocks had little or no life-forms; and in the topmost strata, one can see complex body structures. This pattern has never been observed to be reversed. In other words, no mammal fossil can be seen in the oldest strata that contains trilobites or earlier life-forms.

Fossils of the Missing Links

Many fossils have been discovered that confirm the fact that there were transitional creatures between different species. Initially many people including scientists were skeptical of these discovered fossils' authenticity and their purported claim as to their transitional status. But over the years, as more and more of these transitional forms are discovered, it has been accepted as a fact that these creatures are the "found links" from the missing links of evolution.

The famous creature in this category is the Archaeopteryx, a creature who had features of the dinosaur and the bird. (Archaeo in Greek means "ancient." Pteryx means "wing or feather.") Discovered in 1861 in a limestone quarry in Germany, believed to have been alive 155-150 million years ago. This had features of dinosaurs like jaws with teeth, three fingers with claws, long bony tail, hyper extendable second toe (killing claw), and claws on edge of wings. This also had features of the birdlike wings and feathers. (see pictures 3A and 3B)

Picture 3-A: Diagram of Archaeopteryx
Notice claws on the wings

Picture No. 3-B: Archaeopteryx Lithograph
Source: Wikimedia Commons

Since then, new specimens of birds from China, which are thirty to forty million years younger than Archaeopteryx, have been discovered showing features more like birds, with shorter tails and reduced claws. The Chinese location revealed new dinosaurs with feathers.

These show clear transition forms between dinosaurs and birds (6).

Recent discoveries give examples of transitional forms between fish and amphibians.

The species called Tiktaalik roseae lived 417-375 million years ago. The fossil was discovered recently on Ellesmere Island in Canada (7). It had a skull, neck, and ribs like animal (tetrapod) as well as primitive jaw, fin, and scales like a fish. It was nine feet long.

Anatomical Similarities (8)

A single-celled protozoa, or a highly complex organism with billions of cells, all start as a single cell and grow by cell division process. Then they grow old and die. All living things on earth share the common ability to create complex molecules out of carbon and other elements. Ninety-nine percent of the proteins, carbohydrates, fats, and other molecules of living things are made from six to ninety-two most common elements. Plants and animals get their characteristics from their parents, from the common biological ingredient called DNA. DNA makes proteins by connecting different amino acids in different places. This genetic code and the system of information transfer are found in all living things. All have the capacity to generate energy from sunlight and food that the animals consume.

The upper extremity of humans, the forelegs of dogs and cats, the wings of birds, and the flippers of whales and seals all have same type of bones (humerus, radius, and ulna) because of their common ancestry (6). All living things (whether a single-cell organism or large-bodied animal) have a system of ingesting a source of energy and a process of metabolism to manufacture energy, distribution of the energy to body parts, excretion of waste products, and a structure to protect the contents of the cell (cell wall) and a structure (skin) to protect the body. This may be primitive in early life-forms and elaborate in higher animals. If we cut the body of a human being and a monkey or a rat, all have similar organ structure, namely, a heart, lungs, intestines, kidneys, brain, liver, and a bony case to hold everything in and a covering layer to protect the contents (the skin).

In the case of monkeys and humans, it will be more identical except the size of the brain, which is larger in humans.

Biogeography

Biogeography relates to the study of the distribution of different species, which appear similar but different, species wise, due to adaptation and modification. This is due to different environments and its influence on the organism.

Darwin's finches on Galapagos Islands were similar to those on the mainland but were different species due to evolutionary changes (9).

Evolution of Systems Function

One can see the progression of complexity and efficiency in the animal kingdom:

Example:

The Circulatory System:

Earlier organisms like mollusks pump a bloodlike fluid called hemocoel with a rudimentary heart. The oxygenated and the deoxygenated blood cannot be separated. This inefficient system was altered, in that the fluid was enclosed in a vessel in later organisms. The actual fluid evolved into blood by first having molecules which carried oxygen and the cells which specifically contain this oxygen-carrying molecules. Each of these steps improved efficiency and can be seen in different animals. Arthropods still have an open circulatory system.

Another example of comparative anatomy is that of vestigial organs (10), which are structures that have no known function.

Example:

Whales are often times born with femurs (leg bones) despite the fact they are marine creatures and don't have to walk. It is believed that these rudimentary bony structures represent evolutionary remnants, which are due to the fact they are evolved from a land-living ancestor, probably bovine species

(11). Another is the human appendix, which is thought to be a vestigial cecum (an organ found in many herbivores which helps digest plant material). It has no known function in the human body. Other examples include molar tooth, small hip bone in whales, blind eye in cave fish, wings in flightless birds, and in the human beings the presence of a curved mucus membrane in the eye (nictitating membrane), muscles in the human ear lobes and the tonsils.

Comparative Embryology

The idea that "ontogeny recapitulates phylogeny" popularized by Ernst Haeckel (12) in 1866 implies that different stages in early development correlate with embryonic form of the organism's ancestors. It was called the biogenic law.

Example:

In humans, gill slits (not true gills) are visible in early development, which indicates fish as an ancestor of humans. Animals in early development look extremely similar; as development progresses, they diverge in appearance. The earlier the divergence occurs, the more distant will be the relation of species (Haeckel's diagram. Picture No.4).

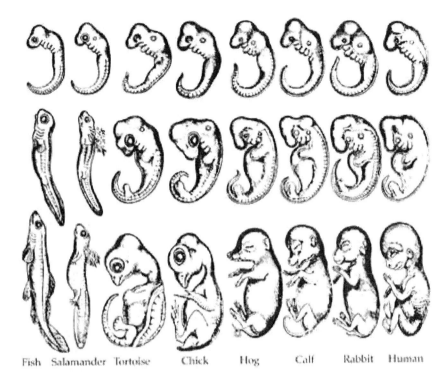

Fish Salamander Tortoise Chick Hog Calf Rabbit Human

Haeckel's drawings

Source: Romanes's 1892 copy of Ernst Haeckel's allegedly fraudulent embryo drawings
(this version of the figure is often attributed incorrectly to Haeckel).[1]

1. Richardson and Keuck, "Haeckel's ABC of evolution and development," p. 516

The human embryo has a tail which eventually becomes the sacrum, suggesting our ancestral relation with apes (13).

Comparative Biochemistry (14)

The biochemical makeup of most animals is remarkably similar. Certain molecule like cytochrome C, which is essential for cellular respiration, is almost identical in vastly different animals. Cytochrome C is a single peptide of 104 residues. It plays a role in the mitochondrial electron transport. It is present in all aerobic organisms and is essential for life. Without it, the organism will die.

This is considered as an evidence for evolution.

A wide variety of organisms like flies, worms, mice, or man has similar sequence of genes that are active early in development, which influences the body segmentation. Similarity in these genes in doing similar things in diverse organisms is believed to be due to their presence in their common early ancestor.

Molecular Biology

The DNA present in every cell has nucleotide sequences, which is translated using a special code to create amino acid sequences to produce different kinds of proteins. This code is essentially the same in all organisms. The proteins in every organism are made out of the same group of twenty two amino acids. These similarities argue for a common early ancestor for all living things.

Endogenous retroviruses (15)

One percent of human genome,is occupied by retroviral genes. These are molecular remnants of past viral infections. Copies of retroviruses' genome found in the host's genome, is called endogenous retroviruses. Retroviruses copy their genome and insert it in the host's genome. If this happens in the germ cells, retroviral DNA will be inherited by the descendents of the host. We share retroviral DNA with the chimpanzee at various locations in our genome. It is impossible for humans and chimpanzees to have same instances of retroviral DNA at the same location on the genome, unless it came from a remote common ancestor for both humans and chimpanzees (16).

In 1959, scientists at Cambridge University in UK (17) studied the three-dimensional structures of two proteins that are found in all multicellular organisms, namely, hemoglobin and myoglobin. Myoglobin has one chain of 153 amino acids wrapped around heme. Hemoglobin has four chains consisting of 144 amino acids in two chains, and 146 amino acids in the other two chains. Each chain has a heme exactly like myoglobin, and each of the four chains in hemoglobin is folded exactly like myoglobin, and it was clear that the two molecules were very closely related.

Subsequently hemoglobin and myoglobin sequences were determined for many mammals. All of these sequences were closely related. From this, a family tree could be constructed for hemoglobin and myoglobin. This tree agreed completely with observations derived from paleontology and anatomy about their common descent.

There is further evidence from molecular biology for evolutionary concept. It has long been postulated that whales descended from land mammals that had returned to the sea. From anatomical and paleontological evidence, the whale's closest relatives seemed to be the even-toed hoofed mammals (cattle, sheep, camels, goats). Comparisons of milk protein genes (beta casein and kappa-casein) have confirmed this relationship and have suggested that the closest relative for whales may be the hippopotamus.

Much of the evidence supporting evolution is the same as Darwin used, namely, fossils and comparative morphology. Since the discovery of DNA, the most important facts that we have learned about evolution come from the study of genetics, molecular biology, and chemistry. It is not surprising that evolution is the change in the genetic code, namely, DNA.

Genes evolve at different rates because some proteins are more tolerant of changes in their amino acid sequences than others. The average rate at which a particular gene or protein (mutates) evolves gives rise to the concept of a molecular clock. Molecular clocks run faster for less constrained proteins and slowly for more constrained proteins. The clock for fibrino peptide runs rapidly; 1 percent of amino acids changes in a little longer than one million years, but for cytochrome C, it is very slow. A 1 percent change in the amino acid sequence takes twenty million years. The molecular clock helps us determine evolutionary relationships among organisms, and also it will point to the time in the past when species started to diverge from one another. Once the clock for a particular gene or protein has been calibrated by reference to some known event, whose time is known, the actual chronological time when all other events occurred can be determined by looking at the gene or protein mutation tree.

The other line of DNA evidence for evolution is in the pseudo genes (18). Pseudo genes are remnants of genes that no longer function and therefore do not code for any amino acids. Still these undergo replication as other functioning genes and are carried over to the progeny. They also undergo mutations, but this does not affect the offspring as they do not code for anything. It is estimated that only 5 percent of the total genes are functioning in the human genome or are needed to be human, and the rest, 95 percent of the genes are pseudo genes and are not functioning (dead genes). Random mutations occur in these genes, and by virtue of the fact they (the pseudo genes) are more numerous than functioning genes, most mutations will be in these dead or pseudo genes and won't affect the off springs. Examining these mutations on these dead genes, one can determine the common ancestry and also the times of divergence of species.

A case in point is the story of vitamin C. This vitamin is essential for primates including humans. Deficiency of it leads to the disease scurvy. Some mammals produce an enzyme protein called LLGO (l-gulono-gamma-lactone oxiase), which synthesizes their own vitamin C. The LLGO gene that codes for this chemical has been identified. Since our diet is rich in vitamin C, we do not need this gene to manufacture vitamin C in our body. Under evolutionary theory, this LLGO gene is inherited from a remote common ancestor. If one of the descendents develops a mutation in this gene and kills it (makes the gene dysfunctional), one might find evidence for this dead gene in the off springs. They will survive because their diet is rich in vitamin C and do not need that gene to manufacture vitamin C in their body. Now scientists have discovered remnants of this once-working LLGO gene in humans and primates.

Any kind of potential defects can kill a gene. So if the defect occurred independently in each primate, then it would be extremely unlikely to have the same error in the same nucleotide sequence or amino acid sequence in all primates and humans. A small segment of the LLGO pseudo gene sequence was recently compared from human and chimpanzee, macaque and orangutan. All four mammals' pseudo genes were found to share a common crippling single nucleotide deletion that would cause the remainder of the protein to be translated in the wrong frame and render the gene nonfunctional. This illustrates the fact that this gene mutation had occurred in a common ancestor who lived in the past and transferred it to its descendents even though this was a nonfunctioning gene (pseudo gene).

Another example of a duplicated dead gene is that of the gene that codes for an enzyme that metabolizes the steroid hormones. Right next to this gene in humans is a defective copy of the same gene that is nonfunctional (dead copy of the still functional gene right next to it). In this case, there is deletion of a particular string of just eight letters (out of thousands of other letters). Chimpanzees have the same dead gene. But what makes it significant is not the chimp has the same dead gene but how it became a dead gene. The fact is that the chimpanzees also have the same exact eight-letter deletion. This points to a descent from a common ancestor in the past with same defect.

What do these dead genes do? Some were active in early embryonic stage and stop functioning later. Some are acquired from ancestors. An example is the embryonic tissue from the jaw of a chicken that was induced to grow teeth in the jaw (19). Genes for teeth are there in the chicken DNA, but they are inactive. When scientists stimulated this nonfunctional gene, the chicken produced teeth in the jaw. It points to the chicken's descent from their reptilian ancestors.

Indirect evidence for evolution can be inferred from the bible and Qur'an regarding the story of the flood of Noah. Before the flood was to occur, God had given instructions to Noah for manufacturing a large boat (the ark) so that Noah can accommodate a pair of every species of animals and birds in addition to his family. God could have ordered Noah to escape in the boat without having to struggle to collect these creatures, put them in the vessel, and feed them till the flood is receded, which took several months. It obviously was a gigantic undertaking for Noah. God could have created all the animals and birds fresh when the flood receded and the Ark landed.

By an act of His command "Be" and it will be done. But that was not the case. God did not undertake a new series of creations; instead God wanted to follow the law of nature as established by Him (to preserve all those life-forms) and not to re-create any species at will, instantly, whenever and wherever needed even though the Almighty has all the power to do so. The existing evolved life-forms were saved by collecting a pair of each species and keeping them in the Ark of Noah, as it had taken billion of years for the evolutionary process to bring forth those live forms that Noah saved, and allowing their propagation to continue the natural way, instead of freshly re-creating the same species.

The final chapter for proof of evolution was written in 2003 when human genomic research team published the DNA sequence of the human being. The oldest code, the code of human life, was revealed. This code is written in just four letters, ATCG (A-adenine, T-thymine, C-cytosine, and G-guanine). These four chemicals make up our genetic code and our life.

The draft of the human genome was published in 2001 (20) along with the sequence of human genome, and the final details of finishing the euchromatic sequence of the human genome in 2004 (21).

Genome is the total genetic material present in a single-cell nucleus. Human beings contain about ten trillion cells. There are three billion base pairs packed into twenty-three chromosomes.

Gene is a segment of DNA that contains information for producing a protein. A gene contains about thirty thousand base pairs. Only 10 percent of these pairs are capable of coding for proteins called exons. The rest is called junk as they have no known functions. There are three to four thousand genes per chromosome.

A more complex organism does not mean it will have more DNA. On the contrary, a human has 2,800 million base pairs. The salamander has 90,000 million base pairs. Lily has 90,000 million base pairs. A bacterium has 4.7 million base pairs.

The chimpanzee, our closest relative, genetically has three billion base pairs. In 2005, scientists completed the chimpanzee genome analysis. Now they can do comparative genomics, and that will tell us what alterations in the chimpanzee genome caused the transformation (evolution) to become a human (the secret of Humanness). The differences in the functional DNA are only 1% and in the wider DNA content are only 4% between a chimpanzee and human. Genetically speaking human and chimpanzee are 98.76% identical. There will be clues why chimpanzees are resistant to Alzheimer's disease, HIV, malaria, and hepatitis. The genome analysis has demonstrated that there are segments in our gene that are similar to many lesser species including bacteria, flies, chicken, mouse, dog, and others. We are only seeing the tip of the iceberg as far as the vast amount of information to be explored by studying the genome and comparative genomics according to the scientists.

By doing comparative genomics, researchers have discovered a surprising number of matching DNA sequences in various vertebrate species including the mouse, rat, chicken, and dog. Since these DNA sequences have not changed over long period of evolutionary history is an indication they are biologically very important. But their (pseudo genes) function in human genome remain a mystery. The DNA bases at 481 regions were completely unchanged. These are called the ultra conserved elements. These elements were found in the genomes of dog and chicken, and two-thirds of them were found in the fish (22).

Recently the Sea Urchin Genome Sequencing Consortium completed the draft genome sequence of the California purple sea urchin and found a surprising number of shared gene sequences with that of human (23) The cattle gene map shows that many genes and even whole chromosomes are configured in the same way as in humans (24).

Scientists have explored only the tip of the iceberg—the human genome. As seen above, the scientists are beginning to see many surprises. The human genome is carrying the DNA sequences of many lower species as seen by many studies so far. We already have seen that there are many more "junk

DNA" than functional DNA in human genome. Why are we carrying these DNA sequences that are not coding for any proteins that we need as human beings? What are their functions? So far, scientists have not been able to detect any useful functions for these junk DNA. Maybe they are contributing certain unknown functions which are yet to be discovered. But prevailing view is that they are unwanted luggage left over by ancestral species that we happen to carry along. Whose luggage is this? Obviously they belong to the bygone species that have gone extinct. If we don't need them, why can't our genome get rid of it?

Every time a sperm fertilizes the egg, the chromosomes in the sperm and egg divide and give half of the genes from both the parents to the embryo. In this process, the junk DNA segments also divide and go to the embryo, and the journey of these junk or pseudo genes continues through generations.

May be these pseudo genes are the biologic repertoire of the history of life. In the long journey of our life, from its first appearance on earth about 3.5 billion years ago, it has passed through millions and billions of life-forms to finally appear in the human body. Comparing our genome to a voluminous book, we can appreciate the fact that each species (those extinct and extant) has contributed a chapter into this "book" called the human genome. The human genome can be called the "Book of Life".

When scientists can decipher the information contributed by different species into our genomic book, by studying the nonfunctioning genes that are similar to the lower species, we will learn how these previous life-forms, our ancestors, were able to continue their life, and if possible why they all went extinct.

In these genetic fingerprints and footprints, there will be hidden evidence for their life and death. We are only beginning to unravel the enormous amount of information hidden in our genome. The genetic Sherlock Holmes will be able to fully explain it in the coming future.

Our life journey being started 3.5 billion years ago can be compared to the perpetual traveler who has collected the blueprint of each and every village and town that he happened to go through for creating its travelogue. The biological traveler, in its "book of life," the human genome, has the blue print of the structure and function of the previous species, extinct and extant (the way stations); either collected by the traveler (life) or was given to it by each way station (extinct life-forms) as a gift for future reference, is immaterial. We are fortunate to have them so that when scientists are able to read the full book of genome, we will have our life story of 3.5 billion years, unfold before us and marvel the beauty and the creativity of nature (God).

It is to be realized that this traveler—Life—even though it started its journey about 3.5 billion years ago and still continues to travel, it has not moved and it remains still, without covering any distance. It changes its vehicle (species) every so often without moving from its station.

These non functional genes (Pseudogenes) will serve as the incontrovertible evidence for evolution as they represent the lower life-forms from whom human species evolved.

Scientists have found that three genes involved in inflammation are deleted in the chimpanzee and that will explain the differences in immunity and inflammatory responses in the chimpanzee and human beings. At the same time, human beings have lost the function of a gene that codes for an enzyme that prevents Alzheimer's disease (25). (The gene caspase-12 is believed to be the gene to prevent Alzheimer's disease and is functioning in the animals). This suggests that the animals that still have this functioning gene are protected against Alzheimer's disease but not human beings. Why did evolutionary process make us vulnerable to Alzheimer's disease by rendering the gene caspase-12 dysfunctional? In evolutionary genetics, this cannot be an advantageous mutation (loss of function of the gene caspase-12) as we are made prone to develop Alzheimer's disease. This mutation definitely is not one that confers any survival advantage, and on the contrary, it makes us prone to the socially dreaded disease. This cannot be explained on the basis of an evolutionary misstep. But it has profound religious and philosophical significance.

As we, the human beings, own the most sophisticated and productive organ in biological history—the human brain—we have been able to achieve what we see and enjoy today. The numerous inventions, scientific advancements for the comfort and happiness of humanity on one hand, the brain also has discovered the means for total eradication of the entire humanity from the face of the world—the atomic bomb. Nevertheless, the brain is a marvel. But it also can be a source of despair, pain, and profound unhappiness. Toward the end of our life, everyone will ponder about our future as to where we are going and look back to our own past life to see what has been achieved in our life time, also we will wonder if there was any useful purpose for our life. Had all those trials and tribulations that we have gone through our life, from childhood onward till death, have achieved anything tangible? We came from dust, and we are going back to be dust again. We have a very short sojourn on earth, and what was the purpose of being here (on earth)? The only lasting legacy for our life in this world is limited to the participation in the propagation of our species by providing the DNA to the off springs.

This saga of life and death continues ever since life appeared on earth 3.5 billion years ago. On the basis of the past evolutionary history, we the human beings cannot be the final evolutionary product, and another species could replace us. In this scenario, we the human beings will be the "visible" link between the yet-to-come new species and the Homo sapiens sapiens that is us. What could be the ultimate purpose of all these present and past biota?

Ever since Adam and Eve appeared on earth, there have been billions of us who came and have gone. The process repeats itself, and we cannot fathom the changes that we may be subjected to, including a change to another species. The purpose of these births and deaths of previous species and individuals of our own species is beyond our comprehension, other than being the participants in the saga of biological evolution. But the question is WHY?

Here we can see a reason for the knocking out of the function of the gene caspase-12, which will enable us to acquire Alzheimer's disease. Those who have Alzheimer's disease will lose cognitive function, self-realization, rumination, thinking about our future, planning, repentance, and all human faculties. Toward the end of life, this may be a welcome change for the reasons enumerated above. The victims of Alzheimer's disease live like an infant without any worry of anything and may be "enjoying a happy life." Which is a better way to exit this world—worrying about the unknown after death or being oblivious of what is going on? Alzheimer's is an anesthetic to the mind as anesthesia during surgery is to remove physical pain. The exceptions are the believers who will have total satisfaction in the impending death as they believe that after death, their journey is to heaven. But still, they are going to a world unknown and have to leave behind their loved ones, and that thought would still be worrisome. In any event, for the majority, death or the thought of impending death, will be the least welcome event. Alzheimer's disease will be the blessing toward the end of our life to be oblivious of anything and everything.

But it will be a burden on the family to care for the demented elderly. But it is a repetition of the parents taking care of the children when the children were without full mental capacity, and one is duty bound to care for the parents when they are reduced into an infantile state.

What are the scriptures saying about the care of our parents in their ripe old age?

Caring for our parents has been ingrained in our culture. Many elders are victims of declining mental faculties and eventually become dependent on others for their daily needs just like children, as dementia sets in. Whether it is a cultural practice or ordained by our genetic imprints that we care for our parents is unclear.

Almost all religions exhort the virtues of caring for our parents. In Hinduism, it has been deemed virtuous. In the four stages of human life, according to Hinduism, it is especially required to take care of the parents in the last two stages, namely, the vanaprastha stage (retirement stage) and the sanyasa stage (preparing for salvation).

Genesis: Exodus 20:12 (26) says, "Honor your father and your mother that your days may be long upon the land which the Lord your God is giving you."

Qur'an 22:5, 30:54, 36:68, 40:67 (27) states, "Many a one of you is reduced in old age to a most abject state, ceasing to know anything of what he once knew so well."

Qur'an:17:23: "And that ye be kind to parents, whether one or both of them attain old age in thy life, say not to them a word of contempt, nor repel them, but address them in terms of honor.

Qur'an:17:24: "And out of kindness lower to them the wing of humility and say "my lord bestow on them thy mercy even as they cherished me in childhood."

In these verses, we can see the plan of the Creator to turn our mind into an abject state of oblivion and make us behave like an infant who has no mental faculties. This indeed is a blessing for the ever-inquisitive mind to be transformed into a docile state when we are about to exit this world by death. For it will be very painful to leave the only place we are familiar with in our entire life and to go to the unknown.

This may well be the reason that the gene caspase-12 has been rendered nonfunctional in the humans unlike in other animals including the apes. In evolutionary theory, an alteration in a gene is usually for a survival advantage. Occasionally it could be a harmful mutation that will lead to the death of the organism. Here we cannot see any survival advantage for human beings by making caspase-12 dysfunctional. This points to a guided evolutionary alteration of the gene for the purpose detailed above.(to be oblivious of the stress and strains of life and the surroundings towards the end of our life)

This lends support for a guided evolution.

References for evidence for biological evolution:

1. Georges Cuvier, paleontologist (1769-1832).
2. Charles Lyell, geologist. proposed uniformitarianism.
3. William Smith (1769-1839), geologist, created first geological map.
4. William Londsale (1794-1871), British geologist and paleontologist.
5. Eukaryotic fossil. Scientific American. Oct. 21, 1999.
6. Wikipedia.http://en.wikipedia.org/wiki/Feathered-dinosaurs.Retrieved 1-17-2009.
7. Nature. April. 2006.
8. Comparative anatomy (need photos).
9. Charles Darwin. Origin of Species.
10. Vestigial Organs.
11. Evolution of Whales. Nov.21. National Geographic.
12. Ernst Haeckel. 1860.
13. Icons of Evolution: Jonathan Wells. (2000), p. 105-107.
14. Converging Lines of Evolution: P. Wesley Edwards. Sep. 2, 2004.
15. Journal of Molecular Evolution, 2:99-116. McLaughlin P. J.; and Dayhoff, M. O. 1973.
16. Evidence supporting biological evolution, Science and creationism View from National Academies of Sciences. 1999.
17. University of Cambridge, UK.
18. Pseudo genes, nonfunctional genes in the genome.
19. Mathew P. Harris. University of Wisconsin. Current Biology, 16:371-377.
20. "The Human Genome." Science, 291:1309-1351.Venter J. C. et al. 2001.
21. Nature, 431: 031-945. "Finishing Eukaryotic sequence of human genome." IHSC.2004.
22. Science, 2004.
23. Developmental Biology. December 1, 2006.
24. Genome Research. Sep. 2000.
25. Alzheimer's disease, a degenerative disease of the brain leading to dementia.
26. The Bible: Exodus 20:12.
27. Qur'an: 22:25, 30:54, 36:68, 40:67.

CHAPTER 18
The Muslim Evolutionists

One of the early scientists to conceive the idea of evolution was a Muslim biologist named Nasir al-Din al-Tusi (1), born 1201 in Tus in Persia. He wrote extensively on biology and is considered one of the pioneers of biological evolution long before Charles Darwin. He begins his theory of evolution with the universe once consisting of equal and similar elements, which themselves consist of elementary particles. As a result of internal contradictions, some substances began developing faster and differently from other substances. He then explains how the elements evolved into minerals, then plants, then animals, and then humans. Tusi then explains how hereditary variability was an important factor for biological evolution of living things (2). The organisms that can gain the new features faster are more viable. As a result, they gain advantages over other creatures. The bodies are changing as a result of the internal and external interactions.

Tusi discusses how organisms are able to adapt to their environments.

"Look at the world of animals and birds. They have all that is necessary for defense, protection, and daily life, including strength, courage, and appropriate tools (organs). Some of these organs are real weapons. For example horns, spear, teeth, and claws—knife and needle, feet and hoofs—cudgel. The thorns and needles of some animals are similar to arrows. Animals that have no other means of defense (as the gazelle and fox) protect themselves with the help of flight and cunning. Some of them for example, bees and ants and some bird species have united in communities In order to protect themselves and help each other."

Tusi recognized three types of living things: plants, animals, and humans. He wrote, "Animals are higher than plants, because they are able to move consciously, go after food, find and eat useful things. There are many differences between the animal and plant species. First of all, the animal kingdom is more complicated. Besides, reason is the most beneficial feature of animals. Owing to reason, they can learn and adopt new, non inherent abilities. For example, the trained horse or hunting falcon—is at a higher point of development in the animal world. The first step of human perfection begins here."

Tusi then explains how humans evolved from advanced animals.

"Such humans (probably anthropoid apes) live in the western Sudan and other distant corners of the world. They are close to animals by their habits, deeds, and behavior. The human has features that distinguish him from other creatures. But he has other features that unite him with the animal world, vegetable kingdom, or even with the inanimate bodies. Before (the creation of humans) all differences between organisms were of the natural origin. The next step will be associated with spiritual perfection, will, observation, and knowledge. All these facts prove that the human being is placed on the middle step of the evolutionary stairway. According to his inherent nature, the human is related to the lower beings, and only with the help of his will can he reach the higher development level."

Al-Jahiz (3). Real name—Abu Uthman Amr ibn Bahr al-Kinani al-Fuqaimi al-Basri.

Born in Basra-781-Dec. 868 or Jan. 869 CE. A famous Arab scholar and author of works on literature, history, biology, zoology, Mutazili philosophy, and theology. Al-Jahiz was one of the earliest figures to conceive the idea of evolution and natural selection. It is believed that his thoughts were very influential on Ibn Miskawayh, al-Biruni, and Ibn Tufail.

Early Life of Al-Jahiz

He was born into a poor family and used to sell fish to help his family. But he was a seeker of knowledge and used to discuss various subjects in the main mosque of Basra. Over a span of twenty-five years, he acquired considerable knowledge in Qur'an and Hadith.

During the Abbasid caliphate (4), a period of cultural renaissance, he was exposed to the Hellenistic philosophy and to the ideas of Aristotle. He had authored about two hundred books. But only thirty books have survived. The caliph al-Mamun wanted al-Jahiz to teach his children but changed his mind when his children got afraid of his boggle eyes. It is said that this was the reason that he got his nickname (al-Jahiz).

His Works

Kitab al-Hayawan (Book of Animals)

In this book, which is considered the most important work of al-Jahiz, he describes over 350 varieties of animals. In this book, al-Jahiz first speculates on the influence of the environment on animals and conceives an early theory of evolution. He describes how the environment can influence their survival and the struggle for survival and the early theory on survival of the fittest (natural selection) (5, 6).

Al-Jahiz wrote,

> Animals engage in a struggle for existence, for resources, to avoid being eaten and to breed. Environmental factors influence organisms to develop new characteristics to ensure survival, thus transforming into new species. Animals that survive to breed can pass on their successful characteristics to offspring (7).

Ibn Miskawayh

The original name: Ahmad Ibn Muhammad Miskawayh Razi was born in Ray, Iran. He was the author of the first major Islamic work on philosophical ethics (Tadhib al-Akhlaq ethical instruction) focusing on practical ethics, conduct, and character. Ibn Miskawah was another early Islamic scholar to clearly describe the idea of evolution (8) in his book, al-Fawz-al-Asghar.

These books state that God first created matter and invested it with energy for development. Matter, therefore, adopted the form of vapor which assumed the shape of water in due time. The next stage of development was mineral life. Different kinds of stones developed in course of time. Their highest form being mirjan (coral). It is a stone which has in it branches like those of a tree. After mineral life evolves vegetation. The evolution of vegetation culminates with a tree which bears the qualities of an animal. This is the date palm. It has male and female genders. It does not wither if all its branches are chopped, but it dies when the head is cut off. The date palm is therefore considered the highest among the trees and resembles the lowest among animals. Then is born the lowest of the animals. It evolves into an ape. This is not the statement of Darwin. This is what Ibn Muskawayh states, and this is precisely what is written in the Epistles of Ikhwan al-safa. The Muslim thinker states that ape then evolved into a lower kind of a barbarian man. He then becomes a superior human being. Man becomes a saint, a prophet. He evolves into higher stage and becomes an angel. The one higher to angel is indeed none but God. Everything begins from him, and everything returns to Him.

Arabic manuscripts of the al-Fawz al-Asghar were available in European centers of education by the nineteenth century, and it is believed to have been read by Charles Darwin. Charles Darwin was a student of Arabic and might have been influenced by this book for his work on evolution (9, 10).

Ibn Khaldun

He was the most important figure in the field of sociology and history in the world. He was the pre eminent Arab polymath. He contributed heavily for the understanding of civilization. He wrote a masterpiece in history and sociology known as Muqaddimah or Prolegomena in Latin. This deals with early Muslim view of universal history. He had few rivals in analyzing world history until Arnold J. Toynbee came along in the twentieth century.

In Muqaddimah (11), Ibn Khaldun wrote the following on biological evolution:

> This world with all the created things in it has a certain order and solid construction. It shows nexuses between causes and things caused, combinations of some parts of creation with others, and transformations of some existent things into others, in a pattern that is both remarkable and endless.
>
> One should then take a look at the world of creation. It started out from the minerals and progressed, in an ingenious, gradual manner, to plants and animals. The last stage of minerals is connected with the first stage of plants, such as herbs and seedless plants. The last stage of plants, such as palms and vines, is connected with the first stage of animals, such as snails and shellfish, which have only the power of touch. The word "connection" with regard to these created things means that the

last stage of each group is fully prepared to become the first stage of the newest group.

The animal world then widens, its species become numerous, and in a gradual process of creation, it finally leads to man, who is able to think and reflect. The higher stage of man is reached from the world of monkeys, in which both sagacity and perception are found, but which has not reached the stage of actual reflection and thinking. At this point, we come to the first stage of man. This is as far as our (physical) observation extends.

Al-Khazini (12)

Abd al-Rahman al-Khazini (1115-1130).A Greek Muslim. Was a scientist, astronomer, physicist, biologist, alchemist, mathematician and philosopher. Born in Merv in the then Persia but now in Turkmenistan.

Robert E. Hall wrote about al-Khazini, "His hydrostatic balance can leave no doubt that as a maker of scientific instruments, he is among the greatest of any time(13)." Al-Khazini wrote about how common people and philosophers of his time in the Islamic world perceived evolution in alchemy and biological evolution.

> When common people hear from natural philosophers that gold is a body which has attained perfection of maturity, to the goal of completeness, they firmly believed that it is something which has gradually come to that perfection by passing through the forms of all other metallic bodies. So that its gold nature was originally lead, after it became tin, then brass, then silver and finally reached the development of gold; not knowing that the natural philosophers mean, in saying this, only something like what they mean when they speak of man, and attributes to him a completeness and equilibrium in nature and constitution—not that man was once a bull and was changed into an ass, and afterward into a horse, and after that into an ape, and finally became a man (14).

Jalal-ad-Din Rumi

The following is a translation of a poem written by Rumi and translated by Sir Muhammad Iqbal (15).

"The Eternal Life"

First man appeared in the class of inorganic things;
Next he passed there from into that of plants;
For years he lived as one of the plants
Remembering naught of his inorganic state so different;
And when he passed from the vegetative to animal state,
He had no remembrance of his state as a plant,
Especially at the time of spring and sweet flowers,
Like the inclination of infants towards their mothers,
Which know not the cause of their inclination to the breast?
Again the great Creator as you know,
Drew man out of the animal into human stage,
Thus man passed from one order of nature to another,
Till he became wise and knowing and strong as he is now,
Of his first soul he has now no remembrance,
And he will be changed again from his present state.

Mawlana Jalal-ad-Din Muhammad Rumi (Sept. 1207-Dec.1273), a widely respected Persian poet, Islamic jurist, and theologian.

Here one can see the scientific curiosity of the early Islamic philosophers and scientists. If these progressive ideas and thoughts were nurtured early in Islam, what happened to these concepts of evolution and the urge to pursue scientific exploration in followers of Islam since the time of those great thinkers and scientists?

After the Prophet's death, many changes crept into the practice of Islam. Early on, there were two schools of thought. The early Muslim philosophers developed the science of citation, the isnad or "backing."

Kalam (17)

There was a period when independent thinkers developed the concept of ijtihad, the willingness to challenge and question authority, recognizing that science and philosophy are both subordinate to morality. In the Kalam School, philosophy separate from Muslim theology, was discouraged.

Independent minds adopting ijtihad sought to investigate the doctrine of Qur'an. Because of individual opinions Ijtihad gave rise to conflicting opinions and was later replaced by a formal procedure of deductions based on Qur'an and Hadith; called "Qiyas" (reasoning by strict analogy).

There were debates between adherents of free will (Qadarites) and Jabarites, who maintained the belief of fatalism (18).

In the second century, Hijra, a new movement arose propounding the principles of Qadarites, called Mutazilite (from itsala, to separate oneself or dissent), developed a rational theology called Ilm-al-Kalam. Those who profess it were called Mutakallamin. They sought philosophical demonstration in confirming religious principles.

The Mutazili school (19) was partly influenced by Greek and Hellenistic philosophy. The Mutazili school was developed in the eighth century. It had basically three principles: (a) God is absolute (tawhid), (b) God's justice (adl), and (c) reward and punishment in the hereafter (al wad-wa-al-waid). It expanded the ijtihad (independent thoughts) to open questions of science and what we call modern philosophy. It had a great influence on the development of modern scientific methods, while isnad is indistinguishable from modern scientific citation. Early Muslim medicine and early Muslim sociology benefited from the Mutazilite concepts, but it led to strong reaction.

Ash'ari school (20)

The Ashari school of theology was developed by Abu-al Hasan-Ashari I (AH 324). This philosophy followed orthodox doctrines and ascribed to dogmatic theology (kalam). This continues to dominate Sunni branch of Islam.

The rise of Asharites put an end to philosophy in the Muslim world but permitted these methods to continue in science and technology. This era was the peak in Muslim innovations. But since then confusion with theology and law had degraded methods. The ulema began to generate a fiqh based on taqlid (emulation) rather than the old ijtihad.

There was the concept of "separation of church and state" during the early Abbasid period (21).

However, later caliphs and dynasties pursued the idea of authority above all, and much thought was not given to scientific or philosophical advancement or ijtihad, and the decline of Islamic scientific advancement began.

Reference for Muslim Evolutionists

1. Nasir al-Din al-Tusi, Wikipedia. March 8, 2008.http://en.wikipedia.org/wiki/Nasir-al-Din-al-Tusi.
2. Farid Alakbaro. Summer 2001. "A 13th Century Darwin? Tusi's View on Evolution," (http://azer.com/aiweb/categories/magzine/92-articles/92-tusi.hotmail). Azerbaijan International, 9.
3. Al-Jahiz. Wikipedia.http://en.wikipedia.org/wiki/Al-jahiz. March 8, 2008.
4. Abbasid caliphate. Wikipedia March 8, 2008.
5. Conway Zirkle: 1941. Natural selection before "The origin of species." Proceedings of the American Philosophical Society 84:1:71-123.
6. Mehmet Bayrakdar (third quarter) 1983, Al Jahiz and the Rise of Biological Evolution.
7. GaryDaegan. Intelligent Design. (http://www.abc.net.au/m/encounter/stories/2006/1656361.htm) Encounter. ABC.
8. Muhammad Hamidullah. From Ibn Miskawayh's Book, al-Fawz-al Asghar.
9. Muhammad Hamidullah and Afzal Iqbal (1993) "The Emergence of Islam. Lectures on the development of Islamic Worldview. Intellectual tradition and polity." p. 143-144. Islamic Research Institute, Islamabad.
10. Ibn Miskawayh, prominent Persian philosopher (932-1030).One of the first to clearly describe biological evolution. Al Fawz-al Asghar.
11. Ibn Khaldun (1332-1406). The north African polymath and Islamic scholar. Book Muqaddimah. Translated by Franz Rosenthal (Princeton University Press, 1981), 74-75.
12. Al Khazini. Born in eleventh century and died in twelfth century. Muslim scientist of Byzantine Greek descent, from Merv the then Persia but now part of Turkmenistan. Wikipedia. http://en.wikipedia.org/wiki/Al-Khazini.retrieved 2-28-2009.
13. Robert E. Hall. 1973. Al-Khazini: Dictionary of Scientific Biography 7:331.
14. John William Draper. 1878. "History of the conflict between religion and science." p. 237. ISBN.1603030964.
15. Mawlana Jalal ad-Din Muhammad Rumi (Sep. 1207-Dec.1275), widely respected Persian poet, Islamic jurist and theologian. http://en.wikipedia.org/wiki/Rumi.
16. cf. E. H. Whinfield (Translation) Masnavi. p. 216-217. Translation of verses 3637-3641 and 3648 of book 4 of Rumi's Mathnavi. cf. Allama Muhammad Iqbal. Observation of these verses in his "Development of Metaphysics in Persia." p. 91.

17. Kalam.An eighth-century school of Islamic philosophy. http://www.muslim philosopohy.com/ip/Kalam.htm.
18. Qadarites and Jabarites. Wikipedia. March 8, 2008;.http://www.sacred-texts. com/isl/moi/moi.html
19. Mutazilli School. Ibid, Wikipedia. March 8, 2008.
20. Ashari school. Ibid.
21. Kevin Staley (1989) "Al Kindi on Creation: Aristotle's challenge of Islam," Journal of the History of Ideas 50 (3): 355-370.

CHAPTER 19
Reverse Evolution

Reverse evolution occurs when an organism returns to the genetic state of its ancestors (1). It is also amazing that the process of evolution is a one-way track. Even though we carry a huge burden of genes, 95 percent of which are not needed for us to be human and are baggage left from earlier species. We are carrying more genes from other species, and they are not needed for being a human. Scientists cannot find a reason for their existence in us, as they are not doing anything that contribute to be a human, or they may be doing something that scientists have not found yet. Regardless, the huge amount of unneeded genes that human beings carry brings up a question that, is it possible that these unneeded genes (pseudo genes) could in some way be reactivated such that human being can be reverted to one of the previous species, from which human beings evolved? When the right pressures and environmental conditions are present, could such a reversal be possible? There is no evidence in the animal world that has ever been documented.

However, it is to be remembered that Qur'an refers to a scenario in which it could have happened (subject to various different interpretations).

Qur'an 7:163 "And ask them about that town which stood by the sea: how its people would profane the Sabbath whenever their fish come to them, breaking the water's surface, on a day on which they ought to have kept Sabbath—because they would not come on other than Sabbath days. Thus did We try them by means of their own iniquitous doings."

7:165;Asad: "And thereupon when those sinners had forgotten all that they had been told to take to heart, We saved those who had tried to prevent the doings of evil, and overwhelmed those who had been bent on evildoing with dreadful suffering for all their iniquities."

7:166 "And then when they disdainfully persisted in doing what they had been forbidden to do, We said unto them, 'Be as apes, despicable.'"

2:65 "For you are well aware of those from among you who profaned the Sabbath, whereupon We said unto them, 'Be as apes, despicable and rejected.'"

2:66 "And set them up as a warning example to their own time and all times to come as well as an admonition to all who are conscious of God" (2).

(The city referred to here is believed to be the city of Ela which was situated on the Red Sea (3). During Sabbath, the people (Jewish) were prohibited from working including fishing, and therefore that day, there will be more fish available as most of them (fisher men) stay away from fishing, and the law breakers had a better chance to collect more fish.

Many commentators describe this incident as a metaphorical statement, in that the Sabbath breakers, (their actions and their thinking) were changed to an inferior status as that of an ape; and they were not physically transformed to an ape. From a practical standpoint, that explanation is credible, as God has not done anything that has a magical touch to it as changing a man to an ape instantaneously in front of the other people there.

But taking the statement literally, that those people were changed to apes, is not an impossibility from a genetic standpoint, notwithstanding the power of the Almighty to transform one form to another at anytime.

Qur'an 2:66 (4) says, "So We made it an example to their own time and posterity." This transformation is limited to a group of people in their generation, in a town who were indulged in certain prohibited activities (fishing on Sabbath day and not to affect all the inhabitants of the area). This memorable event, reverting human beings to apes if that was what had happened, is different from traditional mutation-derived evolution in that usual evolutionary product has some features of survival advantage or the mutant usually becomes a different species. Here the altered humans were inferior to the existing humans and did not have any advantageous characteristics. It was meant as a warning for the rest of human beings around, to think about God's punishment and for the future generation to be reminded of. These mutants (altered ones) might have died out as they could not be a viable race or species suitable to live and propagate in that town, if indeed they were physically transformed to apes or apelike creatures.

What environmental factors or cataclysm caused this presumed "devolution" is unclear. Scientists point to certain climatic alterations or natural disasters or random mutation as a cause of genetic alteration and speciation. In this case, God's displeasure, which, for a believer would be worse than a cataclysm might have triggered this change, in a reverse direction. But why did the process of transformation go the other way (backwards)? Normal mutation if beneficial goes forwards to become a new species. In this instance it was a result of God's anger and had to go in a reverse direction as a warning for wrong doers. It cannot be a new species, as that will not be a sign of God's anger and displeasure.

In the Bible, there is no direct mention of men despised as apes. But in Qur'an 2:65 translation footnote (5), it recognizes the biblical statements in Ezekiel 22:8-11 as behaviorally apelike people (6). The Bible, KJ version in 22:8, says, "You have despised my holy things and profaned My Sabbaths. In you are men who slander to cause blood shed, in you are those who eat on the mountains, in your midst they commit lewdness: In you men uncover their father's nakedness; in you they violate women who are set apart during their impurity.

One commits abomination with his neighbor's wife, another lewdly defiles his daughter-in-law; and another in you violates his sister, his father's daughter"

Is it conceivable that man can undergo reverse evolution to become the next lower species? Certainly we have the genetic makeup of an ape as we have 95 percent of genes compatible with the chimps. If mutation of some sort alters the gene segment that changed in the chimpanzee to make us human (human-creating gene) so that it reverses backwards, then the above mentioned reversal of man to apes becomes a scientific curiosity!

Scientists have grown teeth in the jaw of chicken by manipulating its gene in the embryo (7). The scientists produced these chickens with teeth by providing specially chosen signals to the beak region of developing embryo. This suggests a reversal to their ancestors, the dinosaur, who had teeth.

At the University of Utah Health Science Center, scientists have shown how evolution works by reversing the process (8). They reconstructed a 530-million old gene from mice working through Hox genes. Hox genes are like orchestra conductors directing the actions of other genes during development of the embryo.

Human Reverse Evolution: Is this possible?

If the chicken embryo can be coaxed to grow teeth, is it possible to activate the dormant chimpanzee related genes in human beings and change human to a chimpanzee?

Is there any known episode in history?

The published reports indicate that reverse evolution is possible and that backward evolution spawned apelike people (9).

A researcher from Cukurova University Medical School in Adana, Turkey, has described a family of nineteen in whom several members walk on all fours and speak a primitive language. This is called Uner Tan syndrome. These individuals exhibit prehuman features and represent possible backward evolution.

In the evolutionary history of human beings, the early humanoid species were walking on four limbs (quadrupedalism). Then as evolution progressed, the human species started to walk on two legs (bipedalism). From fossil evidence, looking at the skeletal changes needed for bipedalism, anthropologists conclude that Homo erectus was a bipedal. From that point onward, bipedalism is considered one of the unique characteristics of human species. Therefore, these individuals exhibiting quadrupedal walking may represent a reversal of the evolutionary process, changing from bipedal locomotion into quadrupedal locomotion.

Five of these victims of this syndrome walked on two palms and two feet with extended legs. They could stand up, but only for a short time, with flexed knees and heads. They had a rather primitive language. They spoke to each other using their own language, using only a few hundred words which the parents could partly understand, Tan wrote. They were mentally retarded. They could not count from one to ten. They were not aware of time and space. They were unaware of year, season, day, and time. They had quite strong legs and arms according to the scientist.

The sitting posture was rather similar to an ape. They could not raise their heads to look forward. The head posture was rather similar to the head posture like chimpanzee.

Tan believes that a mutation stripped them off gene or genes that let humans walk upright, returning them to the prehuman state of quadrupedalism.

According to some scientists, to demonstrate reverse evolution, one would have to identify the genetic changes associated with four limb walking (quadrupedalism) (10).

Scientists are mapping the defect causing quadrupedalism to one of the areas of the genome that is most different between humans and the closest primates (10).

And they have mapped the defect to a region of the genome called chromosome 17p, a site of some of the biggest differences between human beings and chimpanzees. Other researchers have linked bipedalism to chromosome 17p (9).

The reverse evolution in the family affected both the mind as well as the body. They were mentally retarded according to the researchers, and the researchers argue that complex traits can both appear and disappear because they involve a single gene or group of related genes, and this supports the theory of punctuated equilibrium, proposed by Niles Eldredge and Stephen Jay Gould (11).

Others have reported on additional members with the Uner Tan syndrome who have quadrupedalism, primitive mental development, curved fingers while walking on fours, and the arm to leg ratio similar to primates. Their MRI images of the brain did not show cerebellar atrophy, except for mild vermal atrophy, which were not unlike in those who were not affected with this defect and were not quadrupeds. This suggests a single gene controlling multiple behaviors (12).

Other scientists assert that genetic research is replete with examples of similar events (13).

Evolution is the process in which occasional beneficial mutation spread throughout the population, as the organism, that have them, reproduce more.

Reverse evolution occurs when an organism returns to the genetic state of its ancestor [1] and could happen when an organism loses genes they had recently acquired through evolution, and are lost again. Alternatively, it could happen when the genes become reactivated after falling to disuse but not lost.

Example is the fish that take up residence in dark caves, which will lose their eyes as they don't use them. But they can re-emerge when the fish resumes life in the surface waters (14). It is hard to prove a reverse evolution. Sometimes the so-called backward evolution may be due to evolution of new genes that produce similar effects, to the old according to the scientists. Some say that there won't be any evolutionary biologist who would subscribe to the notion that reverse evolution is impossible (1).

From these observations, we can postulate that reverse evolution is possible theoretically and factually as described in the Qur'an.

References for Reverse Evolution:

1. Keith Crandall. Brigham Young University of Provo, Utah. World Science. April 29, 2006.
2. Qur'an 7:163; 165, 166; 2:65, 66.Muhammad Asad.
3. Maulana Muhammad Ali's Translation. The Holy Qur'an: 7:163 p. 365.
4. Qur'an 2:66.
5. Maulana Muhammad Ali. The Holy Qur'an. 2:65 p. 34.
6. The Bible: Ezekiel 22:8-11.
7. Mathew P. Harris. University of Wisconsin Current Biology 16:371-77.
8. Mario Capecci. University of Utah Health Science Center. Journal of Developmental Genetics (August 2006).
9. World Science (April 29, 2006). "Backward Evolution Spawns Apelike People. The Uner Tan Syndrome." http://en.wikipedia.org/wiki/Ulas-family.
10. Lawrence Mueller, biologist. University of California, Irvin.
11. Niles Eldredge and Stephen Jay Gould (1972). Punctuated Equilibrium. An Alternative to Phyletic Gradualist, in TMJ Schofp. Ed. Models in Paleobiology. San Francisco. Freeman Cooper. pp. 82-115. Reported in N. Eldredge "Time Frames" (Princeton University Press:1985).
12. Infoclient@inist.fr.
13. Lawrence Mueller. World Science (April 29, 2006). University of California at Irvin.
14. Megan Porter and Keith C. Brigham. Young University. Provo, Utah. "Trends in Ecology and Evolution." (October 2003).

CHAPTER 20

Evolution and Formation of Earth

Planets of the solar system were formed 4.57 billion years ago from the solar nebula. Within this nebula, suns and stars were formed as the dust cloud condensed. A nearby star exploded and sent a shock wave through the solar nebula and caused angular momentum to the condensed dust. As the cloud accelerated the rotation, it flattened to a disk. Most of the mass was in the center and began to heat up. Due to collision of large debris, proto planets began to form. Due to increase in rotational speed and gravity, the center of the disc heated up. Ultimately, nuclear fusion of hydrogen into helium began, and the sun was formed.

Outside the gravitational pull of the sun, large fragments collided and became larger objects and eventually the proto planets. One such accretion is earth, 150 million kilometers away from the sun. Earth is a small planet in the vastness of space. It is one of nine planets that travel through the space around the sun. Earth is home for all living things that we know of, including man. Life is possible on earth because it is at the right distance from the sun. Most living things need the light and heat from the sun. If earth was too far from the sun, it will be too cold for anything to live. If earth was too close to the sun, it will be too hot for any life to survive.

The moon was created from the earth.

The early earth was very different from what we see today.

The outer layer of earth was molten initially, but cooled later to a solid crust when there was enough water in the atmosphere. There were no oceans or oxygen.

174

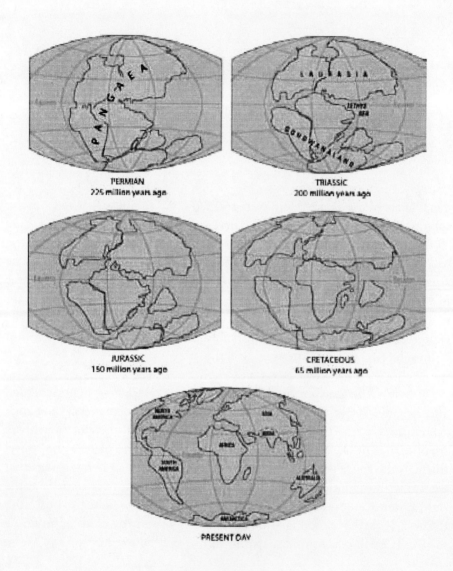

Evolution of Earth

Source. Wikimedia Commons

Soon afterward, a Mars-sized object called Theia hit the earth and as a result, some of the mass of Theia got merged with the earth, but a portion of it was ejected into space and became the moon (1).

Gas emanating from the earth and volcanic activity produced the early atmosphere. During the early years, there were frequent impacts of comets carrying ice. From 4 to 3.8 billion years ago, earth suffered severe asteroid bombardment (2). This ice and condensing water vapor produced the ocean. Over hundreds of millions of years, continents formed and broke up. Occasionally the continents combined to form a super continent. Within 100 million years of early earth, it might have been habitable (3).

About 750 million years ago, the earliest known super continent Rodinia began to break up. Six hundred to four hundred and forty million years ago, these continents recombined to form Pannotia. Later, it became Pangaea (all earth), which again broke apart by 180 millions of years ago.

The ice ages began about forty million years ago. Since then, there were repeated periods of glaciation every forty thousand to one hundred thousand years. The last ice age ended ten thousand years ago.

The geological history of earth can be divided into two periods: the super eon (Precambrian) and the Phanerozoic eon.

The Precambrian period is the longest time encompassing 90 percent of the geological time. It extends from 4.6 billion years ago to about 570 million years ago.

Alfred Wegener proposed that there was a super continent 250 million years ago and called it Pangaea (meaning entire earth in Greek [1]).

Pangaea was a C-shaped land mass that spread across the equator. The body of water enclosed within the resulting crescent was called the Tethys sea. Because of the massive size of the Pangaea, the inland was dry due to lack of precipitation and allowed the terrestrial animals to travel from South Pole to the North Pole as there was no water body separating the poles. The ocean that surrounded the Pangaea was called the Panthalassa.

About 180 million years ago, Pangaea is believed to have broken up into two super continents one called the Gondwana to the south and the other called Laurasia to the north. By the end of Cretaceous period, continents separated and looked very much like the present world (4).

The earth's atmosphere contained ammonia methane, water vapor, carbon dioxide, and nitrogen. Ultraviolet radiation flooded the earth as there was no ozone. Because of lightning and ultraviolet activity in the atmosphere, and the presence of methane, carbon dioxide, hydrogen, and water vapor, organic compounds were formed and collected in the ocean.

Cyano bacteria appeared by 3.5 billions of years ago and produced oxygen by photosynthesis. The earth's crust (the top layer) is not a solid shield. It is broken into large thick plates (tectonic plates), which drift atop the soft underlying mantle. The plates move steadily in relation to one another. The plates are 50-250 miles thick.

In 1960s, plate tectonics were developed (the study of plate structure). The tectonic movements cause earthquakes, volcanoes, and ocean trenches. When boundaries of the plates move apart, it causes seafloor to expand. When they collide, mountains are produced; and when they slip past, earthquakes are produced.

The Austrian geologist Edward Suess believed that there was a large land bridge (5) between South America, Africa, India, Australia, and Antarctica. This area was called Gondwanaland named after a district in India where the fossil tree Glossopteris (tongue like leaf) was found. The same plant is found in South America, South Africa, Australia, and Antarctica. This bolstered the theory of Alfred Wegener that the Pangaea was broken into two super continents during the Jurassic period, the Gondwanaland and Laurasia. Further confirmation of the super continent came from fossil evidence of Mesosaurus, a marine reptile whose fossils are found in both South America and South Africa (6) by a South African scientist, Alexander du Toit. This supports Edward Suess's theory of Gondwanaland, which in turn confirms Alfred Wegener's theory of Pangaea and the continental drift.

This describes the evolution of the earth from a formless mass to the different continents that we see today. The continents still move apart ever so slowly, two to ten centimeters per year.

Evidence from scriptures:

Genesis 1:1: "In the beginning when God created the universe. 1:2. The earth was formless and desolate" (7).

Qur'an 41:11 "And He applied his design to the skies, which were yet smoke."

21:30 "Do not the unbelievers se that the heavens and earth were joined together (as one unit of creation) before We clove them asunder" (8).

Both science and the scriptures point to an evolutionary process (physical transformation) in the formation of the earth as we see it today.

Reference for Evolution of Earth

1. Wikipedia. http:// en. Wikipedia.org/ wiki/ Earth.
2. "Evidence for Ancient Bombardment of Earth." Nature (July 25, 2002).
3. Stephen Mojzsis. Science 2005.
4. Alfred Wegener (1880-1930). On the Origin of Earth and Oceans.
5. Edward Suess.
6. Alexander L. du Toit, South African scientist (1878-1948). "Geological Comparison of South America and South Africa." 1927.
7. Genesis 1:1, 1:2.
8. Qur'an 21:30, 41:11.

CHAPTER 21

The Evolution of The Atmosphere

The atmosphere is a layer of gas surrounding the earth and retained by the earth's gravity.

The history of earth's atmosphere prior to one billion years ago is poorly understood.

Since there were different elements in the atmosphere in its evolution, the present atmosphere is sometimes called the third atmosphere. Like everything else in the universe, the atmosphere also has evolved. The original atmosphere was primarily a mixture of helium and hydrogen. Heat from the still molten earth's crust, the sun and solar wind dissipated this atmosphere.

The earth's surface began to cool about 4.5 billion years ago. The volcanoes released steam, carbon dioxide, and ammonia. Mostly it was carbon dioxide and water vapor with little bit of nitrogen and no trace of oxygen. This was called the second atmosphere.

It is generally believed that the high levels of carbon dioxide and methane created a greenhouse effect and kept the earth from freezing.

The atmosphere was originally without oxygen. Without oxygen, most life-forms will die. The oxygen was gradually formed by a process of photosynthesis by the early bacteria called cyan bacteria or the green-blue algae. The atmosphere is essential for the existence of life on earth. It protects us from the ultraviolet radiation, from the vacuum of space. It is the atmosphere that protects us from falling meteorite. Several meteorites fall in to earth every year, but they are either burnt up in the atmosphere or reduced into very small objects that create only minimal damage. The atmosphere also provides a moderate climate. It is divided into seven layers, depending on chemical contents, temperature, movement, and density. It is retained by earth's gravity. Its contents are 78 percent nitrogen, 21 percent oxygen, 0.93 percent argon, 0.03 percent carbon dioxide and 1 percent water. There is no clear boundary between atmosphere and the space. At 75 miles from earth, during reentry of space vehicles, the atmospheric effects become noticeable. The Karman line at 62 miles from earth's surface is regarded as the boundary between the earth's atmosphere and space (1).

What are the functions of the atmosphere? The earth's atmosphere gives us a moderate temperature. In the space above the atmosphere, the temperature is—270 degree centigrade. The ozone layer of the atmosphere protects the life-forms on earth from ultraviolet radiation from the sun. The magnetic radiation from solar flare is blocked by the magnetosphere or the Van Allen Belt. Just one solar flare can emit the energy equivalent to one hundred atomic bombs. The atmosphere protects us from falling meteorites. It also gives us rain. It is a protective canopy for earth's life-forms.

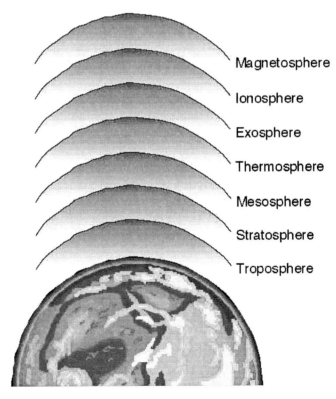

Earth
Layers of atmosphere
Source: Wikimedia Commons

Based on temperature (thermal characteristics), chemical composition, density, and magnetic force the atmosphere is divided into several layers.

There are seven layers to the atmosphere (2, 3).

1. Toposhphere. Up to 10 miles from earth's surfac
2. Stratosphere: 10-30 miles. Temperature decreases with height. This layer contains the ozone layer.
3. Mesosphere: 30-50 miles high. Temperature decreases with height. Most of the meteorites burn up here.
4. Thermosphere: 50-60 miles high. Here temperature increases with height, up to 441 degrees Fahrenheit. The shuttle orbits here.
5. Ionosphere: Ionized by solar radiation. Influences radio propagation to different parts of the earth. Important for atmospheric electricity.
6. Exosphere: 600-650 miles. Free particles move in and out of the solar wind.
7. Magnetosphere: About 650 miles high. This protects the earth's life-forms from the lethal charged solar particles or plasma, blasted off from the sun (4).

Qur'an refers to the atmosphere in several verses (5): 2:22, "Who (God) has made earth a resting place and the sky a canopy."

2:29 "He it is Who created for you all that is on earth. Then He applied His design to the heavens and fashioned them into seven heavens (firmaments, tracks)."

21:32, "And We have made the heavens as a canopy well guarded."

41:12 "So He completed them as seven firmaments (Heavens) in two days (Eons) and He assigned to each heaven its duty and command and We adorned the lower heaven (nearest to earth) with lights and provided it with guard."

65:12, "Allah (God) is Who created seven firmaments and of earth a similar number."

67:3. "He who has created seven heavens one above the other, no want of proportions wilt thou see in the creation of Allah (God)."

Scientists have discovered the seven layers of the atmosphere which could be the seven heavens mentioned in the Qur'an. It is described as a canopy that acts as a shield of protection from the sun. It is provided with guard to protect us from harmful radiation from the sun, and it provides rain.

Qur'an describes the heavens (atmosphere as one above the other). Qur'an says, "And of the earth a similar number (earth has seven layers as the seven layers of the atmosphere)."

The earth also has seven layers.

1. The crust: 6-40 kilometers.
2. The upper mantle: 40-400 kilometers.
3. Transition region: 400-600 kilometers.
4. Lower mantle: 650-2,700 kilometers.
5. Upper mantle: 2,700-2,890 kilometers.
6. Outer core: 2,890-5,150 kilometers.
7. Inner core: 5,150-6,370 kilometers.

These verses in Qur'an clearly indicate that the Seven heavens mentioned in it are none other than the seven layers of the earth's atmosphere and do not indicate seven or several universes or solar systems.

The expression "to guard" in verse 41:12 could imply the protection that the atmosphere gives us from ultraviolet radiation and other harmful effects from the sun, and the meteorite impact. The atmosphere also gives us a controlled temperature. These layers have given certain duties as described above and each layer has given certain functions to guard all the life-forms on earth including man. Science may yet have to discover many more beneficial attributes these layers may have.

Qur'an says the lower heaven (or the heaven close to earth) is adorned with lights. We are able to see the moon, the sun, and the stars in the sky from earth. If these firmaments are indeed the layers of the atmosphere, then these lights cannot be the sun, moon, or the stars as they are above the layers of the atmosphere. Then what could be the meaning of adorning the lower heaven with lights? Does it mean that there are seven solar systems or universes and the lower one (solar system) is adorned with light? But in space, there cannot be a lower or higher of anything. We can only use higher or lower in relation to earth, where we are.

Scientists have discovered several solar systems in the galaxy, but they can't say that these are similar to our solar system (6, 7). Nevertheless, when Qur'an says, "the lower heaven" is adorned with light and we assume it is referring to our solar system as it has the sun, and the moon with reflected light. In the galaxy, higher and lower solar system loses meaning as there cannot be higher or lower of anything in space. One can have a central and or peripheral one as the universe is expanding in all directions. Therefore, the lower heaven described in Qur'an can't be a solar system as it cannot be described as lower or higher. With this in mind, we have to conclude that the reference to the lower heaven must be the lower layer of the atmosphere (ways or tracks-heavens). The atmosphere can be described as having lower and higher heavens-(layers, firmaments, tracks or ways) with respect to the surface of earth.

In space above our atmosphere, there is no light. In space, in spite of the sun and several stars, shining light is negligible as there are no objects or dust to reflect light. Light from the sun passes through space, but space itself is dark as there is nothing to reflect or gravity to bend it. In order to see the sun's light, it has to be reflected from an object or scattered or bent. Light from the sun will travel like a laser beam or like the beam from the flashlight. One can only see the source of light and any object it can reflect from. We will not see the rays of light between the source (laser or flashlight) and the screen it is projected on. In other words, the beam of light between the source and the screen is invisible. Had it not been for the atmosphere, we will not be able to see the sunlight or the objects on earth and the natural scenes around us that we see when we look outside. If there was no atmosphere, one cannot see under a bridge or a tree as there is nothing to scatter the sunlight as it hits the earth in a straight line, and light rays cannot by themselves get under the bridge or the tree as light rays cannot bend to get under. It has to be scattered or reflected from. Similarly, we may not be able to see the stars as good as we see it now if there was no atmosphere.

Because of the atmosphere, we are able to see the luminaries in the sky with the twinkle as we see them now. Had it not been for the presence of atmosphere, scientists say the sun will be brighter. The atmosphere scatters the sun's light and gives the blue hue of the sky and make the objects around us in the attractive colors we see. And this may be the reference to the lower heaven being adorned with lights. The troposphere is the lowest layer of the atmosphere and contains 80 percent of the atmosphere. It contains dust particles and water vapor, which help in scattering sunlight. Light travels in straight line and unless it is scattered or bent, we may not see the light. In the troposphere, these scattering occur. On earth, there are objects like trees, grass, fruits, and flowers which either absorb or reflect back certain wavelengths of the sun's white light and enable us to see different colors. Indeed our surroundings are colorful due to the different spectrum of light as seen in the rainbow. The different colorful flowers and fruits give the color due to the presence of these colors in the sunlight even though sunlight itself is white. These objects absorb certain spectrum of light and reflect back certain other spectrum. The red rose reflects back the red color and absorbs the rest of the colors in the sun's light As we know, the sun's light have seven colors (the eponym VIBGYOR). This may be the reference in Qur'an 41:12 that the lower heaven is adorned with lights.

"He set on the earth mountains standing firm high above it, and bestowed blessings on the earth, and measured therein all things to give them nourishment in due proportion, in four days, in accordance with the needs of those who seek sustenance. As this verse tells us that God bestowed blessings on earth and means of subsistence or nourishment to all things. As discussed earlier, for any living creature to survive on earth the atmosphere had to be there before the living beings were introduced on earth Therefore in this explanation the two days (eons) mentioned in verse 41:12 for the creation of the atmosphere (seven firmaments) should be included in the four days (eons) mentioned in 41:10 so that the atmosphere was created, before the earth could be prepared to have life forms and give sustenance to all creatures. Verse: 41:9: already mentions the creation of earth in two days (eons).

In the verse: 41:11; He Comprehended in his design the sky and it had been as smoke: and said to it and to the earth" come together" willingly or unwillingly. They said we do come together in willingness. Yusuf Ali.

Asad's translation of the verse: 41:11: "And he applied His design" to the skies, which were smoke and He it is who said to them and to the earth, "Come (into being) both of you, willingly or un willingly" to which both responded 'We do come in obedience". What is the significance of this statement regarding the coming together of the skies and the earth. Scientists believe, early in earth's formation a planet called Theia hit the earth (the giant impact theory) and after hitting the earth part of it broke off and was expelled back to space and became the moon. This could be one explanation. The only other thing that could have come together with earth could be the interstellar matter. We cannot see any other objects in the space to come together with the earth other than the meteorites impacts. Could these impacts served any purpose? Possibly. Some scientists believe the oceans were formed on earth due to the meteorite impacts and also they believe that organic materials for the formation of life may have been brought by these meteorites. Therefore meteorite impacts had positive and negative effects. The negative effect being the high temperature brought up on earth due to the impact could have wiped out all life forms.

This may be another explanation.

The concept of the interstellar matter coming together with the earth makes it more scientifically feasible. The interstellar matter which was spread out after the big bang through out the space, consists of 93% hydrogen and rest helium and dust particles.

Scientists believe that the early earth had a reducing atmosphere with no oxygen. Oxygen came much later from green algae. According to science a reducing atmosphere is needed for the origin of the pre biotic molecules for the formation (creation) of life. If there was oxygen in the pre biotic earth's atmosphere these organic molecules would have been destroyed and there won't be any chance for life to appear on earth. In that sense when God asked the skies (the interstellar matter) and earth to come together we have the interstellar matter to surround the earth and becoming a reducing atmosphere consisting of hydrogen, methane and ammonia all of which need hydrogen for their formation. By this process a reducing atmosphere was established for life to begin. Over the ensuing two days (eons) the seven layers of the atmosphere (seven heavens) were formed.

Therefore the statement about coming together of the skies and earth may be these events that had occurred during earth's early evolution-the impact of the planet Theia to form the Moon, bringing interstellar matter to create a reducing atmosphere and the meteorite impacts to create the ocean and for the introduction of organic molecules on earth for the origin of life.

God asks the earth and the skies to come together (Yusuf Ali) willingly or unwillingly. The meaning of this order from God is not fully understood. as God does not need their permission in the creation of all the phenomena in the universe. Why was God asking for their permission? This might be one of those ambiguous statements that God has given to us in Qur'an. 3:7;Yusuf Ali: He it is Who has sent down to thee the Book; In it are verses basic or fundamental (of established meaning).They are the foundation of the Book; Others are not of well established meaning.—But no one knows its true meaning except Allah (God).

The lights referred to in verse 4:12, was to "adorn" the lower heaven as a decorative phenomenon. The different colors (the seven colors of light) are indeed a decoration on earth. And without light and the atmosphere's lower layer—the troposphere (the lower heaven), these different light colors will not come into existence as light has to be scattered or bent by the particles in the atmosphere for the light to be visible. These seven heavens do not appear to represent seven galaxies or seven planets or seven universes. Because none of these can be qualified as lower heaven. For human beings, the reference to lower and higher must be with reference to earth. In space, one cannot describe anything as lower or higher, and the lower heaven referred to in Qur'an most likely is the troposphere, which is the lowest layer of the atmosphere. Moreover the solar systems or galaxies already have light sources in them.

The lower heaven (troposphere) enables us to gaze the stars and the moon in their wonderful shine and twinkle, which in the absence of the troposphere, may not be as beautiful as it is when viewed from earth (adorned with lights).

In conclusion, we see the process of evolution not only in biological species but in the formation of earth as well as in the formation of the atmosphere. The seven heavens (atmospheric layers) were created in two days or (eons).

References for Atmosphere:

1. Wikipedia. http:// en. Wikipedia.org/wiki/earth-atmosphere.
2. Limited Fine Mesh Model 11
3. Michael Pidwirny. "Atmospheric Layers." 1996. University of British Columbia.
4. 4 Wikipedia. http://en.wikipedia.org/wiki/Magnetosphere.Retrieved Jan 21-2009.
5. Qur'an 2:22, 2:29, 21:32, 41:12, 65:12, 67:3.
6. World Science (November 2007).
7. AAAS (American Association for Advancement of Science.).

CHAPTER 22

Time line—geological

Time in
Millions of years.

1. 4600. Formation of Earth.
2. 4300. Melting of Earth, formation of earth structure.
3. 4300. Water vapor dissociates into oxygen and hydrogen. Ozone layer forms.
4. 4000. Bombardment of earth by comets and meteors cease.
5. 3800. Earth crust forms and rocks begin to form.
6. 3800. Water vapor condenses and oceans form.
7. 3500-2800. Primitive cells appear.
8. 3500-3800. Photosynthesis begins by Cyanobacteria (Blue-green algae). Oxygen builds up and ozone layer thickens.
9. 1500. Eukaryotic cells appear.
10. 1500-600. Multi cellular organisms appear.
11. 545. Cambrian Explosion of hard bodied organisms appear.
12. 517-515. Burgess Shale fossilization.
13. Fish appears, the first vertebrates.
14. Algae appear on earth.
15. First land animals—millipedes.
16. 375. First sharks appear.
17. 350 300. Appearance of amphibians.
18. Primitive insects appear.
19. First plants with roots.
20. Reptiles appear.
21. Insects with wings evolved.

22. 250. Permian period extinction.
23. Evolution of bees.
24. Super continent Pangaea breaks up.
25. Crocodiles evolved.
26. Mammals appear.
27. Archaeopteryx appears on earth.
28. Modern sharks appear.
29. 65. Extinction of dinosaurs.
30. Rats and mice appear (mammals).
31. 50. Primitive monkeys appear.
32. 20. Parrots and pigeons appear.
33. Chimpanzees and hominids appear.
34. 4. Bipedalism developed.
35. 3.5 Lucy's appearance.
36. 2 Stone tools being used.
37. 1.6-0.2.Homo erectus lives, uses fire.
38. 0.2-0.03. Neanderthals live.
39. 0.05-0. Homo sapiens sapiens exist and move across the globe.
40. 0.025-0.01. Last glaciation.
41. 0.012. Domestication of animals in Far East.
42. 0.01 Homo sapiens sapiens settlements.
43. 005 Sumerians develop writing in Sumer and Babylon.

CHAPTER 23

The Spiritual Implications

Scriptures:

Genesis (1) describes the creation of living creatures on earth. According to science, fishes came first then land animals and mammals, then birds and finally the human beings. According to the Genesis, the birds appear before animals, which is in variance to the order of the appearance of species according to science.

Genesis 1:11 says, "Let the earth produce all kinds of plants that bear grain and those that bear fruit."

1:20: "Let the water be filled with many kinds living beings and let the air be filled with birds. So God created the great sea monsters and all kinds of creatures that live in water and all kinds of birds."

1:24: "Let the earth produce all kinds of animal life domestic and wild large and small."

1:26: "And now we will make human beings."

1;27: "So God created human beings making them to be like Himself."

2:7: "Then the Lord God took some soil from the ground and formed a man out of it" (2).

From these revelations, one thing is clear that all living things has a common source of origin that is the mud and water. The birds were to fill the air probably after being evolved or created from earth (formed from earth is not mentioned in the Genesis).

In the Qur'an, the description of the creation (evolution) of human beings has been addressed in several verses.

Origin from water (3):

> 21:30: "We made from water every living thing. Will they not then believe."

> 24:45: "And Allah (God) has created every animal from water."

> 25:54: "It is He who has created man from water."

Origin from earth (4):

> 20:55: "From the earth did we create you and unto it shall we return you."

Origin from dust (5):

> 3:59: "He created him from dust."

> 18:37: "Dost thou deny Him who created thee out of dust, then out of a sperm drop. Then fashioned thee into a man."

> 30:20: "Among His signs is this. That He created you from dust."

> 35:11: "And Allah (God) did create you from dust."

> 40:67: "It is he Who has created you from dust."

Creation from clay (6):

> 6:2: "He it is Who created you from clay and then decreed a stated term for you."

> 15:26: "And indeed we have created man out of sounding clay, out of dark slime transmuted (Asad)."

> 23:12: "Man We did create from a quintessence of clay."

> 32:7: "He began the creation of man with [nothing more than] clay."

37:11: "Them have created out of a sticky clay."

38:71: "To the angels, 'I am about to create man from clay.'"

55:14: "He created man from sounding clay like unto pottery."

55:15: "And he created Jinns from fire free of smoke."

Scientific research has entered the sphere of searching for the origin of life. Recent research and the results point, time and again, to clay as an important mineral that help produce most important basic molecules needed for the origin of life.

Both Genesis and Qur'an give us the clear indication that human beings and for that matter, all living things on earth were created from clay (mud) and water. Now we have seen the progress made by science in exploring the mechanisms by which life originated on earth. They believe there may have been different proto life systems present in the primordial earth, but only the ancestors of the carbon-based model prevailed, and the other forms might have perished. Alternatively, the carbon-based model could have been the only life-form ever originated on earth.

The origin of life debate is still raging. Creationists believe it was an act of God, and looking for clues if ever possible as to how God created life is tantamount to denying the Almighty and it will be sacrilegious. But science, as a faculty, always wants to find out the hows and whys of any phenomenon. Science can only prosper on developing hypotheses, theories, and experiments to unravel the mystery of any phenomenon and understand the working of the universe. And in the universe we have "life-forms," and it is prudent in trying to understand how it was formed.

This scientific effort should not be construed as an attempt by atheist scientists to uproot the time old belief, in a Creator, and His divine intervention.

On the contrary, let us look at what kinds of attributes, qualities, and capabilities God has conferred on human beings and what does God want us to do.

Genesis:

> 1:26, "Then God said, 'And now We will make human beings; they will be like Us and resemble Us, they will have power over the fish, the birds and all animals, domesticated and wild, large and small."

> 1:27: "So God created human beings, making them to be like Himself. He created them male and female."

This clearly tells us we, the human beings, are endowed with unimaginable capabilities next to God himself but not quite. But we know that our capabilities are not unlimited. It may be so, for now. History shows the unquestionable scientific advancement that human beings have achieved over the last several decades in chemistry, physics, biology, astronomy, and more importantly in genomic research. As God has said, human beings are created in His image, we are duty bound in the onward march in seeking the ultimate truth about the origin of the universe and of ourselves. Our generation may not be that fortunate people who will unravel all the unseen secrets of the universe. In about ten thousand years, we have come from the hunter-gatherer nomads to be the benefactors and the beneficiaries of the twenty-first century civilization. In the 3.5 billion history of our earth, ten thousand years is only a fleeting moment. If we could achieve those tremendous advancement in the past several decades, imagine what could happen in the next century.

It is just in our lifetime that we began the search outside of earth into the space and beyond. It was in our recent memory that human beings landed on the moon and said, "That's one small step for man and a giant leap for mankind" (8).

Referring to man, Qur'an says,

> 2:30 (9), "Behold thy Lord said to the angels, 'I will create a vicegerent on earth.'" The vicegerent is translated as a trustee on earth (or one who inherits the earth).

> 2:30 (10), "One who shall inherit the earth." In his commentary, he notes "establish on earth a successor. The term khalifa derived from the verb khalafa—means "he succeeded another."

The dictionary (Webster's) meaning of vicegerent is a "deputy" (11).

The above-referred passage in the Qur'an clearly implies that God has given the human creature capabilities next to God himself but not quite.

A deputy or vicegerent should have most, but not all the capabilities and knowledge of the one who deputes. Since we, the human beings, are the vicegerents (khalifa), we should have some of the qualities of God. Certainly it will not be our generation who will exhibit those godly qualities. We probably are not "human enough" to realize those capabilities and to claim to be the real vicegerents. It may be the next race (generation) as Qur'an has indicated (76:28) (12).

"It is We Who created them and made their joints strong. But when We will We can substitute like of them by a complete change."

Qur'an further directs human beings to explore and expand our knowledge.

29:20 (13), "Travel through the earth and see how Allah (God) did originate creations, so will Allah (God) produce a later creation, for Allah (God) has power over all things."

This is another call from the Almighty for mankind to explore the earth and possibly the universe to unravel the secrets of the creation of the universe and the gradual progression of life from inanimate materials to a proto cell and from that to the human being.

In this verse, the thrust is to explore the" earth" to understand the process of the origin and of the creation of life and that of man. This passage may be intended to indicate that life was created (evolved) on earth and not in an extraterrestrial location as some scientists believe. Scientists are not sure if life originated on earth or in an extraterrestrial location as discussed in the chapter "Origin of Life." God wants us to ravel and explore the earth. It is an implication that the evolution (creation) of life and its gradual progression through different life forms, till man appeared, is hidden in the earth for us to explore and learn. They are the markers of early life hidden in rocks and stromatolites, fossils of different species buried in different parts of the earth, which will help us understand the process of evolution. The statement to travel through the earth is very significant in that the fossils of different species are scattered in various regions of the earth, as each earlier species were confined to isolated small regions (niches) of the earth. The bacteria and cyano bacteria are all over the place, but most of the earlier species, were isolated to certain regions other than homo habilis that had presence in different parts of the world. There fore traveling through the earth is the only way to unearth those fossils of the different species that lived in different parts of the earth to understand the evolutionary process.

This further strengthens the theory of evolution as opposed to the creationist view of making man out of a clay effigy (the sculptured creation concept). If it were the sculptured creation concept there is no need to travel through the earth to learn how man was created, as clay is present in every part of the earth.

One such traveler and explorer was Charles Darwin, who undertook the voyage to the Island of Galapagos and observed the finches there and formulated the theory of evolution

For a nonscientific mind, it is apparent that there is life in both the land and water, and some are movable and some are not. All forms of life require food and water to survive. They all have a process of eliminating their waste products. If an average explorer happens to dissect the body of an animal small or large, he or she will be amazed to see how similar their internal organs are. Though of different sizes, yet very similar to that of human beings.

Some of our ancestors were interested in fossils (14, 15), and in their journey in search of fossils they came across some thought-provoking phenomena when they examined strata after strata. The deeper or older the strata, they could not find any fossilized life-forms. This suggested that early in earth's history (3.5 billion years ago), there were no life-forms that could leave fossils. This does not mean there was no life on earth at that time, but the life-forms that existed were very primitive ones without a shell or bone to leave fossils. They were soft-bodied ones.

But in the strata laid later in the upper layer, they began to see shells or skeletons of very small creatures. And in the newer strata, they could see more complex fossils of larger creatures. In the topmost strata, they could see fossils of more advanced species including that of humanoids. They took particular note that none of the fossils they found in the newer strata (top-most) were never found in the older strata. This suggested to them that gradual evolution (transformation) of simpler organisms to larger and complex forms have occurred over billions of years.

Chemists and biochemists realized that the building blocks of life, the amino acids, are the same in all living organisms, whether a bacteria or human being, suggesting that all life-forms must have had a common ancestor. Through exploration and experimentation by molecular biologists and geneticists, it was discovered that the basic code of life, the DNA, is identical in a bacterium or a mammal or man.

Science has given us the knowledge about the basic ingredients necessary for the origin and evolution of life and life-forms. This is a result of the accumulated scientific knowledge over the years or the evolution of science itself.

Scientists have already begun the retrieval and study of the DNA from Neanderthals and the Cro-Magnons. It is believed that the Neanderthals have not contributed any genetic materials to the modern man, and the DNA of the Cro-Magnons is identical to us. One day, they might be able to study the left over DNA of the extinct species that might be lurking around somewhere, either on earth or elsewhere, and when that happens, we will have a better understanding of the evolutionary process.

In order to study the evolutionary process, if at all, it is essential, to create life in the lab, and scientists are working on it. It will be pertinent to point out that the Genesis and Qur'an in particular, repeatedly refers to clay/mud as the origin of all life-forms, and hopefully the life scientists will take a serious look at clay for the creation of life in the lab.

Qur'an refers to a later creation in 29:20. Some authorities believe it refers to resurrection after death. Could this also be reference to a second creation like the one that led to the present-day humans? A re-doing of the entire process of creation (evolution) of the universe and man. If it is a re-doing, the life again has to go through a similar low beginning and by evolutionary process, attain human status. Starting with the bacteria, fungi, fish, rodents, and other animal forms before becoming a human being. This scenario is reminiscent of the Hindu philosophy of reincarnation (as opposed to resurrection) In reincarnation, the life of the wicked and non-God-fearing people will go through cycles of reincarnation through various low life-forms until the soul (life) get emancipated after entering in the human being again, and having that person living a righteous life.

If it were a re-doing, it will take billions of years for human beings to appear again unless a shorter course of evolution will be decided by the Almighty (nature).

The only remnants of the flora and fauna that had participated in the biological evolution that are visible to us are the fossils left behind, and God wants us to travel and see how He created the living creatures.

As mentioned in verse 29:20, "Travel through the earth and see how Allah did originate creation." Human beings need not be afraid of to investigate how life was created. Whether we, the present generation, will achieve the goal of creating life is unknown. If not by our generation, may be the next generation or race will be able to accomplish it. In 76:28 (12) it says, "We can replace them entirely with others of their kind."

In this regard, let us read what the early Muslim scientists (evolutionists) wrote in the thirteenth century.

Nasir al-Din al-Tusi (16), a thirteenth century Muslim evolutionist, wrote, "Such humans (probably anthropoid apes) live in the Western Sudan and other distant corners of the world. They are close to animals by their habits, deeds, and behavior. The human has features that distinguish him from other creatures, but he has other features that unite him with the animal world, vegetable kingdom, or even with the inanimate bodies. Before the creation of humans, all differences between organisms were of the natural origin. The next step will be associated with spiritual perfection, will, observation, and knowledge. All these facts prove that the human being is placed on the middle step of the evolutionary stairway. According to his inherent nature, the human is related to the lower beings and only with the help of his will can he reach the higher development level."

As Tusi remarked we, the present generation, may be in the lower level in the ladder of evolution and as we reach the upper level (by evolution), we may indeed be the real vicegerent as God has envisaged. At that time period, we will be able to understand the process of creation and will be able to do some creating of our own.

Ibn Miskawayh (17) in the tenth century in his book, Al-Fawz al Asghar wrote, "That God first created matter and invested it with energy for development. Matter, therefore, adopted the form of vapor which assumed the shape of water in due time. The next stage of development was mineral life. Different kinds of stones developed in course of time. Their highest form being mirjan (coral). It is a stone which has its branches like those of a tree. After mineral life evolves vegetation. The evolution of vegetation culminates with a tree, which bears the qualities of animal. This is the date palm, it has male and female genders. It does not wither if all its branches are chopped, but it dies when the head is cut off. The date palm is therefore considered the highest among trees and resembles the lowest among animals. Then is born the lowest of animals. It evolves into an ape." This is not the statement of Darwin. This is Ibn Miskawayh's statement and this is precisely what is written in the Epistles of Ikhwan al Safa. The Muslim thinker states "that ape then evolved in to a lower kind of a barbarian man. He then became a superior human being. Man becomes a saint, a prophet. He evolves in to a higher stage and becomes an angel. The one higher to angel is indeed none but God. Everything begins from Him and everything returns to Him."

This may be the advancement of human being in a spiritual sense. But the potential that human being can evolve into a higher species, spiritually, mentally, and every other which way is alluded to here. And at that higher stage of development or evolution, human being can enter into a state of perfect knowledge that at present only God possesses.

In this vast universe, human being is no more than a tiny creature among the other billions and billions of living organisms on earth. The vast majority of them are beyond our eyes' perception. Yet this speck (human being) in this vast universe is phenomenal in having the ability to control everything on earth to a large extent. Human beings always wonder where did we come from and where are we going from here. What is our purpose, or do we have one? Are we here as an accidental by-product of evolution as are many other life-forms whose purpose is not at all clear? Similarly, many millions of species went extinct. Why did they come into being and roam around and disappear? Apart from the earliest hominids, did they contribute anything for our emergence as human beings?

The extinct species must have been a temporary receptacle or vehicle for "life" in its journey from the primordial cell to the present day human being. This may be indicated in our genome by having the genetic blueprints of earlier species. (pseudo genes)

The world is always in a state of flux and change. The earth is constantly moving under our feet ever infinitesimally slow. Over millions of years, the continents have broken and regrouped, oceans separated, mountains formed and worn away. Biological species also change. These small changes are not discernible over the lifetime of a generation. For biological evolution, it is necessary that new species appear and old ones disappear. Species extinction is a natural phenomenon.

There had been at least five mass extinctions in the history of life and four of them in the last 450 million years. Many species disappeared in a short period of geological time. The most recent event took place sixty-five million years ago, at the end of Cretaceous period, and wiped out all the non avian dinosaurs among others.

Causes of Extinction

Many causes can contribute to extinction of species. Any species that is unable to survive or reproduce in its environment and unable to move to a new environment where it can do so dies out. A typical species become extinct within ten million years of its existence (18). But some species called the living fossils survive, unchanged for hundreds of millions of years (bacteria). Only one in a thousand species that existed remain today (19).

The question whether the extinctions seen in the fossil record were caused by evolution or natural catastrophe is a subject of discussion. When concerns about human extinction have been raised, Sir Martin Rees (20) states, "Those concerns lie with the effects of climatic change or technological disaster."

Will there be a credible explanation as to why so many species went extinct and what role the extinct species had in the process of evolution? Especially those who did not directly contribute genetically in the propagation and evolution of one species to the next and eventually to human evolution. Or their disappearance could have given the new and existing species a survival advantage as the available resources did not have to be shared with them. Certainly if every species that ever appeared on earth survived, then there will be extreme scarcity of resources, and all would perish unless species like the humans arrive and control the environment and the resources wisely. But the events did not progress in such a way of chaos. Species after species died out long before human beings appeared as if all these extinctions were necessitated by the rules of a guided evolution. It is believed that after the dinosaurs disappeared, there was a sudden spurt in the multiplication of mammals, and there is speculation that if the dinosaurs did not disappear, the evolution of mammals into higher species will be in doubt. These borders on the speculation that human beings are a result of an accident (the catastrophe that wiped out the dinosaurs 65 million years ago that caused mammalian evolution—and the Toba volcano, 75000 years ago that created a bottle neck, spurting evolution) rather than predestined.

There is a valid question that if the dinosaurs were not extinct, then the mammals would not have the opportunity to flourish in a favorable niche and evolve in to higher species including man. Does this point to the notion that the appearance of human beings was a chance occurrence, or was the disappearance of the dinosaurs a phenomenon of guided evolution? (directed and guided by God) It is also possible that the scenario of mammalian evolution may have a different explanation. I believe in the process of a guided evolution.

References for Spiritual Implications:

1. Genesis 1:11, 20, 24, 26, and 27.
2. Ibid., 2:7.
3. Qur'an 21:30, 24:45, 25:54.Yusuf Ali.
4. Ibid., 20:55.Yusuf Ali.
5. Ibid., 18:37; 30:20; 35:11; 40:67.Yusuf Ali.
6. Ibid; 6:2; 23:12; 32:7; 37:11; 38:71; 55:14-15; Yusuf Ali. 15:26, Muhammad Asad
7. Genesis 1:26.
8. Neil Alden Armstrong. NASA. Apollo 11. July 20, 1969.
9. Qur'an 2:30.
10. Ibid., Muhammad Asad. The Message of Qur'an.
11. Webster's Ninth New Collegiate Dictionary.
12. Qur'an 76:28.
13. Ibid., 29:20.
14. George Cuvier (1769-1832), geologist.
15. Charles Lyell (1797-1875), geologist.
16. Nasir al-Din Tusi. "Thirteenth Century Darwin: Tusis's view on evolution." Farid Alakbarov. Summer 2001. Azerbaijan International 9.
17. Ibn Miskawayh. In his book, Al-Fawz al-Asghar.
18. Newman Mark. A Mathematical Model for Mass Extinction. Cornell University, May 20, 1994.
19. Raup, David M. Extinction: Bad Genes or Bad Luck? W. W. Norton and Company: New York, 1991. p. 3-6.
20. Sir Martin Rees. Our Final Hour. 2003.

CHAPTER 24
What Is Life?

Life as we know it, defies a simple one-sentence definition. Scientists so far have been avoiding a definition and instead are content with describing a set of properties or behaviors that the living organism exhibits to call such an entity "living."

One can recognize life without defining it. Looking at a tree, a bird, a cow, a man, and a rock, one can say which one is alive and which one is not. Why are the life forms (living creatures) on earth appear in different shapes and forms is due to the fact that each living organisms have different and complex body structures and "life" make them function differently and the nonliving of course does not have life as we know, in it.

Scientists believe that life originated on earth 3.5 billion years ago and still goes on defying a credible and simple definition. The Penguin Dictionary of Biology, "Life," defines life as "complex physico-chemical systems whose two main peculiarities are (1) storage and replication of molecular information in the form of nucleic acid, and (2) the presence of enzyme catalysis (except in viruses)."

The properties-oriented definition of life maintains that an entity that shows these properties can be called living. They are (1) structural and behavioral complexity, (2) reproduction, the ability to replicate, (3) growth and development. A biological instruction manual to make the organism grow and exhibit the characteristics of the parent species, (4) creation and utilization of energy from sources outside, (5) responsiveness to external stimuli, (6) homeostasis, the ability to maintain a stable internal environment even when the external environment fluctuates, and (7) adaptation. Adaptation to the environment and modification leading to evolution.

This is only a descriptive term, as scientists before Lavoisier described water as a liquid, transparent, thirst-quenching, and a good solvent. The scientists, at that time, did not know that water was made of oxygen and hydrogen. The alchemists took the solvent characteristic as the major property and considered nitric acid as aqua fortis and hydrochloric acid as aqua Regis (1).

This definition makes the status of a virus in doubt as it cannot replicate without the help of the host cell. It also defies the living status of a eunuch or a castrated person as they cannot reproduce but are alive.

This definition is a functional and structural description of a living thing as we know it, and there could be other kinds of life whose structure or function is unknown to us. In the Bible and Qur'an, there are references to angels and Satan (jinn). In Qur'an, it is mentioned that the jinns are created out of fire, and the Hadith says that the angels are made out of light. Understandably, it is difficult to define life.

The life that we are familiar with is based on carbon and water.

And as such, searching for life as we don't know it will be difficult as well.

The earth was formed a little over four billion years ago, and initially it was inhospitable for any life-forms as we know it. After the appearance of this wonderful and complex phenomenon called "life" about 3.5 billion years ago, it changed the phase of earth from a barren place to this panoramic landscape consisting of myriads of life-forms.

The basic ingredient of life is the DNA. Its composition and function are the same in both the animal and plant life. It has remained unchanged since its appearance 3.5 billion years ago.

It is fascinating to see the fact the fundamental blueprint for life is the same, the DNA that we see in millions and millions of different life-forms in both the animal and plant life. The diversity that we see is due to natural selection and descent with modification preceded by mutations in the DNA.

Even though the organisms are vastly different, the basic blueprint for the DNA is the same.

The phenomenon we call life is the same whether it is in a mouse, man, or monkey or whether it is in a rose or an oak tree.

We call our (the human being's) life as superior to the other life-forms, ignoring the fact that the life is the same whether it is in a worm, a palm tree, mouse, man or monkey, but it is the physical structure of the organisms that differ.

It can be compared to the energy given by electricity. If electricity is applied to a fan it turns and gives us air. If it is applied to a refrigerator it gives us cold temperature, and if it is applied to a TV set, it gives us pictures and sounds. If electricity is applied to a microwave, it gives us heat.

These different life-forms appear different due to the difference in their structure and form, but the basics of "life", the DNA in these different life forms (species) is the same

Similarly, the life of a yet to be born child is already existing now in his or her parents (in the ova and sperm) or has traveled through his or her great-grandparents. The life we carry today was born 3.5 billion years ago and has traveled through millions of species extinct and extant and will continue to travel incessantly.

Scientists are attempting to create artificial life. They have created all the elements that one sees in a living cell including the cell wall, DNA and, RNA. But life, as we know it has not been created in the lab yet. A recent report indicates that self replicating RNA has been created in The Scripps Research Institute in California which could be the beginning of the creation of artificial life.

The medical profession and the health industry in general are hard at work in the preservation and prolongation of life. From time immemorial people have been doing this practice, yet we or the scientists cannot say exactly what "life" is. The physicians are engaged in this on a daily basis. But what are the physicians preserving? We know that "life" is in our body but where, and what it is, is imperfectly understood. The obvious question then will be that if one does not know what exactly he or she is preserving (life) how can it be effectively preserved?.

Billions of dollars are spent in the business of preservation and prolongation of "life" and very little is done to find out what exactly life is.

It is interesting to note that the Hindu philosophy talks about the recycling of the human soul through different lower animal species till such time when the soul redeems itself from the punishment from God and eventually obtains salvation by appearing in a perfect human being. And the recycling comes to an end. This could be an implication of life's journey through lower and primitive species through evolution until it got inside the human body, since its first appearance on earth 3.5 billion years ago. The Hindu philosophy indirectly supports the theory of evolution. Whether being a human creature, itself attests to the emancipation of the soul (life) is unclear. But in human beings, with the advanced human body and brain, life finds vast avenues of expression of thought and retrospection, which we, the human beings, assume to be nonexistent in lower animal species.

Reference for what is life.

1. Carol Cleland. Philosopher, University of Colorado, Astrobiology Science Conference. March 2006.

CHAPTER 25
The Origin of Life

The human being, the most advanced life-form on earth, has always been curious to find answers to the mystery of his origin, and the reality he lives in. One of the profound and enthralling arenas is the search for answers to how he (she) came into being, how the universe originated, and how and when human beings and all the living creatures emerged from the original matter after the big bang.

"Life" is the most elemental to all living things. Even though we claim that one can distinguish a living and a nonliving thing "life" defies a precise definition.

It is believed that life originated on earth sometime between 4.4 years ago when water vapor on earth's surface liquefied and 3.5 billion years ago (1, 2). By 2.4 billion years, molecular biomarkers indicate photosynthesis (3). Also possible is extra planetary or extraterrestrial origin of life thought to have occurred some time over the last 13.7 billion years, in the evolution of the universe since the big bang (4).

When earth formed 4.6 billion years ago, it was lifeless. One billion years later, the earth was teeming with early life-forms, the green algae (5). In the seventeenth century, people believed that the higher animals including man was created by God and lesser creatures like the worms, flies, and frogs were originated from waste and rubbish and other decaying materials.

In 1859, a French scientist Louis Pasteur (1822-1895) (6) disproved the belief of spontaneous generation of life by an experiment sponsored by the French Academy of Sciences in 1859. Pasteur filled a long narrow flask with meat broth. Then he heated the neck of the flask and bent into an S shape. The airborne organisms were trapped in the neck of the flask. Pasteur then boiled the broth. After a while, examination of the broth revealed that there were no organisms growing in the broth. Later the flask was tipped so that the broth reached the bent neck where the trapped germs came in contact with the broth. Then the broth quickly became cloudy due to growth of the microorganisms. This disproved the notion of spontaneous generation. It is to be remembered that the primordial life did come into being from inanimate materials through chemical and organic evolution spontaneously according to scientists. But the creationists believe otherwise. The scientists are wondering and experimenting to find out how life began on earth. The creationists' view was and still is that life was created by God.

Since the events led to the origin of the big bang is not explained by the scientists ,the creationist view that life was "created by God is very valid, as the ingredients needed for the origin of life was put in place by the Creator at the time of the big bang .The evolutionists only deals with what happened to life forms once it appeared on earth.

Charles Darwin (7) before writing the Origin of Species was a theological student at Christ College in Cambridge, England. In later editions of the Origin of Species, Darwin wrote that the "creator originally breathed life into a few forms or into one." Then by evolutionary process endless forms of life appeared. But later he suggested that life might have originated from certain chemicals available in the pre biotic earth in some "warm little pond with all forms of phosphoric salts, heat, light, etc., all present."

With this thought in mind, scientists are investigating the possibility of life emerging from organic compounds.

There are several theories for the origin of life:

Few notable theories are mentioned here.

Charles Darwin in 1871 wrote to his friend Joseph Dalton Hooker (8) that the original spark of life may have been originated in "a warm little pond with all sorts of ammonia, phosphoric salt, light, heat, electricity, etc., present so that a protein compound was chemically formed, ready to undergo still more complex changes." He added that "at the present day such matter would be instantly devoured or absorbed, which could not have been the case before living creatures were formed." The presence of life itself on earth, makes the search for life to be conducted only in sterile lab. The atmosphere 3.5 billion years ago was a reducing one and the organic molecules from which, scientists believe that life originated, could only happen in a reducing atmosphere, and such organic compounds could not form again as they will be instantly destroyed by the oxidizing atmosphere that is present now.

Till 1924 not much was heard until Alexander I. Oparin experimentally showed that atmospheric oxygen prevents synthesis of organic molecules necessary for life (9). He argued that the primordial soup of organic molecules could be created in an oxygen-free atmosphere through action of sunlight. These would combine in more complex fashion until dissolved into a coacervate droplet. These droplets will grow by fusion with other droplets and reproduce through fission into daughter droplets and some have a primitive metabolism, in which those factors which promote "cell" integrity survive, and others become extinct.

At the same time, J. B. S. Haldane (10) proposed that the pre biotic ocean, very different from now could have formed a "dilute soup" in which organic compounds, the building blocks of life, may have formed. This is called bio poesis (life from nonliving).

There is not one model, but many theories about how the building blocks of life might have emerged, and many scientists have created in the lab, amino acids that constitute proteins, primitive cell membranes, and even artificial DNA. But still we do not have a living cell manufactured in the lab. In other words, we have not found "life" yet.

Theories of formation of the basic organic compounds needed for the origin of life.

Planet earth is approximately 4 billion years old. Immediately after the formation of earth, there was continuous bombardment of earth by meteorites and asteroids for about seven million years. Due to the extreme energy and heat released by these impacts, it was sufficient to evaporate any oceans and destroy any life-forms that could exist on earth's surface at that time. These impacts eventually stopped and the evidence for life appeared in the fossil record about 3.5 billion years ago (11).

It was through a complex chain of evolutionary process that life was believed to have emerged on earth. The pre biotic earth had a reducing environment without oxygen. The presence of oxygen would have prevented the biological molecules from making any chemical bonds and also would have oxidized the primitive organic compounds.

The reducing atmosphere was conducive to the formation of complex polymers from existing organic monomers. These monomers were either formed on earth as discussed below or acquired from outer space through meteorites' impact (12, 13).

Scientists believe that the origin of life required a combination of elements, compounds, and environmental-chemical conditions that allowed cells to assemble in less than a billion years (14).

Over time, simple molecules became more complex ones and eventually led to the development of early cells.

Further evolution and modification led some cells to develop the process of photosynthesis. This event changed the atmosphere completely in an irreversible fashion in that the accumulation of oxygen caused the atmosphere to become an oxidizing one from a reducing atmosphere. And except anaerobes, all living creatures need oxygen for metabolism. This alteration from a reducing atmosphere into an oxygen-rich atmosphere by the process of photosynthesis used by earliest bacteria-the cyan bacteria - caused two major effects. One is the proliferation of present-day living organisms, and the other is the total elimination of the pre biotic organic molecules from which scientists believe the life originated and the earlier life-forms came to being.

Because of the elimination of those pre-biotic molecules and the impossibility of these organic molecules to form again in an oxidizing atmosphere, we are shut out from any chance of seeing any new life-forms originating, as our ancestral life-forms originated from the organic molecules that existed on the pre biotic earth. Had it not been for the elimination of those organic molecules and the little warm ponds as Darwin perceived, could there have been one or more different forms of life? Originating from the same source of organic molecules as we did?

Was this a chance occurrence that only one lineage of life-form emerged from that organic pool and evolved into the present biosphere? Or was this due to a Divine Designer that caused the selection of one and only one, the present-day biosphere (only one lineage-carbon based), which through a process of evolution culminated in the appearance of the creature we call human?

The Ozone Layer:

This transformation (the change from a reducing atmosphere into an oxidizing one) had a great impact on the present-day life-forms, in that the ozone layer protected the life-forms on earth from ultraviolet injury from the sun. This oxidizing atmosphere also completely destroyed the prebiotic molecules (not the life-forms) from which we are believed to have evolved. As a criminal trying to wipe out all incriminating evidence from the crime scene, the oxygen destroyed the organic molecules of the pre-biotic world, from which scientists believe that life was formed. Therefore, we cannot see any trace of the substances from which the early life-forms originated about 3.5 billion years ago, and eventually, by evolutionary process transformed into present-day biota including us.

Therefore, scientists have to speculate, experiment, and synthesize a scenario under which the origin of life was possible and to create life anew in the laboratory.

Even if the presumed pre biotic molecules appear anywhere on earth, it will be wiped out by oxygen and/or eaten up by the present, existing life-forms on earth.

We all wonder why there is no new life being formed, as our ancestral life-forms once did, from organic molecules? The abovementioned reasons will explain why. We are left with the fact that any new life-forms that may appear in the future have to come only by mutation and evolution from the existing biosphere.

Scientists believe that for life to start, three essential ingredients were needed in the pre biotic earth:

Water
A source of energy
A source of organic compounds

Water:

All live forms need water for survival. Sixty percent of our body and cells are made of water. It is highly improbable to have life as we know it, to exist without water.

How did water appear on earth? It is believed that after the hot and molten earth cooled, the water vapor cooled and precipitated from the atmosphere. It is also claimed that water came from space when meteorites carrying ice from the solar debris impacted the earth (1).

It is believed that the first fossilized microbes were estimated to have lived 3.5 billion years ago, and water had to be present before that (15, 16).

Energy:

In order for evolution of life to proceed, first the small molecules have to become more complex molecules by a process called polymerization. This requires energy. This energy was provided by sunlight, lightning, volcanoes, and the very intense UV radiation that penetrated the atmosphere due to lack of protection from ozone, which came much later.

Scientists have been experimenting with chemicals believed to have been present in the pre biotic earth, in order to produce simple organic molecules, which forms the basic ingredients for life and to see if life can be created (originated) in the lab.

Organic Compounds:

The Miller-Urey experiment:

By the 1950s, scientists were in the pursuit of the origin of life. In 1953, a graduate student at the University of Chicago (Miller) and his professor Harold C. Urey (17) conducted an experiment in their lab using molecules believed to have been present on earth's atmosphere in the pre biotic era. These were methane (CH_4), ammonia (NH_3), hydrogen (H_2), and water (H_2O). These were put in a closed system, and electricity was passed continuously for a week. Electricity was used to simulate energy from lightning that might have bombarded the primitive earth. Later the sediment was examined by chromatography and found that 10 to 15 percent of the carbon was in the form of organic compounds and 2 percent in the form of amino acids including thirteen of the twenty-two amino acids that are used to make proteins present in the present-day organisms. Glycine was the most abundant. Additionally sugars and some of the building blocks for nucleotides were also formed.

In 1961, scientists (18) produced amino acids from hydrogen cyanide (HCN) and ammonia in aqueous solution. He also could generate the nucleotide Adenine as it is one of the four bases in RNA and DNA. It is also present in ATP, which is important in cellular energy production. Others also have generated RNA and DNA bases in a reducing atmosphere.

Recently studies have been done on Old areas in old genes (defined—as that is found to be common to organisms from several widely separated species, assumed to share the last universal ancestor [LUA] of all extant species). These studies found, products of these areas are enriched in those amino acids that were also most readily produced by Miller-Urey experiment. This suggests that the original genetic code was based on a smaller number of amino acids—only those available in pre biotic nature—than current one (19).

Cell Membrane:

1. Phospholipids can spontaneously form lipid layers, a basic component of cell membrane.
2. Polymerization of nucleotide into random RNA molecules might have resulted in self replicatory ribosome (RNA world hypothesis).
3. Selective pressure for catalytic efficiency and diversity results in ribosome, which catalyze peptidyl transfer (forming small proteins since oligopeptides complex with RNA to form better catalysts). Thus the first ribosome is born.
4. Proteins out compete ribosomes in catalytic ability and therefore become the dominant biopolymer.

The basic chemicals from which life is believed to have originated are

Methane (CH_4),
Ammonia (NH_3),
Water (H_2O),
Hydrogen sulfide (H_2S),
CO_2 or CO (carbon dioxide or carbon monoxide), and
Phosphate (PO4).

It is believed that molecular oxygen or ozone was absent, because these gases are oxidizing and the organic molecules will be destroyed by these. As of today, no one has synthesized a proto cell, which is the basic unit for life, with "life" in it. Some are working on it (20) called the bottom up theory. Others are working on a "top down" approach (21). Scientists at the Genomic Research and others are doing engineering with existing prokaryotic cells with progressively lower genes, attempting to learn at which point the minimal requirement for life were reached.

Biologist John Bernal coined the term biopoesis (22) and suggested several stages in the origin of life.

Stage 1: Origin of bio molecules.
Stage 2: Biological polymers.
Stage 3: Evolution to cell.

But how did these simple organic molecules—the building blocks—polymerize and form complex structures leading to a proto cell? In aqueous environment, hydrolysis will prevent formation of complex molecules.

In 1950s and 1960s, scientists showed that amino acids could spontaneously form peptides (23). These amino acids and peptides could be encouraged to form closed spherical membranes called micro spheres. They called them proto cells that could grow and reproduce.

Wachtershauser's hypothesis (24):

In Miller-Urey experiments, they had to rely on an external source of energy for the synthesis, like electricity. But Wachtershauser showed that sulfides of iron and other minerals can release energy from red ox reactions and that can be utilized to synthesize organic molecules and also can help formation of oligomeres and polymers. These could evolve into autocatalytic sets of self-replicating metabolically active entities that would predate the life-forms.

But they noted that these dipeptides hydrolyzed rapidly under these conditions.

A modified version of the iron-sulfide theory was proposed by others (25). They proposed that the first cellular life-forms may have evolved in the so-called black smokers in the seafloor spreading zones in the deep sea. These are micro scale caverns that are coated by thin layer of membranous metal sulfide walls. This could solve the problem with Wachtershauser's formulations.

1. Micro caverns can concentrate newly formed molecules that increases chance to form oligomeres.

2. The steep temperature gradients inside a black smoker allows for establishing optimum zones of partial reactions in different regions of the black smoker (monomer formation in hotter zones and oligomerization in colder zones).

3. The flow of hydrothermal water through this structure provides a constant source of building blocks and energy (freshly precipitated metal sulfides).

4. This model allows for different stages of cellular evolution, (pre-biotic chemistry, monomer formation, oligomere synthesis, peptide and protein synthesis, and locates the LUCA inside a black smoker rather than assuming a free living form of LUCA. [last universal common ancestor]). The last evolutionary step would be synthesis of a lipid membrane that finally allows the organism to leave the micro cave system of black smokers and start independent life. This is a postulated synthesis of RNA world and DNA world in a single structure. This model, late acquisition of the lipid wall, is consistent with presence of completely different types of membrane lipids in archaic bacteria and eubacteria, with highly similar cellular physiology of all life-forms, in most other respects (26).

From Organic Molecules to Proto cells

It is a still unanswered question, how did the simple organic molecules manage to create a proto cell? There are some theories:

The Gene First Model:

"RNA world" hypothesis:

Short RNA molecules could have spontaneously formed that were capable of catalyzing their own replication. Early cell membrane could have formed spontaneously from proteinoids (protein like molecules) that are produced when amino acids solutions are heated—when present at correct concentrations in aqueous solutions. This will form micro spheres, which are observed to behave like membrane-enclosed compartments.

Other possibility is a chemical reaction with clay substrate or pyrite rocks.

Short RNA molecules, which can duplicate others have been artificially produced in the lab (27).

Metabolism First Model:

Some reject the idea of "self-replication" of "naked gene" and postulate the emergence of a primitive metabolism which could help in the replication of RNA. This was first proposed by A. I. Oparin in 1924 (8). Recent variations are proposed by investigators (25) such as the iron-sulfide world theory, in which they propose that evolution of biochemical pathways as fundamentals for evolution. Scientists propose that early chemistry of life occurred not in bulk solutions in the ocean, but on mineral surfaces near deep hydrothermal vents, in an anaerobic, high temperature, high-pressure atmosphere. Similar models were introduced by others, based on chemistry of thio esters (28).

The Bubble Theory (29)

Waves breaking on the ocean shores create a delicate foam composed of bubbles. By this way, organic molecules could be concentrated on shore lines. Phospholipids were believed to have been prevalent in the pre biotic sea. These can form lipid membranes. When the bubble bursts, its contents are released and these molecules can form prokaryotes, eukaryotes, etc. Recently scientists suggested that the enclosure of an autocatalytic non enzymatic metabolism within a proto cell may have been one way of avoiding the side reaction problem that is found in the metabolism first model (30).

Other Models:

Auto catalysts (31):

Scientists also believe that auto catalysts as a potential explanation for the origin of life as indicated in the book, The Ancestor's Tale. Auto catalysts catalyze the production of themselves and act as simple molecular replicators. This has been experimentally done by investigators (32).

Clay: As Origin of Life

In 1985, a University of Glasgow chemist proposed clay as the basis of the origin of life (33). This theory was supported by others as well (34) in the book The Selfish Gene pages 21-23. This postulates that complex organic molecules arose gradually on a pre-existing non organic platform-silicate crystal in solution. Complexity in companion molecules developed as a function of selection pressure on types of clay crystals and is then led to serve the replication of organic molecules independently of their silicate launch stage.

Deep Hot Biospheres:

Nanobes (filamentous structures smaller than bacteria) may contain DNA and was discovered in deep rocks. Scientists believe that life developed not on surface of the earth but several kilometers below the surface (35). It is now known that microbial life is plentiful up to 5 km below earth's surface in the form of archae.

Other Places Where Life Might Have Originated:

Organic compounds are common in space. Comets are encrusted by a tar like material composed of complex organic material formed by irradiation by ultraviolet light and this could have been transported to earth by these comets (36, 37) and became the ingredients for origin of life.

The Lipid World:

Proponents of this theory believes that the first replicating object to be lipid like (38). Phospholipids spontaneously form bi layers in water the same structures as in cell membranes. These layers may expand by acquiring additional lipids and under stress may split and become two progeners. The molecular composition of the lipid bodies is the preliminary way for information storage, and evolution led to the appearance of polymer entities such as RNA or DNA that may store information favorably.

It has been suggested that lipid molecules have hereditary potential, like proteins and RNA for catalytic capabilities (30). Based on this, it is postulated that lipids and amphiphilic molecules constituted the first systems capable of information storage, inheritance, and selection (41).

Scientists have demonstrated (41) that extract from the Murchison meteorite contained amphiphilic molecules, which are capable of spontaneously forming stable membrane vesicles with defined composition and organization, capable of selective permeability.

Cell Membrane (42)

The earliest forms of life needed a cell membrane to keep its contents in and to protect from outer harmful agents. The modern cell membranes are made of phospholipids, but it is unlikely to have such complex structures in the early cells. It is postulated that simpler membrogenic amphiphilic molecules served as a precursor and gradually evolved into the complex structure seen in the present-day cells. Amphiphilic molecules have the property in that one end favorably interacts with water (hydrophilic), and the other end that does not (hydrophobic). This allows them according to scientists, to self-assemble into vesicles and bi-layers. It is speculated that these amphiphilic molecules were abundant in pre biotic environment. Like other primordial organic molecules, these compounds have an earthly source or an exogenous source. These are capable of spontaneously forming stable membrane vesicles with defined composition and organization.

Early Membrane Characteristics:

When amphiphilic molecules self assembled into membranes, this creates a barrier between the interior and the aqueous environment outside (43).

The selective entry of the early membranes that formed the boundary of primitive cells permitted the entry of essential nutrients. They could have been impermeable to larger polymeric molecules such as the precursors of nucleic acids and protein polymers. In order to encapsulate the larger molecules, the membrane gets disrupted, allowing their entry and then resealed to trap the molecules.

Laboratory simulations of hydration dehydration cycles in inter tidal zones or of an evaporating lagoon on early earth have verified the ability of early membranous boundaries to encapsulate functional macromolecules. This property of the early membranes was the only way to entrap bio molecules in the cell. As evolution advanced a population of these bio molecules advanced in metabolic complexity. This was followed by controlled cell growth and ultimately, to the cell growth as we see it today.

There is evidence that membrane vesicles are the intermediate between pre biotic cells and the first cells capable of growth and division (44).

From the dilute organic compound in the water, the inherent self aggregation of amphiphilic molecules would have contributed to local high concentrations. Once formed, the cell membranes have the capacity to maintain a concentration gradient providing a source of free energy that can drive transport processes across the membrane boundary.

The origin of life required a combination of elements, compounds, and environmental, physical-chemical conditions. The ability to form membranous microenvironments underlies some of the significant events in the origin of life. A number of questions remain unanswered as to the fundamental chemical and physical environments that were necessary for the origin of life.

References for Origin of Life:

1. Wilde, S. A. et al. Nature 409, and No. 6817 (January 2000): 175-178.
2. Schopf, J. W., et al. Nature 416, no. 6876 (March 2002): 73-76.
3. How and when did microbes change the world. Phil. Trans. R. Soc. B. 361. (1470) 845-850.
4. The Big Bang.
5. Mckinney, et al. Current perspective in Geology. 2000. p. 22.
6. Louis Pasteur (1822-1895). Spontaneous Generation of Life Forms.
7. Charles Darwin (1809-1882). Origin of Species (1859).
8. Sir Joseph Dalton Hooker (1817-1911), botanist-biographer-traveler.
9. A. I. Oparin. The Origin of Life, Moscow, Worker. 1924.
10. J. B. S. Haldane (1892-1964). Origin of Life. New Biology. (16) 1954.
11. Campbell, N. Biology. Benjamin/Cummings Publishing Company, Inc., 1996.
12. Franchi, M. and E. Gallori. "Origin, persistence and biological activity of genetic material in pre biotic habitats." Origin Life Evol. Biosph. 34, no. 133 (2004).
13. Pzzareloo, S. "Chemical Evolution and Meteorites: An Update." Origin Life Evol. Biosph 34, no. 25.
14. Trevors, J. T. "Early Assembly of Cellular Life." Prig. Biophysics mol Biol. 81, no. 201 (2003).
15. Pizzareloo. Ibid.
16. Miller, S. L. "A Production of Amino Acids under Possible Primitive Earth Conditions." 193. Science 117:528.
17. Miller, S. A. Ibid.
18. Juan Oro (1961).Evolving code net. Origin of life scientist.
19. Brooks, D. F., Fesco, J. R., Lesk, A. N., Singh, M. Evolution of amino acid frequencies in protein over deep time. Inferred order of introduction of amino acids in to genetic code. Molecular Biology and Evolution⊗19)1645-55.
20. Steen Rasmussen, Los Alamos Lab, and Jack Szostak of Harvard University.
21. Craig Venter. Genomic Research Center. TIGR. Rockville, Maryland.

22. John Desmond Bernal: Biologist. Wikipedia: http://en.wikipedia.org/wiki/Origin-of-life;Origin of life.1969.Winefield and Nicholson.

23. Sidney W. Fox. In the Origin of Pre biological Systems and Their Molecular Matrices. New York Academy Press. 1965.

24. Gunter Wachtershauser. Science 289 (2000): 107-1308.

25. William Martin and Michael Russell. "On the Origin of Cell." Philosophical Transcriptions of the Royal Society of Biol. Science 358 (2002): 59-85.

26. Wikipedia.http://en.wikipedia.org/wiki/Iron-sulfur-world-Theory. retrieved—3-20-2009

27. W. K. Johnson; P. J. Unaru; K. S. Lawrence; M. E. Glasner and D. P. Bartel. "RNA catalyzed RNA polymerization. Accurate and General Templated Primer Extension." Science 292:1319-2001.

28. Gunter Wachtershauser. Ibid.

29. Christian De Duve, American scientist. Sep./Oct.

30. Louis Lerman, D. Stanford University, Hertz Foundation Scholar.

31. Fernando and Rowe. www.cugs.susx.ac.uk/users/ctf20/dphil.2005.publications. html.(retrieved 2007-07-10).

32. Richard Dawkins. The Ancestors Tale.

33. Julius Rebek et al. Scripps Research Institute, California.

34. Dr. A. G. Smith. Life Puzzle. On crystals and organisms and the possibility of a crystal as an ancestor.

35. Richard Dawkins. The Selfish Gene.

36. Thomas Gold. "Deep Biosphere." Proc. National Academy of Sciences 89, No. 6045.

37. Weizmann. ac.il//molgen/members/lancet/doron-publications.html.

38. Segre, D. and D. Ben-Eli; W. Deamer and D. Lancet. "The Lipid World." Origin life Evol. Biosph 31, No. 119 (2001).

39. Segre, D. and D. Lancet. 2000. Composing Life EMBO Rep 1:217.

40. Deamrer et al. Murchison meteorite.

41. Monard, P. A. and D. W. Deamer. "Membrane Self Assembly Processes. Step towards the First Cellular Life." Anat. Rec. 268, No. 196 (2002).

42. Segre, D., et al. Ibid., 39.

43. Svetina, S. and B. Zes. "Shape and Behavior of Lipid Vesicles as the Basis of Some Cellular Processes." Anat. Rec. 268, No:. 215 (2002).

44. Martin Haczync and Jack Szostak. Howard Hughes Medical Institute. Massachusetts general hospital, Boston. 6.4.2008.

CHAPTER 26
When Did Life Begin on Earth and where

It is believed that the earth was formed about 4.5 billion years ago. No one knows exactly when and where life originated on earth except to say the microfossils of bacteria dating back to 3.5 billion years ago have been found. The events that led to the origin of life is least understood by the scientists.

Scientists have to depend on paleontology at present to decide when life started on earth. The oldest and accepted evidence for life are found in Western Australia dating from 3.4 to 3.5 billion years ago. They were single-celled organisms capable of photosynthesis resembling modern cyanobacteria. Since photosynthesis takes a long time to evolve, some believe that life must have started a considerable time before that.

Rock like mounds in Western Australia of varying sizes from a fingernail to that of the size of a man were analyzed and found to have been created by stromatolites. Stromatolites are produced by microbes mainly photosynthesizing cyan bacteria that form thin microfilms which trap mud and debris. Layers of these mud/microbe mats can build into layered rock structures called stromatolites.

Stromatolites are still produced today. These modern stromatolites are remarkably similar to the ancient stromatolites, which provide evidence for some of the earliest life on earth. Microfossils of ancient cyan bacteria can be found in them. Some stromatolites are recovered from South Africa also.

These are produced layer by layer when dirt sediments mix with carbon dioxide emitted by the microbes, water, and minerals trapped in the sticky mucilage of these microbes. These were dated back to 3.4 billion years ago.

Researchers at the Australian Center for Astrobiology believe that "it is an ancestor of life, if one thinks that all life arose on this one planet, perhaps this is where it started" (1).

"It is the last bet for evidence of oldest life on earth" according to scientists at the NASA Astrobiology Institute, in Moffett, California (2).

Sedimentary rocks found in Greenland dating back to 3.85 billion years ago is believed to contain evidence for life, in the form of traces of carbon with altered isotope ratios indicative of biological activity (3). If this finding is well corroborated, then the origin of life in Australia will be in doubt.

References for When Did Life Originate:

1. Abigail Allwood. Australian Center for Astrobiology. Nature (June 2006).
2. Bruce Runniger. NASA Astrobiology Institute, Moffet, California. Nature (2006).
3. Mojzsis, S. J. et al. "Evidence for Life on Earth before 3.8 billion years ago." Nature 384, no. 55 (1996).

CHAPTER 27

Location Where Life First Started

The solar system is believed to have been formed about 4.5 billion years ago. During this time, for about seven hundred million years, the planets were subject to severe bombardment by debris from interplanetary space. Bombardment of earth by asteroids and meteors continued throughout the geological history including the meteorite impact that is believed to have caused the extinction of the dinosaurs. However, the severity of these impacts decreased since 3.8 billion years ago.

What do these impacts have anything to do with origin of life? It is determined that these impacts can wipe out all forms of life on earth, and therefore, one needs to examine the secret niches in which life-forms could have hidden to survive.

Sleep et al. has studied the effects of such impacts (1). An impact of a body 500 km in diameter would wipe out the atmosphere and replace with a thick blanket of rock vapor at a temperature of three thousand degree centigrade and will boil the oceans and create a steam blanket that takes for months to rain out. Biological life will be impossible for about ten thousand years. The earth surface will be sterilized, and extreme temperature will seep into the earth's crust.

Even though Charles Darwin hinted at a warm little pond where life might have originated, that seems in doubt due to these adverse effects of meteorite impact.

Many of the molecules made by Miller-Urey experiment (organic compounds, including glycine) are known to exist in outer space. On September 28, 1969,a meteorite fell over Murchison, Australia (2) Only about one hundred kilograms were recovered. Scientific analysis showed it was rich in amino acids. Over 90 amino acids have been identified so far by researchers. Nineteen of these amino acids are found on earth. Early earth is believed to be similar to many of these asteroids and comets still traversing the space. If the amino acids are able to survive in outer space under extreme conditions, then amino acids must have been present when earth was formed. Alternatively, the earth might have acquired the amino acids from falling meteorites.

Thermal vents: discovered in 1979.

Scientists have discovered life-forms in the unfathomable depths of the seas and land. The submersible vessel Alvin detected a complex ecosystem deep in the Pacific Ocean in 1977 (3). These were found around volcanic vents also called black smokers due to the dusky effluent spewing out of these chimneys like structures. The fluid is extremely hot as high as 350 degree centigrade, but this won't boil due to the high pressures at these depths.

There, they detected microbes of the class called chemo trophs that derive energy from chemicals and heat rather than sunlight. Some of these microbes can survive in temperatures as high as 100-113 degree centigrade. They are also called hyper thermophiles.

Because they found life in places where it was presumed to be impossible for life to exist, scientists are looking at the possibility that these thermal vents may be the place where life might have originated. The chemicals found in these vents and the energy they provide could have fuelled many of the chemical reactions necessary for the origin of life. Further more, using DNA sequencing of modern organisms, biologists have tentatively traced the most recent common ancestor (MRCA) of all life forms to an aquatic microorganism that lived in extremely high temperature-a likely candidate for a hydrothermal vent inhabitant. But deeper than the thermal vents, the ocean drilling program has recovered rocks deep from the ocean, one kilometer below and detected microbes there. It is believed that up to five kilometers below the ocean floor life can survive (4).

ALH 84001:Allan Hills, Antarctica (5)
A 4.5—billion-year-old meteorite was found in Allan hills in Antarctica which fell to the earth about thirteen thousand years ago. Discovered in December 1984 by ANSMET. Inside the meteorite, scientists found

tiny tracks and along these tracks found evidence for what is considered as fossilized bacteria. It also contained aromatic compounds, which are complex organic compounds. But some scientists argue that these bacterial elements might have come from contaminated earth's bio film. This debate continues. Scientists believe that this meteorite is one of the oldest pieces of the solar system, thought to have crystallized from molten rocks 4.5 billion years ago. It is believed to have originated from Mars. Age of the rock was determined by radiometric dating techniques.

A similar story is found beneath the surface of land. In 1980s, during oil drilling in Sweden found evidence for living organisms in granite several kilometers below the surface (6). Subsequently drilling in the Columbia River basin in the U.S. confirmed these findings (7).

Paul Davies (8) hypothesizes that these hyper thermophiles probably are the ancient life-forms.

To support this, fossil microbes from the so-called black smokers dated back to 3.26 billion years ago have been discovered (9).

It is also argued that the microbes might have buried deep from the surface to escape the harsh bombardment of the earth's surface by meteorites.

It is also felt that Mars was hospitable for life in its early years with water, and from Mars through meteorites, life landed on earth. These life-forms can be protected from heat, radiation, and ultraviolet damage by situating inside a meteorite as seen from Martian meteorite ALH 8400. Studies on radiation resistant bacteria inside a rock in space have shown a lifetime of up to millions of years of durability (10).

Alternatively, microbes can become spores, which have high degree of protection against these offenders. If the meteorite impact will sterilize the earth surface, how could the microbes survive? Some suggests that the impact would have propelled pieces of rock into space with bacteria inside, and after sojourn in space, it would have returned to earth at a time when condition on earth was hospitable.

Panspermia (11) was introduced a century ago by a Swedish biochemist and Nobel Prize winner who proposed that the space is teeming with microbes, propelled across the galaxy at high speed under the effect of the pressure of light from the parent star. When a microbe encounters a suitable planet, he thought the microbe will colonize it. Life was ready-made in space.

Other proponents of panspermia include Sir Fred Hoyle (12) and Chandra Wickramasinghe (13).

Proto cells in space:

Researchers working with NASA's Ames Astrobiology Lab (14) used simple chemicals in their experiment to produce proto cells in space.—ices from water, methanol, ammonia, and carbon monoxide. They were zapped with ultraviolet radiation in a vacuum to simulate space conditions. This produced solid materials which, when immersed in water, spontaneously created soap bubble like membranous structures that contained both an "inside" and an "outside" layer. They were not alive though.

The formation of these biological compounds by irradiating simple interstellar ices show that some of the organic compounds falling to earth in meteorites and interplanetary dust might have been born in the coldest regions of interstellar space.

Scientists working on Extraterrestrial Intelligence Institute believe that all life-forms as we know it on earth use membrane structure (cell wall) to separate and protect the chemistry involved in the life process inside, from the outside (15).

This discovery proposes that the early life-forming molecules do not need already-formed planets. Instead, they seem to take place in deep space long before planet formation. This supports the panspermia theory, though the microbes referred to in the pan spermia theory have not been produced artificially yet. Scientists have known for a long time that the building blocks for life exist in outer space (16).

The concept of panspermia does not indicate where life began, but proposes that the galaxy is full of microbes and when they find a suitable planet, they settle and multiply there.

So it is possible that life arose on earth or Mars or interstellar space and cross-contaminated and flourished on earth , as it is the only place in the universe , that we know of , capable of sustaining the form of life that we are familiar with.

There will be life-forms with different structure and function and origin in the universe that we cannot see or appreciate. Reference to such life-forms is evident in the scriptures, namely, Satan and angels in the Bible and Qur'an. The Jinns are said to be made from fire, Qur'an:55:15(17). "And He created Jinns from fire free of smoke."

Qur'an does not mention the origin of angels. But Aisha (r) reported a hadith, "The messenger of Allah said, 'The angels are created from light, just as the Jinns are created from smokeless fire, and mankind is created from what you have been told about'" (Reported by Muslim no. 2996 [18]).

It is learned that the angels and Jinns were created long before man.

Whatever this wonderful yet un definable process that we call "life" is, it is propagated through reproduction from generation to generations, establishing its residence in the new life-forms and continuing in the previous life-forms till they die. This phenomenon (life) is the only everlasting biological process indestructible in the present world as we know it. Its journey had started about three to four billion years ago and will go on for infinite time into the future. It had resided in creatures of various shapes and sizes, both mobile and immobile. Its composition is known as DNA. Its functional blue print remains unchanged ever since it appeared 3.5 billion years ago on earth. The DNA bases can get damaged several times in a cell every day, but they are repaired constantly. Some DNA eventually become senescent. But it (life) is still going. Even though scientists know its structure and function, how it was put together and what made it "live" and off and running is still a mystery and is under research. In the human body, is there a hierarchal chain of command to get the "life" going? Every system that we (human beings) have created, has a command and control center. In the living organisms including man, if there is a command and control center, where is it? Is it a particular organ or a cell, which is controlling our "life"?

The creationists believe that life was created by the supernatural force (God), and it will be sacrilegious for human beings to investigate its origin or to attempt to create life artificially. Some scientists believe that one does not need to invoke the supernatural to explain the phenomenon of "life."

But we need not to worry about the perceived violation of the Divine Authority in the search for life. The scriptures give us the implied capacity and authority to pursue the events and phenomena around us and to understand how God has created us and the universe from a theological standpoint. In fact, God has asked mankind to explore and find out how He has created the life and other things in the earth. And possibly the universe.

Genesis 1:26 : "Then God said, 'and now we will make human beings; they will be like Us and resemble Us."

Gen 1:27 says, "So God created human beings, making them to be like Himself. He created them male and female (19). These statements clearly elevates human beings to a higher level close to God and the implication is that presumably we will be able to acquire the knowledge and wisdom like that of the Creator himself."

Qur'an goes further and states,

> 29:20 "Travel through the earth and see how Allah (God) did originate creation, so will Allah (God) produce a later creation. For Allah (God) has power over all things" (20).

> 2:30 (21): "Behold, thy lord said to the angels, 'I will create a vicegerent on earth.'"

> 38:26 (22): "O David! We did indeed make thee a vicegerent on earth."

Muhammad Asad's c commentary states that the term khalifa was derived from verb khalafa, which means "he succeeded another" (established on earth a successor).

These passages from the Bible and Qur'an clearly implore the mankind to explore any and all avenues to find out how God created life on earth, and being the vicegerent of God, we will have the ability and capacity to create "life" itself as we are made in His image, and we are the vicegerents of God.

This must be an imperative to all mankind to seek the truth and investigate the origin of our past, and follow the path of evidence ascertained by science. One has to follow the path of truth wherever it takes us. We are given the capacity to search, but whether we will be successful in creating life is a different matter. Maybe our own generation or the future generation (the another race into which we might be transformed into as mentioned in Qur'an 76:28 (23) will be able to acquire the knowledge that is necessary to get to the bottom of the tree of life and to understand how God created it.

If we do not pursue this course of exploration as we are asked to do and disregard the instruction and prohibitions as prescribed in the scriptures, there is no guarantee that we will not be destroyed like many generations before (Qur'an 19:98 [24]); and a new creation will be in place, who will do what God has instructed us to do, but we did not.

We have inherited and possess this un definable and indescribable phenomenon that is called life, which is a little over 3.5 billion years old.

In spite of its (life's) old age, it does not exhibit any sign of aging. It moves from one container to the next through a process of reproduction. (From one species to the other through mutational changes in the genes, and from one pair to the next generation within species through the process of reproduction). Its capacity to keep its container(body) alive for a limited time, generation after generation goes on undiminished. Its intricate mechanism of functioning remains the same as it started off 3.5 billion years ago. Its modus operandi remains unchanged. Even though some damage and repair is needed for the aging DNA, "life" itself remains an entity that does not need repair and it goes on unchanged. In other words "life" itself does not get "old." But its functional secret remains unchanged. The mechanism of life that we observe in the unicellular organism is the same as it is in us, the human beings and other gigantic multi cellular organisms. To a large extent, its inner mechanism was a mystery, until Francis Crick and James Watson figured out the structure of DNA (25).

Even though a lot of information have been gathered about the basic structure of life, we have not yet produced "life" in the lab yet. Life has been a mystery. Any system that is man-made needs repair or replacement. Life's (DNA) means of communication within the cell or the language it uses, the nature of the communicator, the messenger or the recipient of the message is the same ever since it appeared on earth 3.5 billion years ago.

It has been so far unable, for the scientists, to decode the language or decipher its "letters" used for its communication with the messenger RNA. It communicates in the same "language whether it is in China, Russia, Europe, Asia, or South America. Such a universal system of communication between DNA, mRNA and ribosome, etc., within us and around us has baffled the scientists so far as to its mystery.

It is to be remembered that we have reached this stage through evolution from the primordial cell. But why the lineage that we evolved from alone got this chance for survival through evolutionary processes leading to the present-day humans? and other lines if they existed, were left in the cold and perished. We see archaec-bacteria still around, believed to be the cousins of the ancient progenitor cell of mankind. Was it an unexplained random phenomenon, or a divinely directed process, that enabled the primordial cell to change and acquire new capabilities to evolve and create all these species?

The believers consider this as a divine act. Why did God discriminate , in that , some species were left behind to perish and another got progressed by evolution?

Or is it that God's system will appear to us as discriminatory when there may be another way to look at it that we do not know. Look at our own distant cousins, the chimpanzees, they still are sitting on the tree.

It appears that even among humans, God has given preference to certain individuals for reasons beyond our comprehension. A case in point is the prophets, who are close to God but selected out of the general population. Consequently the believers are told that the prophets will be in heaven but our fate is uncertain. We can only say that it is the way of God, and we may never understand it. Many are impoverished while others are well provided for. Some die young, others live longer. Some are afflicted with deadly diseases, others are unscathed. Trials and tribulations abound and are around us.

Life's journey stared 3.5 billion years ago and through a process of evolution and extinction , newer species are brought in, and it is still traveling. Many a species have fallen by the way side never to be seen again. One can only look back with awe and disappointment, that myriads of our ancestral species have disappeared or were destroyed for the sole purpose of installing the most advanced species—the human beings—on earth We may not be the final chapter in this saga of evolution. We may also be counted as an extinct species over time or remain as a living fossil co-existing with the newer species (human) yet to come As mentioned in the Vedas and Qur'an this universe will be destroyed and another will be created or formed and this cycle continues—BUT WHY?

The purpose of our existence and the ultimate goal of humanity is a mystery.

References for Where Life Originated:

1. Sleep, N. et al. "Annihilation of Ecosystem by Large Asteroid Impact on the Early Earth." Nature 342, no. 139.
2. Murchison meteorite.Australia.September, 1969. Meteoritical Bulletin.No.48. MoscowThe Meteoritical society. Wikipedia:http;//en.wikipedia.org/wiki/ Murchison-meteorite
3. ALVIN. National Oceanic and Atmospheric Administration Wikipedia:.http:// en. Wikipedia.org/wiki/ Hydrothermal-vent.
4. http://www2jpl.nasa.gov/snc/news27.html.

5. Alh 84001.Allan Hills, Antarctica. David Mckay. NASA. Science (August 1996).

6. Parkes, R. J. "Deep Bacterial Biosphere in Pacific Ocean Sediments." Nature 371, No. 410 (1994).

   Mckinley, J. P. et al. "D.O.F. Seeks Origin of Deep Subsurface Bacteria. E.O.S. Transactions of the American Geophysical Union 75, no. 385 (1994).

7. Gold, T. "The Deep Hot Biosphere." Proc. Nat. Acad. Sci 89, no. 6045 (1992).

8. Paul Davies. Origin of Life.

9. Walter, M. R. 1996. In Brock, G. and Goode, Jeds. Evolution of Hydrothermal Ecosystems on Earth and Mars. Wiley, Chichester, p. 112.

10. Martian Meteorite. Meleikowsky, C. et al. Icarus 145, no. 391.

11. Svate Arrhenius. Panspermia.http://en.wikipedia.org/wiki/Swante-Arrhenius.3-2-2009.

12. Fred Hoyle, (1915-2001). The Intelligent Universe. London: Michael Joseph Limited.1983.

13. Chandra Wickramasinghe et al. 2000. "Balloon Experiment to Detect Microorganisms in the Outer Space." Astrophys. Space. Sci. 285, no. 2:555-562.

14. NASA's Ames Astrophysical Lab. University of California, Santa Cruz.

15. Dr. Jason Dworkin. Search for Extraterrestrial. Intelligence Institute, California.

16. Monica Grady. Natural History Museum, London.

17. Qur'an 55:15.

18. Aisha (R). Prophet's wife. Hadith. Reported by Muslim no. 2996.

19. Genesis 1:26-27.

20. Qur'an 29:20.

21. Ibid., 2:30; 38:26; 15:29.

22. Ibid., 38:26.

23. Ibid., 76:28.

24. Ibid.,19:98.

25. Francis Crick and James Watson. Discovery of DNA. Nature.April. 1953.

CHAPTER 28

Origin of Life: The Clay Connection, Science and Scriptures

Science:

The origin of life:

As of today, scientists have no credible definition to the phenomenon called life. Scientists can only describe what a living organism does. We are only familiar with the life-forms on earth and therefore cannot say if life exists elsewhere beyond our planet. Nor scientists know if there could be living creatures made of different ingredients (building blocks) unlike that on earth.

Even though scientists do not know what life is, they are trying to figure out how life might have originated on earth.

There are several theories about the origin of life on earth apart from the creationist view that God created the life. According to the Bible, God took some soil from the ground and made Adam out of it. Then instilled the life-giving spirit into his nostrils, and he became alive. In Qur'an it is mentioned that God made Adam out of mud/clay.

The debate between the creationists and evolutionists, to a large extent, centers along the creation or evolution of Adam and Eve. But we need to realize that life and living creatures were already there before Adam came around and the question should be when did God create life and in what form. Evolutionists are primarily concerned with what happened to life after life appeared (created) on earth. Even those who believe in the spontaneous generation of life (life from non-living materials-abiogenesis) cannot discard the fact that the ingredients needed for the formation (creation) of life from non-living compounds were made available by the big bang fifteen billion years ago. But the events that led to the big bang remain a mystery for scientists so far. The creationists can vehemently argue that the big bang indeed was the handiwork of God and He had sowed the seeds for life in the form of inorganic materials at that time and from which life became a reality.

The scientists are investigating the possibility of creating artificial life and exploring the facts about how life began on earth.

One theory is the Darwinian (1) concept of a "small little pond with organic molecules" from which life might have originated with energy provided by lightning and heat. This theory was further revived by Haldane (2), and Oparin (3). It speculates that cells formed first, then proteins (catalysts) and then nucleic acids, which contain genetic information.

The second theory is that of an RNA world, wherein the RNA appeared first and then the rest of the cell and its contents. These are the most popular concepts of most life-searching biologists.

A third theory was proposed by the British chemist Graham Cairn-Smith (4) called the clay hypothesis. He believes that clay can accelerate the formation of organic molecules, which are the basic ingredients for the origin of life. He further believes that life originated on clay, and later there was a genetic takeover by the DNA. The clays are capable of replication, mutation, and storage of genetic information. Richard Dawkins (5) has endorsed this concept in his book, The Selfish Gene.

The clay can dissolve in water and precipitate out again. The crystalline forms utilize the rarer elements within itself to structure themselves into different shapes. These different shapes can act as templates to produce more shapes of the same kind, building up on top. If a crystal breaks, each piece of the crystal can act as a template for further growth. It can be safely said that these clay forms (crystals) *can replicate or reproduce* in the biological sense. Clay is the only substance on earth nearest to a silicon-based life-form capable of replication and be able to piggyback other chemicals. The carbon compounds naturally stick to the crystal surfaces and the crystals can catalyze organic reactions as described by A. G. Smith. This polymerization causes the molecules to become large chains and by this process, amino acids can become proteins; simple bases can connect together and become RNA, DNA, and other nucleic acids.

In 1996, Jim Ferris (6), a chemist, described an experiment in which he added montmorillonite clay to the chemical mix and found long RNA chains attached to the surface of the clay crystals. A. G. Smith believes that in the pre biotic era, it was a clay life, which became the present-day life on account of a "genetic takeover" by the DNA. This, according to Smith, is a silent transition from inorganic chemicals to organic life.

Scientists have observed that when dilute solution of organic molecules were dropped on to hot clay or rock, polymerization takes place. Because various polymers bind to charged site on clay particles, clay might have concentrated various organic monomers. The metal atoms like zinc and iron present in the clay, catalyzes the reaction in making polymers from monomers.

Hence, clay might have had a significant role in the creation of life as indicated in the Bible and Qur'an. As mentioned above, hot and dry clay absorbs water and concentrate the organic molecules to form the monomers and in to polymers, which are the building blocks of life.

Qur'an:55:14: "He created man from sounding clay like unto pottery". (when clay is heated, it becomes hard like pottery and it acquires the red hue)." This passage clearly shows the importance of hot clay, which has been shown to remove water and concentrate the organic molecules and to catalyze the formation monomers and polymers which are required to make complex molecules in the origin of life as proposed by A. G. Smith and others.

Mr. Smith eloquently proposed for the first time, that clay crystals were the first "**living organisms**." He proposed that the first organisms were "naked replicators" rather than cells. Recent research increasingly point to clay as a catalyst for RNA replication rather than carbon-based compounds. The clay crystals grow using conventional crystal growth processes and would have divided when mechanical stress causes them to break into pieces. Information is replicated across the layers during crystal growth. Specifically the fault structure, domain structure, and cross-sectional shape are all copied.

When the crystals break, the information is exposed in both ends of the resulting crystals. It is this information that forms the heritable information of the crystals and acts as the basis for genetic evolution. The surface grooves of the crystals would have played a role in catalyzing reactions among other compounds in the solution. Heredity in crystals appears to be a simple, natural occurrence. Therefore, crystals appear to be the most plausible **self-replicating agent** in a pre biotic world.

When the correct conditions are present, crystal growth reveals a form of natural error correction. This is the only type of error correction known to occur naturally outside of modern biology.

The high efficiency with which the crystals can transmit information between their layers make them the most likely and natural candidates for *the first living organisms* (8).

In mythology, from time immemorial, clay has taken the center stage as the primal material in the creation of man. Starting from Sumerian times (9) through the Babylonian era, clay has been believed to be associated with the creation of humans. One can perhaps understand this line of thought. Clay is present in all parts of the world and although formless itself, forms can be readily made out of it or imposed on it. Clay has been used to make lifelike sculptures. In the Bible and Qur'an, it is stated that God created man from mud and/or clay, many people believe that perhaps God, the great sculptor, first made man and the animals literally by taking some clay from the ground and sculpturing them into their respective shapes and later made them alive. As scientists are experimenting with minerals in the pursuit of the origin of life, this imagery of God creating man from clay may have a grain of truth in it.

Many scientists believe that indeed clay minerals are likely to have been involved in the origin of life, not in the sense of a sculptured creation concept, but as catalysts in forming the building blocks of life, namely, the RNA, DNA, and the cell wall.

The Bible mentions that Adam was created from mud/clay. Qur'an frequently refers to clay as the substance from which man was created. The clay was originated after earth was formed. and clay is referred to as the origin of man. But actually the earth and clay were formed "out of nothing" from the big bang period fifteen billion years ago (scientists have no idea how this big bang originated). From the standpoint of creation of life on earth, clay, an ingredient on earth, is referred to as the material from which human being was created (formed) not withstanding the fact that clay also came into existence from the big bang, (the singularity) or the pre bang "nothing".

Qur'an refers to this truth in verse 19:67, "But does not man call to mind that We created him before out of nothing"(10). Life as we know it is a carbon based entity. The earliest visible life form, either an archaeon, a virus or a bacteria all got started from organic compounds present on earth, most likely the clay. But the root cause of all these was the big bang when everything started from.

Scientists indicate that Mars exploration space craft (Mars Express) (11), which carried an instrument, the OMEGA, has detected sulfite and phyllo silicates or clay on Mars suggesting there was water on Mars in the remote past. Scientists involved in Mars exploration expressed the belief that "clay materials seems to be the most favorable, to have hosted life's emergence" because they are good at preserving organic matter (4).

It was reported that science backed up religion in a study that suggests life may have indeed sprung from clay—just as many faiths teach. A team of scientists at the Howard Hughes Medical Institute and Massachusetts General Hospital in Boston have shown materials in clay, specifically a clay mixture called montmorillonite, not only helps form little bags of fat and lipids but helps cells use genetic material called RNA. That, in turn, is one of the key processes of life (12).

Scientists have found clays could catalyze the chemical reactions needed to make RNA from building blocks called nucleotides.

They also showed that when fatty acids and RNA were mixed with clay, vesicles [balloons] were formed with RNA trapped in it. A process like this may have led to the primordial cell. Earlier scientists have shown that clay can help the formation of RNA (12). They found the clay sped along the process by which fatty acids formed little baglike structures called vesicles. The clay also carried RNA into those vesicles. A cell is, in essence, a complex bag of liquid compounds.

Clay as a "Primordial Womb"

Geochemists at the Arizona State University have discovered that certain clay minerals under conditions, at the bottom of the ocean, may have acted as incubators for the first organic molecules on earth.

Their article "Organic Molecules Formed in a 'Primordial Womb'" was published in the November issue of Geology (13). Their research suggests that the fundamental materials necessary for life might have come into existence deep in the ocean. It has been discovered that there are hydrothermal vents along the lines where tectonic plates converge on the ocean floor. The vents are fissures in the seafloor that spew out super-hot water, like an underwater volcano.

Earlier work has shown that with high enough temperatures and pressures, volcanic emissions could produce the chemical compound methanol. However, scientists did not know how methanol could survive the temperatures of 300-400 degree centigrade. Methanol gets destroyed at these high temperatures and something has to protect the methanol from these high temperatures, as high temperatures should break down methanol. The answer was that the common clay mineral was the protector. (Methanol has been used to create the organic compounds-the building blocks of life).

They hypothesized that the expandable clay surrounding the hydrothermal vents might have served as a "primordial womb" for the infant molecules, sheltering them within its mineral layers.

They then devised an experiment that would test whether the organic compound methanol would be protected between the clay layers.

The team of scientists simulated the intense heat and pressure of the ocean floor within a pressurized vessel. Over a six-week period, the reaction of clay and methanol was monitored. The team found that the expandable clay not only protected the methanol, but also promoted reactions that helped form more complex organic compounds. The reaction between the clay minerals and methanol promoted production of new organic compounds.

Scientists speculate that the diverse organic molecules protected within the clay might eventually be expelled into an environment more hospitable for life, leading to an "organic soup." What makes the finding very exciting is that the experimental conditions reflect scientists' best estimation of the simplest conditions that might have existed when life first began, according to the investigators.

The scientists speculate that as long as there is water and the right chemical ingredients, common clay minerals can help produce the ingredients for bio molecules (chemical components used by living organisms).

Additional experiments are planned to find what chemical conditions would be required to form the building blocks of life.

According to the investigators, scientists have only started investigating the influence of clays on the origin of life.

Jon Bernal, the British scientist, postulated that adsorption of molecular intermediaries on clays or other minerals may have concentrated these intermediaries, and such concentration could offset the tendency of water to break down polymers of biologic significance (14).

These experiments show us the importance of clay in the formation of the basic building blocks of life and point to the origin of life from clay and water as mentioned in the Bible and Qur'an. We can call clay, the crucible of life and the "Primordial womb" of mankind.

Scientists have demonstrated that , not only can clay and other mineral surfaces accelerate vesicle assembly, but assuming that the clay ends up inside, at least some of the time, provides a pathway by which RNA could get into vesicles.

"The formation, growth, and division of the earliest cells may have occurred in response to similar interactions with mineral particles and inputs of materials and energy," the researchers wrote in their report published in the journal Science.

The scientists are not claiming that this was how life was started, but they have demonstrated growth and division without any biochemical machinery. Ultimately, if scientists can demonstrate more natural ways this might have happened, it may begin to give us clues about how life could have actually gotten started on the primitive earth (12).

Two of the crucial components for the origin of life—genetic material and cell membranes—could have been introduced to one another by a clump of clay according to a new experiment (15). The study of montmorilonite clay by scientist at the Massachusetts General (Science, October 24, 2003) Hospital in Boston revealed that it can accelerate the formation of membranous fluid-filled sacs. These vesicles or "proto cells" were made to divide by forcing them through small holes. This caused them to split into smaller vesicles with minimal loss of their contents. The researchers admit that in nature, the vesicles will rarely be forced to divide, and they are searching for different mixtures of membrane-forming molecules that might divide spontaneously (11).

Previous work has shown that the same simple mineral can help assemble the genetic material RNA from simpler chemicals. "Interestingly, the clay also gets internalized in the vesicles" (16).

The genesis of cell wall and the emergence of genetic material are of paramount importance in the origin of life research. The cell membrane is an important key for the physiologic function of cell as it protects its contents, concentrates chemicals to promote chemical and metabolic function, and isolates successful genes from unsuccessful ones. "It's clear that one really needs both of these elements to get evolution off the ground and running," according to scientists (11).

Scientists know that some of the building blocks for RNA like molecules and membranes are spontaneously created by chemical reactions in conditions that might have existed on primordial earth. But how these subunits were assembled was unknown.

One theory regarding RNA formation revolves around the unusual properties of montmorillonite clay. The negatively charged layers of its crystals create a sandwich of positive charge between them. This becomes an attractive environment for RNA subunits to concentrate and join together to form long chains.

Scientists demonstrated that clay caused a hundredfold acceleration of vesicle formation. Once formed, the vesicles often incorporated bits of clay and were able to grow by absorbing more fatty acid subunits.

Naked RNA molecules can't copy itself. It needs to be enclosed in a thin envelope, a bubble of fat that keeps out harmful substances while letting in beneficial ones. Once protected by a membrane, RNA could evolve quickly. Scientists have made an RNA molecule capable of bonding amino acids together. The next step is to link them together into the so-called peptides. Combining peptide together will produce proteins. In the hot springs on the ocean floor, a primitive one-celled creature called an archeon was recently discovered. Its genes show that it shares a common evolutionary heritage with us, but not with bacteria. The consensus is that both archeons and bacteria came from a common, even simpler creature. But even this one-celled organism is far more complicated than the first living thing, according to the scientists.

A lot of evolution has to occur before RNA, working alone, could have evolved into a cell complete with proteins and genes, conclude the scientists.

Viruses are the only organisms that now have genes made of RNA. DNA took over that vital function very early in evolution, even before the ancestors of archaeons and bacteria.

Some scientists (12) believe life on earth started with RNA molecules that stored genetic information and catalyzed the chemical reactions needed to make proteins and hundreds of millions years later, these two functions became specialized. DNA now stores these genetic blueprints that make an organism, an amoeba, or a human. Proteins catalyze all of life's chemistry, including the replication of DNA that passes from parents to off springs.

Details of how earth went from an RNA to a DNA world are lost forever in the natural record, since all traces of the origin of life have long been destroyed by chemistry, geology, and the biology of more complex more voracious creatures. Scientists' hope of recreating life now is limited to lab experiments as naturally occurring organic compounds cannot exist outside as they will be instantly destroyed by oxygen and the existing life forms. First, scientists have to make something that everyone agrees is "alive", to go further with origin of life research (12).

Over the past fifty years, researchers have known that mineral surfaces may have played important roles in organizing or activating molecules that would become the building blocks of life like the amino acids and nucleic acids. But scientists are perplexed with the fact that they don't know which of the countless possible combinations of bio molecules and mineral surfaces were the key to this bio molecular evolution.

Researchers have developed protocols for adapting DNA micro array technology to rapidly identify molecule/mineral pairs.

Some twenty two amino acids form life-essential proteins. "In a quirk of nature, amino acids come in two mirror image forms—left and right handed, or called chiral molecules. Life uses the left-handed variety exclusively. Non biological processes, however, do not usually distinguish between left and right variants. In order to have a transition from a chemical to biological era, some process has to separate the left from the right-handed variety and concentrate. This step, called chiral selection, is crucial to forming the molecules of life (17)."

Like amino acids, some minerals have pairs of crystal surfaces that have a mirror relationship to each other, called left and right faces. Calcite, one such mineral, is common today and was prevalent during the Archean era when life first emerged. In 2001, Hazen and colleagues performed the first experiments showing that the left-handed amino acid, aspartic acid, preferentially adhere to left faced-calcite. This demonstrated one process by which left-handed amino acids can be selected out from a mixture of right-handed and left-handed amino acid in the primordial soup. But of the countless bio molecule/mineral surface interactions which are the likely candidate in the formation of life?

To find which molecules stick and which don't, they are using Time-of-Flight Secondary Ion Mass Spectrometry (ToF-SIMS). This will allow the detection of the organic molecules that bind most strongly to mineral surfaces (18).

In the scientific endeavor of searching for the origin of life, many advances have been made as described above. We have created amino acids, the building blocks, proteins, RNA, DNA, a cell wall, all the basic ingredients for life, but we have not succeeded in creating a living cell. But in this great research, scientists have demonstrated the multifaceted qualities of clay and minerals as an integral part of the production and catalysis of the building blocks of life, whether it is RNA, DNA, or the cell membrane. It is important to look at the divinely revealed scriptures to understand the beginning of life and the frequent reference to clay as the substrate for the origin of life, and its obvious implication in the evolution of life itself.

A great many followers of Judeo-Christian-Islamic faiths strongly reject the idea of evolution. But they all accept the lowly origin of man from earth or clay in the sculptured creation model (concept), but not the evolutionary model.

References for Origin of Life: the Clay Connection:

1. Charles Darwin. The Origin of Species.
2. J. B. S. Haldane. Origin of Life. New Biology.
3. A. I. Oparin. Origin of Life. Moscow Worker. 1924.
4. Alexander Graham Cairn-Smith. The Life Puzzle: On Crystals and Organisms. (1971).
5. Richard Dawkins. The Selfish Gene.
6. Jim Ferris, Chemist. (1996).
7. Qur'an 55:14.
8. Tim Tyler/contact/http://originlife.net.
9. The Sumerians, an ancient civilization.
10. Qur'an 19:67.
11. Mars Express. OMEGA. Jack Mustard. Brown University. Mars Exploration. Astrobiology Magazine (April 2006).
12. Sozstak, et al. Life Science 312:678.
13. Lynda Williams. Arizona State University. "Clay as a Primordial Womb." Geology (November 2005).
14. John Desmond Bernal, Biologist. *http://folk.ntnu.no*. fossumi. Physical phenomenon in clays. John Otto Fossumi. Dep. of Physics. NTNU. Trondheim. Norway.
15. Philip Cohen. 2003 New Scientist. Com Science Reporter.
16. Leslie Orgel. Origin of Life Expert. Salk Institute for Biological Sciences. San Diego, California.
17. Robert Hazen, scientist. Carnegie Institution's Geophysical Lab
18. ToF-SIMS.Time-of-FlightIonMass Spectrometry.http://www.phi.com/ techniques/tof-sims.html.3-1=2009.

CHAPTER 29
Hominid Evolution

Science:

A hominid is any member of the biological family hominidae—the great apes including the extinct and extant human species, chimpanzees, and gorillas. A human is a member of the genus Homo. The classification of species resulted in our position in the genus homo sapiens sapiens or homo sapiens idaltu. The human being is also a primate of the family of Hominidae characterized by upright locomotion (bi pedalism), opposing thumb and fingers, increased brain size, language, and culture.

The study of human evolution or anthropogenesis is intended to find out how the Homo sapiens evolved as a separate species from other hominids, the great apes, and placental mammals. This includes the study of fossils, linguistics, and genetics.

More anthropomorphic primates of the Hominini tribe are placed in the Hominina sub tribe. They are characterized by the evolution of an increasingly erect bipedal locomotion. The only extant species is homo sapiens.

The fossil record indicates that this sub tribe branched off from the common ancestor with chimpanzee lineage 3-5 million years ago. About 2 million years ago Australopithecus began to change into two tracks. One lineage became Paranthropus a plant eating creature with strong jaws, molar teeth and powerful facial muscles requiring a strong cranial crest for muscle attachment. The other track led to Homo sapiens.

The genus Homo includes earlier species like Australopithecines (hominins) from which the divergence that led to the current human species occurred two million years ago in Africa. Both genera coexisted at the same time for about 1.5 million years There were other Homo species like Homo habilis, Homo erectus, and the Neanderthalensis who have gone extinct.

The archaic Homo sapiens evolved in Africa and spread to the world. It was Homo habilis that used tools for the first time in human history, and fire was used first by the next species the Homo erectus. Scientists have speculated the close relationship between human being and the great apes, on the basis of the natural range of the apes, and assumed that these two species shared a common ancestor and the fossils of such common ancestor could be found in Africa as well, and indeed it has been found.

In 1925, Raymond Hart discovered the fossils of what is named as Australopithecus Africanus, which showed evidence for bipedal locomotion. This species is considered a remote ancestor to humans. Long before that, the primates had originated from bats.

The first species of the hominid lineage is Homo habilis.

Homo sapiens otherwise called the wise man, based on usage of tools and brain size (intelligence) appeared between four hundred thousand and two hundred fifty thousand years ago.

Paleoanthropologists believe that human beings were evolved from early primates about six million years ago. Our body parts, cellular structures, and basic genetic makeup are similar to other animals. Unlike other animals, we can populate any parts of the world, can control the environment, and alter a path we are set into. Creationist belief says that every animal is created independently of the others as separate groups. But paleontology, genetics, and molecular biology indicate that all animals have something in common and believe that they are evolved from a common ancestor. The discovery that the genetic composition of chimpanzee and human beings differ only by 2.2 percent based on analysis of base per base variations, argues for close relationship between chimpanzees and human beings.

There is no fossil evidence of the common ancestor of present-day human beings and the chimpanzees. It is believed that this ancestor was a tree dweller capable of walking quadrupedally on the tree branches and capable of climbing. From such an ancestor, one lineage developed long hands so that when they came down to the ground, they used knuckle walking (walking on four limbs and the knuckle) to support their trunk. This is what we see in the great apes like gorillas and chimpanzees. The other lineage developed long legs, short trunk, and a repositioned shoulder joints and eventually developed bipedal locomotion (bipedalism) and eventually became human.

Scientists are studying when and how we got separated from the common ancestor , from whom human beings and chimpanzees evolved separately. One method used to determine the time of divergence is by what is called the molecular clock based on the molecular clock hypothesis (MCH). This is a technique in molecular evolution to relate the divergence time of two species, to the number of molecular differences measured between the two species (DNA sequences). This is also called the genetic clock (2).The DNA mutates at a constant rate. Another method is by mixing two different samples of DNA from two different organisms and measuring the difference in the melting point, allows one to approximate the percent genetic difference. This was developed by Charles Sibley and Jon Ahlquist (3).

About six million years ago, an ape-man appeared in the fossil record. This creature was able to walk without using the hands (apes usually use both hands and legs to move—knuckle walking). It had hands like apes and legs looking more like man, was not totally upright but bent forward while walking. But not totally humanlike either. This ape-man or man-ape was named Australopithecus (southern ape).

About three million years ago, two separate man-ape species evolved, namely, Australopithecus robustus and Australopithecus Africanus. But the former did not survive.

The Australopithecus Africanus evolved into Homo habilis so named because there was evidence that they used tools (handy man). These tools were made of stone and wood.

About 1.7 million years ago, a fully upright form of hominid appeared in the fossil record and was named Homo erectus. There is evidence that they used fire. They were very strong so that they could travel long distances due to their strong lower limbs. It is claimed that they were the fastest animals to cover a distance of over 100 km. This helped them to colonize the entire world. This is believed to be during an ice age, and due to ice formation, the sea level was very low. The low sea level uncovered several land bridges connecting different continents and could walk across without the need for a boat.

About five hundred thousand years ago, Homo sapiens (wise men) appear in the fossil record. The earliest is called the Neanderthals. They flourished from five hundred thousand years to thirty thousand years ago and became extinct.

The anatomically modern humans appear in the fossil record about one hundred thirty thousand years ago. The fossils of the most modern humans appear thirty-five thousand years ago. They are called the Cro-Magnons. They had great innovations. They built watercrafts, bows and arrows and spears for close hunting. They wore jewelry, had artwork and had musical instruments. They disappeared ten to fifteen thousand years ago from the fossil record.

Human beings living today are called Homo sapiens sapiens. We belong to the genus, Homo. A genus can contain several species that have certain common features. The hominids are the early human species. In the continuum of biological evolution, it will be difficult to characterize a particular species as human. Nevertheless, certain characteristics are associated with being human, namely, social life, language, culture, and God consciousness. We call ourselves human beings, but where is the line of demarcation between human beings and sub-human beings? For the followers of the Judeo-Christian-Islamic faith, this demarcation has already been done by God Himself. God had made Adam the first man and Eve as the first woman who were husband and wife, and thence all the descendents of this pair are rightfully called human beings.

Scientists call us (the present day humans) the most modern human beings in the long line of hominid evolution, on the basis of fossil characteristics and the size of the cranium, which contains the brain. Many of the pre-Adamic population look like us From the fossils, but had smaller brain size except the Cro-Magnons. Short of that, the differences between us and them on the basis of fossils, is not much and it will be difficult to say which one is a human being and which one is a sub-human. That is why the scientists call us the most modern human beings and the previous creatures as less modern. Scientists have already established the features of the less human creatures called the archaic humans or early hominids on the basis of fossils. Anthropologists conclude that the Cro-Magnons are identical to ourselves, and the recent DNA analysis confirms that genetically, the Cro-Magnons are identical to us. In all respects they were human beings (according to our definition) but God did not give them the status of the full human beings for unclear reasons to us, probably their brain capacity was not developed enough to entertain full God consciousness. It was Adam who is considered the fully developed human being according to God and he appeared between twelve thousand and ten thousand years ago. At this time the then existing species, the Cro-Magnons were on the way out to extinction.

Scriptures:

At this juncture, let us look at what Qur'an is saying (4) 2:30, "Behold thy Lord said to the angels, 'I am about to establish up on earth one who shall inherit it (vicegerent).

The angels said, 'Wilt thou make therein one who will make mischief There in and blood shed.' The angels must have seen the blood shed created by the hominid species that were living on earth before Adam, to make such a statement as discussed before. Angels do no have the capacity to predict what the future human beings will be doing. They can only relate to what they have seen and witnessed.

This testifies to the fact there were creatures like human beings on earth who were brutish and created bloodshed by infighting. The anthropologists believe there was cannibalism among the early hominids demonstrated by tooth marks on the fossil bones believed to have been left by the act of biting on the bone with flesh on it (human tooth marks). We have words from the angels testifying before God and paleontological evidence for humanlike beings, being present on earth before Adam was created.

Qur'an 6:133, (5) "If it were His will, He could destroy you and in your place appoint whom He wills, as your successors, even as He raised you up from "**Other People's Seeds**".

Qur'an 19:98 (6), "But how many (countless) generations before them have We destroyed." Whether these generations pertain to the pre-Adamic people or not is unclear. But nevertheless, we have enough evidence in the Qur'an and the Bible (7) (Genesis 1:26) to believe there were humanlike creatures on earth before Adam, and scientists have shown the immediate pre-Adamic people called the Cro-Magnons were genetically identical to us (Adam and his generation) to be able to intermarry and have surviving children.

Evolutionary sequence based on fossils:

Ardipithecus ramidus. Had more chimpanzee-like features. They might have walked upright and lived 4.4 million years ago. Their fossils were found in 1992.

Australopithecus anamenesis. Walked on feet but the arm bones were like that of apes.

They lived 4.2-3.9 million years ago. Their fossils were found in 1965.

Australopithecus afarensis which includes "Lucy." Discovered by Johanson (8). The leg bones and pelvis and teeth were like humans, but the brain case and jaws were like chimpanzees. Average height was three to five feet. They walked upright and lived 3.5-2.9 million years ago. The fossils were found in 1973.

Australopithecus africanus. Was similar to afarensis, but had a slightly bigger brain cavity and lived 3-2.4 million years ago. The fossils were found in 1924.

Australopithecus robustus. They had large heavy skull and large jaws and teeth. Had a sagittal crest that runs on top of the skull from front to back. This was for attachment of heavy temporal muscles. They lived 2.1-1.6 million years ago. Their fossils were found in 1938.

Australopithecus boisei. Their skull and teeth were larger than that of robustus. Walked upright and lived 2.3-1.1 million years ago. Fossil found in 1959.

Homo habilis (Handy man—first used tools). Their height was about five feet and weighed 100 pounds. The brain was larger than that of Australopithecus. They lived 2.4-1.5 million years ago. The fossils was discovered in 1960.

Homo erectus (Java Man). Original fossil found in Java, Indonesia. Subsequently several fossils were found all over the world. They were the first wide-ranging hominids. Their skeleton is very similar to that of modern man, but very heavier and thicker. The skull was smaller than present-day humans. They were the first to use fire in human history. The use of fire helped them to ward off any predatory animals and protect their caves or residences. They cooked food and might have prevented many infectious pathogens. They lived one million to three hundred thousand years ago. This was in an ice age, and there were several land bridges connecting the continents. Because of these land bridges, these hominids could cross to different continents without the need for a boat.

Homo sapiens (also called archaic homo).

Homo heidelbergenesis. Their brain was larger than that of Homo erectus. Their fossils were found in Africa and Europe. Lived five hundred thousand years before the present to two hundred thousand years before the present. Their fossils were found in 1921.

Homo sapiens Neanderthals. They were adapted to cold climate. Had short limbs and powerful muscles. They stood about 5.5 feet high. Their skull was larger than present-day humans. They lived 300,000 (three hundred thousand) years before the present to thirty thousand years ago. Their fossils were found in 1856.

Homo sapiens sapiens. They were like us. They had advanced tools, spears, arrow and bow, boats, paintings, and early musical instruments. They lived thirty five thousand years ago. Went extinct by ten to fifteen thousand years ago. They were called the Cro-Magnons. Their fossils were discovered in 1868.

Ardopithecus was the common primate ancestor to Paranthropines, Australopithecines, and humans. But this species became extinct four million years ago. There were other species of our genus called transitional hominids, but they all died out. Human evolution is not a straightforward case, one after the other. Several species lived side by side at the same time. Recent evidence shows that Homo habilis and Homo erectus might have lived at the same time (9), but all of them died out except our lineage. Was this a chance occurrence or a guided evolution? The fossils of early transitional hominids were discovered by anthropologists in the Olduvai Gorge in Tanzania in 1960 (10) and named Homo habilis.

Similar fossils were later discovered at East Lake Turkana in Kenya by the same anthropologists. The later fossils were called H. Rudolfenesis (the former name for Lake Turkana)(11).

The disappearance of Cro-Magnons approximately coincides with the appearance of Adam and Eve from biblical time scale and other archaeological evidences as described earlier, and more recently from molecular science as described later. It is appropriate to call all the hominid species up to and including the Cro-Magnons as the pre-Adamic humans, the Cro-Magnons can be called the first generation of most modern human beings that is us. And the population from the time of Adam and Eve onward as Adamic population or the second generation of human beings. The preceding account of this transformation from one species to the next and the physical and mental changes that is commensurate with those transformation is further complemented and elaborated in Qur'an.

Qur'an: 71:14 (12), "He created you in different stages." Some commentators refer to this statement to the steps of the development of the fetus in the womb. The development of the fetus is a continuous process without discernible stages to speak of. The different stages more likely represents the different stages in the biological evolutionary ladder of life's earliest beginning from a proto cell, through mammals to the level of humans through pre-Adamic hominid species including the Cro-Magnons.

Qur'an 71:14 (13) says, "He has created you in various stages."

Verse 6:133(14) further states, "If He so wills he may bring an end to you and thereafter cause whom He wills to succeed you—even as He has brought you into being out of the "SEEDS OF OTHER PEOPLE."

This statement points to our origin (humans) **from the SEEDS** (sperm and ova) of previous generations of pre-Adamic hominids who are extinct now, which includes our recent ancestors, the Cro-Magnons. But humanity did not disappear with the extinction of our posterity (the extinction of the Cro-Magnons) due to the unique feature of this wonderful phenomenon called "life" given to us by the Almighty. Life propagates through seeds (sperms and ova) of humankind, as well as other life forms and it passes on to the next generation.

In this context let us examine the statement in Qur'an about the similitude of Jesus and Adam.

Qur'an:3:59: (15) "Verily in the sight of God, the nature of Jesus is as the nature of Adam, whom he created out of dust and said unto him, "Be" and he is." In this passage there are several implications. This revelation was in relation to the visit of by a Christian delegation who came from Nijran (Yemen) to meet Prophet Muhammad (pbuh) and reiterated their belief that Jesus was the son of God and Prophet told them the truth that he was just a human being. This verse clearly states that the physical nature of Jesus was like Adam who was created from dust and as such there is no basis to believe that Jesus was the son of God. The prophet was demonstrating to the Christian delegation that the physical nature was that of a human and not of God. Some other inferences can be made from this verse. The word in this verse "Mathal" means among other things, nature, analogous, similar, to represent, to bear likeness, copy etc.

As Maulana Muhammad Ali in The holy Qur'an points out in his commentary page 155 that there is no reference to Jesus being brought to existence without the agency of a male parent in the Qur'an. Further more, we know that Jesus was not brought in to existence like the traditional belief of Adam's creation, in that God took some clay and molded a human effigy and made it alive and called him Adam. There is no mention of clay being used on the spot to create Jesus, similar to the creationist belief of the creation of Adam. If the similarity of these two prophets is extended to their birth we see that Jesus came out of the womb of his mother Mary (Mariyam) and therefore Adam must have had a mother too. This statement clearly negates the traditional belief that Adam was created from a clay effigy. All creatures and human beings were originated from clay or dust as were Adam and Jesus but not from a clay effigy or a clay model.

It is amazing that this biological phenomenon called "Life" never died since its inception on earth 3.5 billion years ago even though many species who carried life went extinct. Thus life goes on and on into the endless future.

This statement in the Qur'an (6:133) [14] and the discussion given above should dampen our belief that we are the final products of evolution (creation) as we may be transformed (evolved) to another species physically or mentally.

Scientists cannot say exactly how these pre-Adamic hominids from Australopithecus including the Cro-Magnons went extinct. Several theories are put forward to explain their extinction. Fighting for survival due to limited food supply or the ones who have some survival advantage will destroy the less advanced species prior to them, are a few reasons among others. Another theory is the susceptibility to infections that the new species would introduce to the existing species and not having resistance to the infection, they perish. The adaptability of the new species to adjust to climatic changes, better techniques of hunting, and gathering and possibly other new traits favors the new species' survival. Whatever the reason or reasons, several pre-Adamic generations went extinct. It might be the will of God for the purpose of establishing and installing the perfect man, Adam.

In the human genome we see the foot prints of the extinct species in the form of Pseudogenes and also the genes of our distant cousins, the chimpanzee, our ancestral race, the Cro-Magnons who went extinct. The genes of the Cro-Magnons are identical to us (16).

In this process of evolution, significant changes have occurred in our brain function and more importantly in our physical structure. Our physical appearance may seem similar to the chimpanzees, but our skeletal structure and muscle attachments and their differential enlargements and strengthening are special to human beings, to make us stand upright and walk on two legs. Without these two important transformations, namely, in the brain and more importantly in the musculoskeletal frame, there won't be human beings as we know them.

These musculoskeletal changes needed for being a human being is described in the Qur'an.

Qur'an gives some thought-provoking statements about the changes made in our body or the gradual remodeling done,, so to speak, to the skeletal structure in the evolutionary process, to enable human beings to walk upright (bipedalism). Our skeletal frame may look like that of the chimpanzee, but significant changes have to happen in order to be upright and be able to walk on two legs.

These observations should reinforce our belief in biological evolution.

Qur'an 76:28 (17) says, "It is We created them, and We have made their joints strong. But when We will We can substitute the like of them by a complete change."

"We created them and fixed their bones and joints (18)."(Ahmed Ali)

This reference to the bones and joints is a profound endorsement for evolutionary phenomenon. We know that Adam was created with full complements of a human being. Qur'an 15:29 (19) (Asad) states, "And when I have fashioned (formed) him fully and breathed My spirit in to him, fall down in prostration," and there was no need to strengthen the bones and joints of his progeny as our physical structure, especially our bones and joints, is perfect for the activities of human species. This suggests that there were some species in the past with weak bones and joints (or bones and joints that were unsuitable for bipedalism, like the apes and early hominids) who were not fully developed human beings. This is born out of fossil evidence as well.

It is believed that about six million years ago, there was a split between the hominid lineage and the ape lineage. Through the process of evolution, the hominid lineage became the present-day human beings, and the ape lineage became the great apes (chimpanzees, gorillas, orangutans). It is to be remembered that the present-day human beings did not get transformed from the present-day gorillas or chimpanzees. The transformation started from a common ancestral creature from whom our lineage split about six million years ago and eventually became human beings, and the other lineage being separated from our lineage six million years ago eventually became the great apes including the chimpanzees. During these prolonged evolutionary transformations, the hominid species became more and more of humans and less and less of apes (ape-man to man-ape) and finally the fully developed human being).

Before Adam and Eve (thirty-five thousand years ago), there were modern human beings like us called the Cro-Magnons. But God conferred the title of the fully developed human being on Adam, ten to fifteen thousand years before present. During this transformation as mentioned above, significant changes have occurred in the physical and more importantly the size and function of the brain. The most important physical change is the ability of walking upright, but with this gift of upright walking came the proverbial curse of the "back pain" that human beings suffer due to the stress and strain of being upright, causing pain in the lower spine (lumbar spine).

The Advantages of Bipedal Locomotion Thermoregulation.

It was in the savannas of Africa where it is believed that these evolutionary changes occurred millions of years ago, had a very hot climate. By walking upright, the total body surface exposed to the sun becomes less; and in the upright stance, more body surface gets exposed to the cooling winds (20). Because of the ability to walk on legs, the hands get free to do other things like carrying food from one place to the other, and the females can carry their babies. Recently scientists have speculated that early in evolution walking to collect fruits from small trees or bushes would have been advantageous instead of getting down on all fours and go to the next tree and climb up again (21). It might have helped brain growth due the development of fine motor skills.

It is to be recalled that over the past several millions of years, several species, including humanoid species, have come and gone; and each new species had changes in both physical characters as well as in the brain capacity.

What are the physical changes that have occurred?

The Skull:

In the base of the skull, there is an opening called the foramen magnum, which is located in the center of the base of the skull. Through this opening, the spinal cord comes out. This position helps human being to balance the head on the spine when upright. In the chimpanzee, the closest biological relative of man, the foramen magnum is located farther in the back so that it can balance the head when in the horizontal posture.

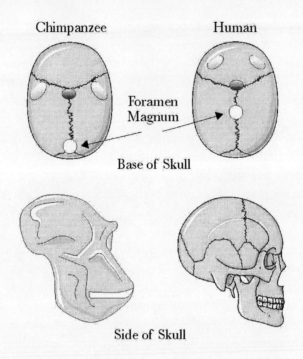

Comparison of Chimpanzee ansd Human Skulls

Figures were produced using Servier Medical Art, www.servier.com.

The Spinal Column:

The spine in the chimpanzee is curved with its convexity to the back or dorsally. It is primarily to suspend the abdominal organs; it functions as a suspension bridge. The human spines have four curves. The curve in the cervical spine is convex anteriorly; in the thoracic spine, the curve is convex posteriorly; in the lumbar spine, it is convex anteriorly; and in the lowest segment of the spine, the sacrum, it is concave anteriorly. This will support the body like a spring when erect. The vertebral bodies are wider in the human than in the chimpanzee and have soft inter vertebral discs to absorb the stress when upright and walking. The size of the vertebral bodies increase in size from the top to the bottom of the spine. The lumbar vertebrae are the largest. The lower end of the spine called the sacrum is attached to the iliac bones with very strong ligaments to give support and stability to the trunk when upright. The lower limbs of human are longer than the upper limbs, and this helps in upright walking.

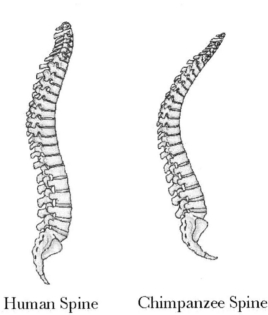

Human Spine   Chimpanzee Spine

Comparison of Human and Chimpanzee Spines

Figures were produced using Servier Medical Art, www.servier.com.

The Pelvis:

The human pelvis shows significant changes from that of the chimpanzee. It is shorter from top to bottom in the human being. The acetabulum (the hole in the hip bone to hold the head of the femur) is placed very low in the chimpanzee pelvis. In human pelvis, it is placed higher, and this gives more stability for the upright stature. The human pelvis is wider, and the hip joints are wider apart, and this subjects the hip joints for considerable stress while walking when weight is taken on one leg, but makes walking more stable.

The Sacrum:

The sacrum is the lowest segment of the human spine. It is connected to the iliac bones with strong ligaments to give stability for the erect body.

The Foot:

The chimpanzee's foot is flat, and weight bearing is uniformly distributed over the sole of the foot. The human foot is arched in its longitudinal direction. The arch is supported by thick and strong ligaments called the plantar fascia. The toes are closer in human foot while the big toe of the chimpanzee is placed away from the rest of the toes, and it is opposable for climbing. The muscles of the hallux are well developed in the human foot to provide a thrust during walking. While walking or standing, the weight in the human is borne by the heel, the front of the foot, and its lateral margin.

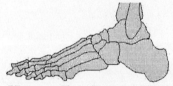

Human Foot Lateral View

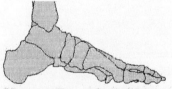

Human Foot Medial View

Chimpanzee Foot

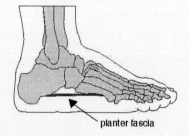

planter fascia

Chimpanzee and Human foot comparison

The Knee Joint:

The chimpanzee cannot extend its knee and lock their leg straight. By extending the knee and locking, we do not have to use muscle power to accomplish it while standing. The chimpanzee has to use a lot of muscle power while attempting to stand up.

In human being, the thighbone (the femur) slopes medially (inward) toward the knee. This helps to bring the feet under our center of gravity so that we won't sway while standing or walking. In the chimpanzee, the hip bone (the femur) does not slope medially toward the knee joint; instead the femur joins the knee joint in a straight line, and consequently the chimpanzee walks with their feet wide apart. The chimpanzee has to rock the whole body from side to side while walking (waddling gait) to keep the center of gravity over whichever leg is bearing the weight. The abductor muscle in the chimpanzee is very weak compared to the human.

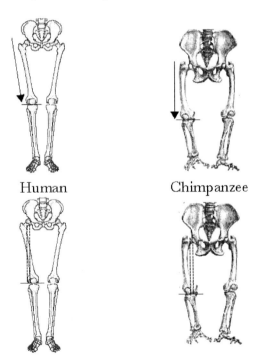

Human   Chimpanzee

Human and Chimpanzee Hip Joints
Human figures were produced using Servier Medical Art, www.servier.com.
Source: Brehms Tierleben, Small Edition 1927, "Skeleton of human (1) and gorilla (2), unnaturally stretched."

Because the hip joints are wider apart in the human beings, the joints take tremendous amount of stress while walking when the weight of the body is borne on one leg. Because of this, several muscles in the hip joint had to be re-arranged and strengthened compared to the apes. The gluteus minimus and the gluteus medius are used in the chimpanzee as extensors of the hip (push the hip backward) and also used for climbing. In the human, these muscles are used as abductors (push laterally, away from the center) to balance the trunk on the weight-bearing leg during ambulation. The gluteus maximus (the thick muscles of our hip) is used to keep the hip in extension during weight bearing. This muscle also helps with abduction and rotation of the hip that has to happen while walking. When one leg is swung forward and touches the ground, that side rotates externally whereas the opposite side rotates internally. These are made possible because of the changes made (re-arrangement) in the skeletal and muscular structure of the hip joints of the human species compared to the previous hominid species.

When standing, we need very minimal muscle activity due to the special character of our skeletal structure and leads to significant energy saving.

Studies have shown (22) that the gluteus maximus is primarily used in running and also to stabilize the hip while bending, digging, and picking objects, which are all activities associated with foraging. When standing, this muscle is relatively quiet in the human.

It is believed that running capacity and the ability to bend down and collect objects and food had significant survival advantage in the evolutionary history. Either running away from the predator or running after the prey. Researchers (22) studied the electrical activity of the gluteus maximus muscle while in resting, standing, sitting, and running conditions and determined that the gluteus maximus is largely silent while standing but becomes very active while running. It is also active while bending or getting up from sitting position and stabilizes the trunk. According to the investigators, the gluteus muscles in the human are primarily for running.

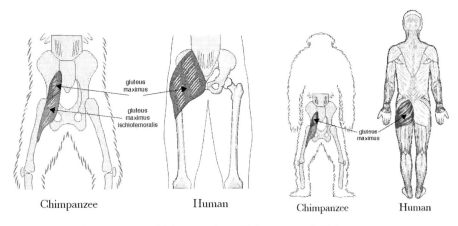

Comparison of hip muscles of Human and Chimpanzee

Source: Journal of Experimental Biology 209, 2143-2155 (2006), Daniel E. Lieberman

Figures were produced using Servier Medical Art, www.servier.com.

As mentioned in the Qur'an, the muscles and joints were made strong than the previous species. In Qur'an 76:28 it implies that there were previous species whose joints and bones were weak or unfit for being upright or walking on two legs. This is what we see in the fossil record according to the anthropologists that the previous species were mostly quadrupedal till early hominids appeared. The above mentioned verse in Qur'an implies an evolutionary transition.

Additionally Qur'an reminds us of our transformation to another kind of people. Qur'an 47:38; 4:133; 11:57 (23) says, "And if you turn back, he will bring in your place another people, then they will not be like you." This suggests the next people who might replace us will be physically different and possibly mentally as well. This is what the anthropologists tell us that there were physical changes in the body of every new species with enlargement of the brain as well, during biological evolution.

The Dating Methods:

Several methods are used to determine the age of the fossils and rocks. These are called the dating methods. Fossils can document the order of appearance and disappearance of groups (dead creatures) and can tell us about the physical appearance of ancient and extinct life forms. It also can show us the results of major catastrophes that had happened in the past.

Sophisticated dating techniques have confirmed accuracy of fossils and their dating. Therefore, the history of life can be learned from rocks with accuracy and confidence.

There are two kinds of dating methods called relative and absolute. The relative methods involve looking at fossils old and new. The absolute techniques utilize the radioactive decay of certain naturally occurring radioactive materials. Based on their half-lives, chemists can determine the age of fossils.

Geostratigraphy is used to date fossils. This is based on the law of superposition originally proposed by Ibn Sina (Avicenna) (24), which states that "sedimentary layers are deposited in a time sequence, with the oldest on the bottom and the youngest on the top." William Smith (25), a geologist, observed long before Darwin that the deepest (oldest) strata did not contain fossils, and as the strata were examined from the bottom to the top, he recognized a pattern of appearance of fossilized creatures. The lower strata, if at all showed any fossils, were of the primitive live forms and as newer strata to the top were examined they found that the successive newer strata contained more and more complex fossils. The most complex and advanced fossils were seen in the newer and newer strata, suggesting gradual development of complex organisms. Mr. Smith was not a believer in evolution at that time.

Absolute dating methods rely on the naturally occurring chemicals with radioactivity. The radioactivity decays at a constant rate to change from the parent radioactive form to the daughter stable form, and noting the proportion of the remaining radioactive parent chemical and the stable daughter chemical, they can calculate the date or age of the fossil and of the sediment, in which it is deposited, based on the half life of the chemical. The time taken for half of the radioactive parent form to become the stable daughter form is called the half-life.

Scientists can use different chemicals for this purpose. The most common and reliable one is carbon 14, which is present in our atmosphere, and plants take it from the atmosphere along with carbon dioxide for photosynthesis, and when the animals including man eat the plant or plant products, they acquire this compound (carbon 14). The half life of carbon 14 is 5,730 years. It cannot be used for materials older than seventy thousand years. The anthropologists prefer this technique.

A third method is radiometric dating by using the isotope series like rubidium/strontium, thorium/lead, potassium/argon, argon/argon, or uranium/lead. But they have very long half-lives ranging from 0.7 million to 48.6 million years.

Subtle differences in the proportion of these isotopes can give very accurate dates for rocks of any age. It is shown that there is only a 1 percent chance of going wrong with these methods, and scientists believe the methods are very reliable.

References for Hominid Evolution:

1. Cheng, Z., et al. Nature 437 (September 2005).
2. The Molecular Clock. Wikipedia (10-16-2008).http://en.wikipedia.org/wiki/Molecular-clock.
3. Charles Sibley and Jon Ahlquist.http://www.d.umn.edu/da/faculty/troufs/anth1602/video/children.htm.
4. Qur'an 2:30.
5. Ibid., 6:133.
6. Ibid., 19:98.
7. Ibid., 1:26.
8. Lucy. Donald Johanson. The Beginning of Humankind (1974).
9. Two coexisting lineages. Nature (August 2007).
10. Louis and Mary Leakey. Tanzania. Olduvai Gorge Excavation. 1971. Cambridge University press.
11. Lake Turkana, Kenya.
12. Qur'an 71:14. Yusuf Ali. The Meaning of the Holy Qur'an.
13. Ibid., Ahmed Ali. Al-Qur'an.
14. Ibid., 6:133. Muhammad Asad. The Message of Qur'an.
15. 3:59:Ibid.
16. Caramelli, D., and G. Bertorelle. Evidence for Genetic Discontinuity. Proc. National Academy of Sciences (2003).
17. Qur'an 76:28. Yusuf Ali.The Meaning of the Holy Qur'an.
18. Ibid., Ahmed Ali. Al-Qur'an.
19. Ibid., 15:29. Muhammad Asad. The Message of the Qur'an.
20. Peter Wheeler. Journal of Human Evolution 13 (1984): 91-98.
21. Kevin Hunt. "Evolution of Human Bipedalism." Journal of Human Evolution 26 (1994): 183-202.
22. Daniel E. Lieberman, et al. Journal of Experimental Biology (2006): 2145-2155.
23. Qur'an 47:38; 11:57; 4:133.
24. Avicenna (Ibn Sina-Abu Ali Sina), the Persian polymath, physician, geologist, astronomer, scientist, and paleontologist. 980 CE. http://en.wikipedia.org/wiki/Law-of-superposition.
25. William Smith (1769-1839), English geologist and stratist. http://cn.wikipedia.org/wiki/William-smith-(geologist).

CHAPTER 30

The Evolution of The Universe

Summation of all particles and energy that exist and the space-time in which all events occur, is the universe.

Why is there a universe? What would have happened if there was no universe (we need only the solar system for our life)? How did it come into being? Does it have a beginning and an end? Is there one universe or many more universes (multiverse)? These are questions being asked by human beings for centuries. Scientists cannot give a clear answer how it began or where will it end.

Philosopher Bernulf Kanitscheider (1) once said, "Out of nothing, nothing comes."

Bertrand Russell (2) says, "The universe is just there and that is all."

It is worthwhile looking at the scriptures, even though many scientists want to convey the impression that there is no compelling reason to invoke the intervention of the supernatural being to explain the phenomenon called the universe. Scientists have concluded that the universe began with the "big bang" (3). What is the big bang? Big bang is an explosion from zero volume at zero time of a hot spot of energy and matter equivalent to the mass, energy, and radiation that now constitute the universe. Everything we see now was once compacted into an infinitesimally small blimp that suddenly exploded and expanded and created the space and time that is expanding into. And the universe is on a course of continued expansion.

There is consensus on this theory of big bang. It is still a theory like many other scientific theories. But scientific theories become facts on the basis of observations and experiments. Prior to Albert Einstein's (4) proposal of the general theory of relativity in 1917, throughout human history, it was believed that the universe was fixed and immutable. Upon this theory, Alexander

Friedman (5) and Georges Lemaitre (6) formulated an expanding universe. In 1929, Edwin Hubble's (7) measurement of the red shift confirmed the expanding universe theory of Friedman and Lemaitre. This Hubble experiment is considered a major discovery. Hubble made observations that he interpreted as showing that distant stars and galaxies are receding from earth in every directions. The velocities of recession increased in proportion with distance. These observations have been confirmed by numerous other measurements. The implication of these findings is that the universe is expanding. Another testable deduction of big bang theory is that the temperature in deep space should be several degrees above absolute zero. This has been confirmed by observations. The big bang theory also predicted the existence of the cosmic microwave background radiation (CMB) (8). Which is composed of photons first emitted during early evolution of the universe. This radiation is thought to be observable at every point in the universe coming from all directions.

In 1964, scientists (8) working for Bell Lab, using a new microwave receiver, discovered cosmic background radiation. This discovery provided substantial confirmation of the big bang theory predictions. The Nobel Prize was awarded for this discovery. In 1989 NASA launched COBE Satellite (9) which also confirmed infra red microwave background radiation. In 1990s, CMB anisotropies were further investigated by ground-based experiments, and the universe was shown to be almost flat by measuring the angular size of the anisotropies. In 2003, Wilkinson Microwave Anisotropy Satellite observation (10), believed to be more accurate for cosmological data, also supported the expanding universe (inflation model).

Observation of the morphology and distribution of galaxies and quasars provide further evidence for the big bang. It is believed that the first galaxies and quasars were formed about a billion years after the big bang. Since then, larger galaxy clusters and super clusters are being formed. Some stars are aging, and others are being formed. The distant galaxies from the early universe appear different from nearby galaxies formed recently. Also the galaxies formed earlier and recently which are of same distance appear markedly different. All these are against the theory of a steady state universe and further support the theory of the big bang.

During the inflation period, space-time expanded so much that any residual curvature associated with it would have been smoothed out to a high degree of precision. Hence, inflation drove the universe to be nearly flat spatially (10, 11).

The BOOMERANG experiment confirms that the universe is flat and resembles a sheet on 2-D (12). Together with other experiments,

BOOMERANG data from 1997 and 1998 determined the angular diameter distance to surface of last scattering with high precision. When combined with complementary data regarding value of Hubble Constant, the BOOMERANG data determined the geometry of the universe to be flat, supporting the supernova evidence for existence of dark energy—dark matter (13).

During the 1970s, galactic rotation curves indicated that there is not sufficient visible matter in the universe to account for the gravitational forces, in and between galaxies. It is also found that the universe is less lumpy and has deuterium than can be accounted for. This led to the conclusion that 90 percent of the matter in the universe is dark matter. In the early phases, there were controversies about dark matter.

Dark matter is the material that gravitates but does not emit very much light to be seen. It has high ratio of mass to luminosity. Dark matter was first detected in 1970 (13). An inventory of the universe reveals that the matter in stars and galaxies is less than 1 percent, matter in neutrinos is 0.4 percent, ordinary (baryonic) energy 5 percent. Rest of the matter is dark. Some astronomers began the proposal and concept of dark matter (14). The missing matter was believed to be within the galaxies. Now it is called dark as it is the light that is missing and not the matter itself. It is there in the interstellar spaces.

In August 2006, through measurement of colliding galaxies in the Bullet Cluster, presence of dark matter was convincingly acknowledged (15). This was observed by the Hubble telescope, Chandra X-ray Observatory, the Magellan telescope, the European Southern Observatory, and others. Dark matter makes it known through its gravitational pull, and it has not been observed in the lab.

Future of the Universe

Before realization of dark energy, there were two scenarios for the future of the universe (16):

a   The big crunch: if the total mass density of the universe is above the critical density, then the universe will attain a maximum size and stop expanding and then begin to contract and would become denser and hotter again, becoming infinitesimally small as it was when it started at the big bang. There is speculation that after the universe shrinks to a dimensionless singularity, it can explode again like the first big bang and start all over again. This scenario is called the oscillating model of the universe.

b. If the density of the universe is equal or below the critical mass density, the expansion of the universe will continue but will slow down, never to stop. The interstellar gas in each galaxy will be consumed and star formation will cease. Stars will burn out. Left will be dwarf stars, neutron stars, and black holes. There will be collision between these, and larger black holes will be formed. The temperature of the universe will approach absolute zero. The universe will become a cold and desolate place (the Big Freeze). Eventually the entropy of the universe will increase, and no energy could be derived from it. This state is called a heat death.

Modern speculation tells that the universe will continue to expand our horizon and go out of contact and go on expanding for an unknown destiny. On the basis of dark energy model, it suggests that ultimately, matter itself will be torn apart including everything else by the ever-increasing expansion, called the Big Rip.

Religious Implications
End of the World in the Scriptures:

Hinduism (17)

Vedas:
Vedas of Hinduism are ancient sacred texts of divine inspirations written in Sanskrit. Veda means knowledge. There are four Vedic books believed to have been written about one thousand years before Christ. The oldest being Rig-Veda which contains reference to the universe and the creation. The universe along with earth and all creatures including human beings go through repeated cycles of creation and destruction. It is eternal and cyclic. The universe is believed to have been created by Brahma, the creator, who in turn is created by God or Brahman.

In Hindu cosmology, a universe endures for 4,320,000,000 years, which is one day of Brahma. Then it gets destroyed by fire or water (this is akin to the big crunch and cold freeze as cosmologists suggest). Then Brahma rests for one night, which is as long as his day.

(In Genesis, God rests on the seventh day of creation, not after destruction.) This event of the destruction of the universe is called Prelayam (cataclysm). This cyclic creation and destruction lasts for one hundred Brahma years, which is 311 trillion human years. The present Brahma cycle is 115 trillion human years old. After Brahma disappears, it takes another one hundred Brahma years until He is born again, and the creation begins, and the cycle repeats. Brahma's life span has one thousand cycles. Maha Yuga is the period where life starts and disappears, and this yuga lasts for 4,320,000 years. The Puranas, another religious writings in Hinduism, mention creation and destruction of the universe and cosmology. Brahman is the source of the universe. Hinduism believes in reincarnation in which all beings on earth and Gods above are subject to this cosmic cycle of repeated creation and destruction.

The Rigveda of Hinduism, in the hymns for Prajapathi, the Creator states "Whence this creation has come to existence, whether He created it or did not, He who is the overseer in the higher firmament, He verily knows or knows not."

Genesis (18) 1:1 says, "In the beginning God created the heavens and the earth." (There is no mention of how or from what.)

Qur'an 7:54 (19) states, "God created the heavens and earth in six days then He established himself on the throne. He created the sun, moon, and the stars." (All governed by laws under His command.)

21:30, "The heavens and the earth were joined together as one unit before We clove them asunder."

30:22, "And among His signs is the creation of the heavens and the earth."

67:3, "He who created the seven heavens one above the other no want of proportion wilt thou see in the creation of Allah (God).

41:11, "He comprehended then, his design to the sky and it had been as smoke and vapor."

51:47, (Asad) "Expanding universe 'And We are expanding it".

21:104, "We shall roll up the heavens like rolling up of written scrolls."

In these statements in the Qur'an, there are similarities to the scientific discoveries about the universe (or multiverse).

Qur'an mentions seven heavens whose significance is not clear. It may be referring to the multiverse as speculated by scientists or to the seven layers of the atmosphere as discussed in chapter 21. Science has not given any clear answer as to whether there is one universe or multiverse.

On the statement that the heavens and earth were joined together as one entity and was later cleaved apart, the scholars give some explanation. The religious scholars (20) comment on the word fatq (in Qur'an), meaning disintegration of a whole into several parts. This is akin to the dispersal of matter and energy by the big bang from one infinitesimally small spot as described by the scientists.

According to science, after the big bang, the universe was filled with dust and matter.

Qur'an (21) 25:59, "God is the one Who created the heavens, the earth and what is in between."(matter ?)

Qur'an (19) 41:11, "God turned to the sky and it had been as smoke and vapor."

Qur'an (19) 21:104 it states that in the end God will roll up the heavens like a written scroll and then God will reproduce it as He had began the first creation.

In this instance, scientists cannot say if after the end of the universe whether another big bang will start all over again. But Qur'an unmistakably states (21:104) the re-creation of the universe as it is a promise binding on God. The cyclic recreation is mentioned in the Vedas also.

There is reference to rolling up the heavens like a written scroll. With regard to this statement, the universe is likened to a flat object to be rolled up. A thing to be rolled like a written scroll doesn't have to be thin like a paper. We can roll a bed, bale of hay, and sod. It only needs to be relatively flat.

Scientists have determined that the universe is spatially flat (11). The human eyes cannot visualize the enormity of our universe, its shape, or its size, except by advanced technology and mathematical calculation, and thereby the scientists have determined that the universe is spatially flat. (This is consistent with the Qur'an statement that God will roll up the universe like a written scroll, [19] as it is spatially flat.)

Taoism (22) was a belief system established in China prior to Confucianism (23). Tao (the way) is indescribable and beyond human perception and understanding. Tao is believed to be the origin of the universe, the basis of existence of all creatures and the development of laws and ruling for all creatures. Tao sublimates to the vital energy and gathers to form the three purities. Taoism believes that the universe is created from emptiness. Tao is an intangible entity. We cannot see, touch, smell, hear, or taste it. But it exists in eternity. Confucianism focuses on morality and good deeds. It's a complex system of morals, social, political, and quasi-religious thoughts. The neoconfucian cosmology laid down by Zhou Dunyi (1017-1079) in his Taiji Tushuo said the origin of the world, both of things and men, was a spontaneous product of interaction between the five agents (water, fire, wood, metal, and earth).

Confucius's view on the origin of the universe is "qi" (matter-energy) as the creative factor than "li" (principles) which is included in "qi."

References for the Universe:

1. Bernulf Kanitscheider, philosopher-scientist. Center for the Philosophy of Science of the Justus. University, Geissen, Germany.
2. Bertrand Russell (1872-1970), British philosopher.
3. The Big Bang. First proposed by a Belgian priest, Georges Lemaitre.http://en.wikipedia.org/wiki/Big-Bang.3-2-2009.
4. Albert Einstein (1879-1955). The Theory of Relativity.
5. Alexander Friedman (1888-1925), Russian scientist. Discovered expanding universe (1922). http://en.wikipedia.org/wiki/Alexander-Friedman.
6. Georges Lemaitre (1894-1966). First proposed the big bang theory in "Hypothesis of the Primeval Atom" (1931).
7. Edwin Hubble (1889-1953). Hubble's Law (1929): Proceedings of the Natural Academy of Science.
8. CMBR. Cosmic Microwave Background Radiation. Wikipedia. http://en.wikipedia.org/wiki/Cosmic-microwave-background-radiation.(retrieved 3-28-08). Arno Penzia and Robert Wilson. Bell Laboratory. 1965.
9. NASA. Cosmic Background Explorer (COBE). 1989.
10. Wilkinson Microwave Anisotropy Satellite. 2001. (WMAP) 2001. Wikipedia: http://en.wikipedia.org/wiki/Microwave-Anisotropy-Probe. Retrieved Jan.21.2009.
11. Nature 2000. BOOMERANG (Balloon Observation of Millimetric Extragalactic Radiation and Geophysics). Heat death. Wikipedia. http://en.wikipedia.org/wiki/Heat-death-of-the-universe.(retrieved 3-28-2008).
12. BOOMERANG (Balloon Observation of Millimetric Extragalactic Radiation and Geophysics)http://cmb.phys.cwnu. 3-2-2009.
13. Dark matter. Physical Review Letters (2007).
14. Scientific American (1998). Fitz Zwiky.
15. Bullet Cluster. Wikipedia. http: //en. Wikipedia. org/ wiki /Bullet-Cluster. (retrieved 3-28-2008).

16. Future of the Universe.Wikipedia.http://en.wikipedia.org/wiki/Future-of-an-expanding-universe. (retrieved 3-28-2008)

17. Hinduism. Rig-Veda and Puranas.

18. Genesis 1:1.

19. Islam. Qur'an 7:54, 21:30, 30:22, 67:3, 41:11, 51:47 (Muhammad Asad), 21:104.

20. Maurice Bacailles: Qur'an and modern science. The French physician and scholar.

21. Qur'an 25:59.

22. Taoism.

23. Confucianism.

CHAPTER 31

Eschatology (End of the World or Universe)

In Judaism, end of the world is called acharit hayamim (1). Tumultuous events will overturn the world and a new order will be created and God is universally accepted as the ruler.

In Hinduism (2), the Puranas say that the world will fall into chaos, degeneration, immorality, and conflict.

"Yada yada Hi ahamasya glamir bharati bharata, abhyuthanam adharmasya tadatmanam srijami aham." (Whenever there is decay of righteousness O'Bharata and a rise of unrighteousness, then I manifest myself.) This avatar will clean up the mess. There are different yugas (epochs) which go on cycling.

We are in the Kali Yuga now according to Hindu belief. Next yuga will be Satya Yuga where righteousness prevails. Then comes Dwapara Yuga, Treta Yuga, and then another Kali Yuga, and it keeps repeating.

In Christianity (3)

Bible: In 2 Peter 3:12, 13 it says, "As you wait for the day of God and do your best to make it come soon—the day when the heavens will burn up and be destroyed and the heavenly bodies will be melted by heat. But we wait for what God has promised. New heavens and a new earth where righteousness will be at home."

Matthew (4) 24:29, "Soon after the trouble of those days the sun will grow darker, the moon will no longer shine. The stars will fall from heaven and the powers in space will be driven from their courses."

Eschatology in Islam:

In Islam as in Christianity, Judaism, Zoroastrianism, and Hinduism, there is an end to the universe and then a resurrection. In fact qiyamam (resurrection) is one of the fundamental beliefs in the Islamic faith. There will be a cosmic rapture at the end of time. Qur'an (5) 21:104, "We shall roll up the heavens as a recorder rolls up a written scroll. As We began the first creation, We shall repeat it."

55:37, "And when the sky is laid rent asunder and become red like burning oil (or red hide)."

70:8, "In a day when the sky will be like molten lead and the mountains will be like wool when is the day of resurrection." In 75:7 it says, "At length, when the sight is dazed and the moon is buried in darkness," 75:9, "and the sun and moon are joined together," 75:10, "that day will man say, 'where is the refuge,'" 81:1, "when the sun is shrouded in darkness," 81:2, "and when the stars lose their light," 81:3, "when the mountains are made to vanish and when the seas boil over and when heaven is laid bare," 69:13, "when the horn is blown once the earth and the mountains will be carried off and crushed, utterly crushed. This is the day when the inevitable event will come to pass."

Qur'an 14:48 (6) says, "The day will come when this earth will be substituted with a new earth and also the heavens, and everyone will be brought before God, the one, the supreme."

This is consistent with the Hindu cosmology of destruction and re-creation of the universe. The same scenario is mentioned in the bible as described above.

The Death of the Sun

Qur'an 13:2 (7), "He has subjected the Sun and the moon to His Laws. Each one runs its course for a time appointed."

36:38, "And the sun runs its course for a period determined for it." (In these two verses, there is a clear indication that the sun will die out.)

75:8-9, "And the moon is buried in darkness and the sun and the moon are joined together."

81:1-6, "When the sun is folded up (shrouded in darkness) when the stars fall losing their luster when the mountains vanish. When the oceans boil over with a swell."

Science: The sun is 4.5 billion years old. It has used up half of its nuclear fuel (hydrogen). In about five billion years, the sun will begin to die. As it grows old, the sun will expand. The core will contract as the hydrogen and later the helium are exhausted. The outer layers will expand, cool, and become less bright and will become a red giant star. When its heat is all dispersed, it will become a cold, dark dwarf. (Because of the compressed carbon, some believe it may be full of diamonds. Of course no one will be around to gather them.)

Scientists believe that in 1.1 billion years, the sun's brightness will increase by 10 percent. This will superheat our planet, and oceans will boil over, and all life-forms will die.

In 6.5 billion years, it will double in brightness and will use up all the hydrogen. Then the sun will begin to swell.

In eight billion years, the sun will swell to 166 times its present size. This giant star will swallow Mercury, Venus, and even Earth.

In twelve billion years, the sun becomes a cold dwarf.

These scientific predictions are clearly enumerated in the above mentioned passages in the Vedas, the bible and specifically in the Qur'an.

References for the Eschatology:

1. Eschatology in Judaism.
2. Eschatology in Hinduism.
3. The Bible. 2 Peter 3:12-13.
4. Ibid., Matthew 24:29.
5. Qur'an 21:104; 55:37; 70:8; 75:7-9 and 10; 81:1-2; 69:13.
6. Ibid., 14:48.
7. Ibid., 13:2.
8. Ibid., 36:38; 75:8-9; 81:1-6.

CHAPTER 32

Our Final Exit (Extinction of Mankind)

As we have seen in the biological and geological time line, the majority of the species have died out. When the new species evolve, the parent species go extinct. There is no clear and conclusive evidence for the causes of these extinctions. There were five major extinctions in the geological history. The causes of these extinctions have been credited with evolution of new species (external cause of evolution). Traditionally five major causes for extinction are described:

1. Impacts
2. Climatic
3. Volcanic
4. Gamma ray exposure from the sun
5. Plate tectonics

It is believed that when large meteorites impacted the earth, it caused climatic changes that led to extinction of species. The K-T extinction that caused the disappearance of dinosaurs was believed to have caused by such an impact from outer space possibly one meteorite or more about 65 million years ago. These impacts can raise massive amounts of dust into the atmosphere and block sunlight and consequently all live forms can perish. This hypothesis is called the Alvarez hypothesis (1) and scientists believe it is the most plausible explanation though it is not without controversy. Due to plate tectonics and continental drift, large bridges appeared and disappeared, and this must have played a role in species extinction. A mass extinction means an event in the history of evolution when more than 50% of all known species living at that time went extinct, in a relatively short time in geological history of two million years or so.

The recent extinction of the Neanderthals is believed to be due to a glaciation and resultant extreme cold temperatures. Similar glaciations have occurred before. Several theories are proposed for these glaciations. It is generally accepted that a global decrease in temperature of four to five degree centigrade and a substantial increase in the amount of snowfall in the sub arctic and arctic regions are necessary for glaciations to happen. The abovementioned catastrophes can cause decrease in sun's heat and radiation and cooling of the earth

The Toba catastrophe theory (2).

It is believed that the Toba volcano that erupted in Lake Toba in Sumatra, Indonesia about 75000 years ago wiped out human population in the world, leaving only a thousand breeding pairs. This is called a bottleneck in the evolutionary jargon.

One of the pioneering theories of glaciations was proposed by the Serbian scientist Milutin Milankovich (3"); there are three components to the earth's orbit about the sun that contribute to climatic changes on earth.

1. Axial shift
2. Eccentricity
3. Precession

Axial shift: The axis of the earth, an imaginary line that passes through the North Pole to the South can be considered as the earth's axis. If one draws a line from the sun to the center of earth, it can be seen that the earth's axis does not run parallel to the line drawn from the sun to earth, and it crosses the sun-earth line; this angle between the line drawn from the sun to earth and the polar axis (line drawn through the North Pole and the South Pole) is called the axial shift. To complete the cycle and reverse its axis, it takes forty one thousand years. It can shift from 21.5 to 24.5 degrees. It is currently at 23.5 degrees. The axial shift causes climatic changes on earth. When the northern hemisphere is farther away from the sun, it gets colder and vice versa.

Eccentricity: The earth's orbital path around the sun is not circular. It is elliptical, and the dimension of the ellipse varies from less elliptical to more elliptical. It changes from zero to five degrees every one hundred thousand years. When the ellipse is more stretched out, the earth becomes away from the sun and is believed to have caused the ice ages.

Precession: During its orbit around the sun, not only it rotates on its long axis, but it also makes a slow wobble. It has a cycle duration of twenty-six thousand years. The direction in the sky to which the axis points goes around a big circle with a radius of 23.5 degrees.

When these three planetary changes coalesce, it can cause alteration on earth's climate and possibly ice ages.

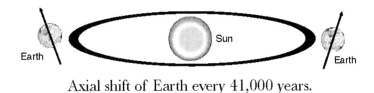

Axial shift of Earth every 41,000 years.

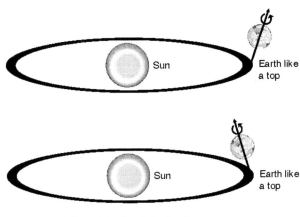

The Milankovich Cycles

Tectonic movement of continents influences the appearance and the disappearance of land bridges, which can adversely affect the survival of species.

Whatever were the causes of the extinction, many species died out, leaving only their fossils and possibly some genetic imprints in the present-day biota. However, we still have the early life-forms around us, like the bacteria, the fungi, and the cyan bacteria who have remained the same since they appeared on earth and are called the "living fossils" It is very curious to know why they did not undergo evolutionary changes in these many years of their time. This also calls into question the survival of the fittest theory. Are human beings more fit than the bacteria? If so, why are these bacteria here still? Why did the evolutionary process bypass these creatures? Obviously these bacteria are not contributing to our survival, or could they? The cyan bacteria generate oxygen that is useful to living creatures.

By looking back, we see a pattern of evolution and extinction. The newer the species have become, the smaller its span of existence. The Neanderthals lived from five hundred thousand years to about thirty thousand years ago. The Cro-Magnons lived from thirty-five thousand years to about twelve to fifteen thousand years ago. The earlier humanoid species lasted much longer, into millions of years before their extinction. This brings the obvious question, how long will the present-day human species survive? From the above history, it seems that we may not be here longer than our recent ancestors, namely, the Cro-Magnons who only survived for close to twenty thousand years. If we take the origin of our species from Adam's time, we already have survived at least ten to twelve thousand years; and if we are lucky, we (our species) may survive another eight to ten thousand years more, based on the life span of our predecessors, the Cro-Magnon race. This span of our existence is like a fleeting second compared to the geological time span. If only we knew the causes of the extinction of previous species, we, the human beings, could devise methods to survive as we have the capacity in ourselves to do so. We also have the capacity to destroy the entire humanity with the weapons that we possess now and we are contributing to the destruction of our environment and to the clean shaving of the rain forests.

The capacities that human beings are endowed with are unprecedented in the history of earth. Many natural calamities can be forewarned and necessary steps taken to avert a disaster. Currently we can predict an earthquake and lay a plan of escape. The weather bureau can advise the arrival of hurricanes and thunderstorms beforehand, to move to safer areas as seen during the Katrina hurricane in Southern United States. Not to mention the nuclear shelters. In the arena of extraterrestrial catastrophes like a meteor impact, the U.S. is developing missiles to strike any incoming meteors and destroy them in space. There are many other potential killers out there, both in the earth and outside. We may control any possible deadly viruses like the Ebola as we have done with the smallpox and malaria. As scientists have noted, many of the external threats for our survival have been controlled and if future threats and catastrophes can be controlled or eliminated, and if evolution is due to the destruction of a species from these threats and resultant bottleneck, then we may be in a position to thwart any external stimulus (catastrophes)) for evolution, and therefore, evolutionary phenomenon may be a thing of the past.

It is also possible to colonize the Moon or the Mars, should the earthly life become impossible due to either some natural catastrophe or man-made disaster as in a large-scale nuclear bombardment. By doing so, we can save our species and re-enter the earth when it is safe to do so.

The last chance for mutation will be the sole, random variety, but the needed natural selection is taken out of the equation as we are capable of preventing and avoiding an external threat. In this scenario, the present-day humans are at a dead end of the evolutionary saga.

If by chance an evolutionary circumstance does arise and there were new species, how will that impact us? We can survive like the "living fossils" of the present (bacteria and fungi) and live subservient to the new masters, or we can be wiped out by the newcomers as probably had happened in the remote past for earlier hominids or coexist with the new arrivals. If they are super humans with more humane thoughts than we are, we may survive. If not, our fate will be like other animals now existing on earth, to provide services for the masters including to be unlucky enough to become a tasty dish for their dinner.

In short, progress of science will be the final blow to biological evolution, and the evolutionary tree will be withered forever.

The Qur'an repeatedly mentions that we may be replaced by yet another creation, if God so wills (Qur'an 4:133; 17:99; 14:19; 29:20; 35:16) (4). Therefore, regardless of any environmental catastrophe, under circumstances deemed necessary, God could transform us into a new race or species. In this warning, it is understood that the existing species will be replaced and will not be left out to be under the mercy of the new species. In other words, there will not be a coexisting scenario.

References for the Final Exit:

1. Alvarez hypothesis.http://www.ucmp.berely.edu/diapsids/extictheory.html.
2. Stanley H. Ambrose:. http://en.wikipedia.org/wiki/Toba-catastrophe-theory.
3. Milutin Milankovich (1879). Canon of Insulation of the Earth and Its Application to the Problems of Ice Ages (1930).
4. Qur'an 4:133; 17:99; 14:19; 29:20; 35:16.

CHAPTER 33
Conclusion

In this book, I have touched upon several aspects of human origin and its future. The creationists believe that each living form was made independently by the creative process dictated by God. The evolutionists believe all the living forms were evolved from a primitive cell or life-form and not individually created. Many believe that these two opposing views are mutually exclusive. But in this book, I have shown that there is no need to mutually exclude one by the other; instead both are in tandem and complementary. The tree of evolution as hinted in the Vedas and the Bible and elaborated in the Qur'an is revisited. One can argue that, God is all-powerful and by saying "Be" it is done, and there is no need for an evolutionary process, passing through various life-forms to come to the level of mankind, and He could have created man instantaneously at will.

Scientists have made great advancement in understanding the process of biological evolution. They are now embarking on the search for artificial life. Human beings by nature are curious about everything and raise questions to find an answer. Why we are here, and how did we come about on earth?

It is to be remembered that these questions sometimes may not yield an answer. If it is the will of God to bring about these phenomena in the universe, it will be. But still human beings like to find out the cause and effect of every phenomenon. Therefore, it is appropriate to raise questions and find the answer, and that is science. It is by finding out the cause of many diseases that created epidemics in the past that we are able to prevent them. There are many areas this search for truth has given big dividends. For any problem, whether natural or individual, this search will eventually shed some light on the reason or reasons for the creation of the universe and mankind. We do not know why we (the human beings) are here in this world or the reason for the formation of the universe.

It appears from the history of life on earth that it is changing from one form to the other and possibly the human beings could be changed to another form (species). The more advanced the creature becomes, he or she may be able to understand the eternal power we call God or may be raised to His level as predicted by early Islamic evolutionists. The same theme is reflected in Hinduism and Buddhism in a different fashion.

Even if we find out the secrets of the universe and of our own life, what will be next? Will we be able to explain why our own life (human form) went through this evolutionary path to reach our present stature? The universe also has gone through this process of transformation from the time of the big bang. Even if the future generation were to find the secrets of the universe and of our own existence, the question still remains—WHY.

INDEX

S

T

U

V

W